UNIVERSITY OF NORTH CAROLIN.
DEPARTMENT OF ROMANCE L.

NORTH CAROLINA STUDIES
IN THE ROMANCE LANGUAGES AND LITERATURES

Founder: URBAN TIGNER HOLMES

Distributed by:

UNIVERSITY OF NORTH CAROLINA PRESS

CHAPEL HILL

North Carolina 27514

U.S.A.

NORTH CAROLINA STUDIES IN THE
ROMANCE LANGUAGES AND LITERATURES
Number 185

THE *CORT D'AMOR*

A THIRTEENTH-CENTURY ALLEGORICAL ART OF LOVE

THE *CORT D'AMOR*
A THIRTEENTH-CENTURY ALLEGORICAL ART OF LOVE

BY

LOWANNE E. JONES

CHAPEL HILL

NORTH CAROLINA STUDIES IN THE ROMANCE
LANGUAGES AND LITERATURES
U.N.C. DEPARTMENT OF ROMANCE LANGUAGES
1977

Library of Congress Cataloging in Publication Data

Cort d'Amor.
    The Cort d'Amor: a thirteenth-century allegorical art of love.

    (North Carolina studies in the Romance languages and literatures; no. 185)
    The text is that included in MS. M. 819 in the Pierpont Morgan Library
and is here accompanied by the English translation.
    Bibliography: p.
    Includes index.
    I. Jones, Lowanne E.   II. Series.

PQ1453.C585 1977   841'.1   77-2898
ISBN 0-8078-9185-1

I.S.B.N. 0-8078-9185-1

IMPRESO EN ESPAÑA
PRINTED IN SPAIN

DEPÓSITO LEGAL: V. 2.928 - 1977   I.S.B.N. 84-399-7622-4
ARTES GRÁFICAS SOLER, S. A. - JÁVEA, 28 - VALENCIA (8) - 1977

ACKNOWLEDGEMENTS

I am greatly indebted to the Fulbright-Hayes Commission for making it possible for me to spend a year in France researching this study, and I am equally indebted to Professor Charles Camproux of Montpellier whose generous advice and assistance during that year were invaluable.

I would also like to thank Mr. Antoine Vidal for his help in using the facilities of the Bibliothèque des Lettres de l'Université Paul Valéry, Montpellier, and Professor André de Mandach of Berne, Switzerland, and Mr. William Voelkle of the Pierpont Morgan Library in New York, for their kind assistance in reading the illegible passages of the manuscript. Adam Rodriguez has earned my special thanks for his cheerful assistance in technical matters.

I greatly appreciate the support of Dean Arthur Adams and the College of Humanities at the Ohio State University who ensured the preparation of this edition with two substantial grants-in-aid.

I am also very grateful to my friends and colleagues of the Division of Comparative Literature at the Ohio State University, especially my husband, Professor Frank Rodriguez, whose confidence and good humor have been steadfast.

Finally I am most happy to express my sincere thanks to Professor Hans-Erich Keller whose gentle enthusiasm and patient encouragement inspired and sustained me in the preparation of this edition.

TABLE OF CONTENTS

INTRODUCTION

I. Manuscript of the Cort d'Amor

The *Cort d'Amor* occupies folios 31r through 46v of manuscript M. 819 in the Pierpont Morgan Library in New York City, the only manuscript in which it is preserved. The manuscript was formerly owned by Sir Thomas Phillipps (1792-1872), and remained in his library in Cheltenham, England where it bore the number 8335 until it was purchased by the Morgan Library on July 1, 1946. The earliest owners of M. 819 were the Gonzaga, dukes of Mantua in the fourteenth and fifteenth centuries and it remained in their library where it was used by Mario Equicola (1470-1525) and Cardinal Pietro Bembo (1470-1547), librarian of the Marciana Library in Venice. There is no further trace of it until 1816 when the manuscript belonged to Count J. MacCarthy-Reagh at Toulouse. It was purchased from the Mac-Carthy collection by Richard Heber (1773-1853), who sold it to Sir Thomas Phillipps. [1]

M. 819 contains 293 pages with 3 blank leaves and measures 10¼ by 7½ inches with two columns to a page, each with 27 lines. The folios were misnumbered originally and in the description, table and extracts published by H. Suchier, "Il Canzoniere Provenzale di Cheltenham," *Rivista di Filologia romanza*, 20 (1875), pp. 49-52, 144-172, but a revised and corrected index was given by Curt F. Buhler, "The Phillipps Manuscript of Provençal Poetry," *Speculum*, 22 (1947), 68-74. Léopold Constans published a description of this manuscript in the *Revue des Langues Romanes*, 20 (1881), 130-138, Part I of his article "Les Manuscrits provençaux de Cheltenham." Brief descrip-

---

[1] Unpublished Morgan Library File, MS M. 819, p. 14.

tions of M. 819, long known as Manuscript N, may also be found
in Alfred Jeanroy, *Bibliographie sommaire des chansonniers provençaux* (Paris: Champion, 1916) *CFMA* 16, p. 10, and in A. Pillet
and H. Carstens, *Bibliographie des Troubadours* (Halle: Saale, 1933),
p. xviii, and in Clovis Brunel, *Bibliographie des manuscrits littéraires
en ancien provençal* (Paris: Droz, 1935), p. 4.

This manuscript in quarto on vellum in an eighteenth century
French binding, was copied and illuminated at Padua, Italy, near the
end of the thirteenth century, and not in the fourteenth century as
A. Jeanroy believed (*Bibliographie*, p. 10), although it does include,
as he pointed out, later additions in Italian hands of the fourteenth
and fifteenth centuries. M. 819 is most easily dated through the
miniatures it contains by an artist (or artists) of the atelier of Giovanni
Gaibana, curate of the cathedral at Padua where he was buried on
his death in 1293. [2] The miniatures include 28 historiated initials,
39 pages with marginal illustrations, mostly line drawings in ink, and
four illuminated initials. "The style of the miniatures dates it at the
end of the XIIIth century and includes M. 819 within a group of
North Italian MSS, chief of which is a Lectionary at Padua, dated
1259, and signed by Giovanni da Gaibana.... Professor Jan Kvet,
in his discussion of Gaibana's MSS and influence (*Italske vlivy*)
considers them the work of several painters, schooled in the same
place and style, to which he applied the term 'style gaibanesque.'
Their locale was in the patriarchate of Aquileia, that is, Aquileia
itself, Padua, Trieste and Venice, in the second half of the XIIIth
century. The date of M. 819 can be fixed between 1285 and 1300
by certain details of costumes, iconography and calligraphic ornament.
Among these are the types of costumes, the fillet worn by the women
on their brows, the chain armor and shields, the shape of the bishop's
mitre (f. 55); the type of filigrane ornament, and the modelling and
posture of Christ on the cross on folio f. 65. These are all before
1300." [3]

Unfortunately folios 31r through 46v are completely without illustrations. Of a certain interest, however, are three drawings along
the margin of folio 66v depicting the lady sitting in judgment, the
poet being conducted to her court, and the poet accepting her de-

---

[2] *Ibid.*
[3] *Ibid.*

cision. They accompany the text of a poem composed by the Monk of Montaudon but erroneously attributed in the manuscript to Arnaut de Mareuil, "Aissi con cel c'om mena al iuiemen," not the *Cort d'Amor,* but one cannot help recalling the seigneur of Love also sitting in judgment. In the miniatures of M. 819, Love is personified six times (folios 56, 58v, 61v, 64, 73, and 211), but each time as a cherub and not once as the royal lady described in the *Cort d'Amor.*

MS M. 819 involved the work of five different scribes, and the *Cort d'Amor* was copied by two of them: "Hand II" of the Morgan Library classification is found in folios 31 through 35r, and "Hand IV" in folios 35v through 46v. [4] The script is gothic miniscule book hand and both hands are very similar to the North Italian hand of MS Venice VII (V7) of the *Song of Roland,* published in photostat by Raoul Mortier, *Les Textes de la Chanson de Roland* (Paris: La Geste Francor, 1942), vol. V.

Both scribes copying the *Cort d'Amor* used a considerable amount of punctuation including period, comma, apostrophe, and cedilla. The use of abbreviations is nearly identical, consisting of — above a vowel to indicate nasal *m* or *n; p* to represent *per*; p⋅, t⋅ to represent *pri, tri*; and the Italian form 9 to represent *co, com, con.* The second copyist of the *Cort d'Amor* tended to use abbreviations much less sparingly than the first and his script is slightly larger. The second scribe also uses q³ for *qe,* while the first uses q̄ or spells out *que.* It is also possible that the text was dictated to the scribes. One finds *plus ma* (l. 595) for *pluma* which is an aural error, not a visual one, and suggests that the scribe did not have a copy of the text before his eyes. In the same way *gaire* (l. 614) is probably also an aural misunderstanding of *gaia.*

The orthography also bears certain resemblances to that of Upper Italy in the second half of the thirteenth century.

> *ci* (l. 561), *ce* (l. 804), *c'era* (l. 747), *ceran* (l. 994): *c* for *s* before *e* is attested as early as 1228 in a Cremonese document (Monaci, *Crestomazia*, no. 60, l. 93), and in the early fourteenth century in a Venetian document (Monaci, no. 145, l. 5).

---

[4] *Ibid.*

diçon (1. 738), *plaçers* (1. 1590): *ç* for *s* or *z* is attested in a manuscript of a Bolognese dialect in 1242 or 1243 (Monaci, no. 34, 1. 7).

qart (1. 1553), *qarta* (1. 391), *qeron* (1. 824): *q* for *qu* is attested early in the thirteenth century in a Cremonese manuscript (Monaci, no. 62, 1. 52).

francha (1. 1457): *ch* for *c* before *a* is attested in 1233-1243 (Monaci, no. 37, 1. 2).

seignor (1. 353): is attested in the twelfth century in a Gallo-Italian sermon (Monaci, no. 18, 1. 2). The following spellings of this word are also found in this text: *seinor* (ll. 1, 124, 127, 496, 979), *seinors* (1. 101), *seingner* (1. 97), *seiner* (ll. 881, 1575), *senior* (1. 871), *sener* (1. 1125), *seihner* (1. 992), *seinhor* (1. 1645), *sejnor* (1. 1431). Levy *PD* cites *senhor, senher*.

ja (1. 1488), *za* (ll. 9, 491), *ia* (ll. 80, 199); *zutgament* (1. 34), *jutguament* (1. 834), *jutgat* (1. 423), *zuzatz* (1. 29); *zauzia* (1. 1670); *zou* (1. 1618), *iou* (1. 286), *joy* (1. 272), *ioi* (1. 137), *iois* (ll. 109, 263), *zoi* (ll. 42, 118), *zor* (ll. 36, 69), *jonrs* (1. 1603), *zorns* (ll. 1425, 1557), *iorn* (1. 1220): *z* for initial *j* is attested in the poetry of Bonevesin de la Riva (b. 1240-1250, d. 1313) (Monaci, no. 146[2], 1. 182), and in the fourteenth century in the story of "Rainardo e Lesengrino" (Monaci, no. 145T, 1. 25). The use of *i* for *j*, especially in the initial position, and vice versa, is common in medieval manuscripts, and in MS. M. 819, the scribes seem to have used *i* and *j* interchangeably in this position.

asaiar (1. 501), *preiar* (1. 214), *cuiaria* (1. 1540), *cuzon* (1. 1473), *cujon* (1. 1702), *cuza* (1. 295), *haza* (1. 28), *endompneiatz* (1. 1445); *enozos* (1. 1682) which rhymes with *zoios* (1. 1683): *i* for intervocalic *j* is attested in the first half of the thirteenth century (Monaci, no. 35, 1. 148); *z* for intervocalic *j* is attested in 1281 in a Bolognese manuscript (Monaci, no. 138, 1. 12).

envez (1. 190), *envei* (1. 168); *mez* (1. 54), *mei* (1. 312); *rej* (1. 1594); *gaz* (1. 1453); *estaz* (1. 32), *estai* (1. 429); *ieu haz* (1. 82), *ieu haj* (1. 184), *eu hai* (1. 230); [*eu*] *saz* (ll. 237, 1427), *eu soj* (ll. 501, 1489); [*eu*] *sai* (1. 1429); and all of the following in the first person singular: *faj* (1. 1463), *vaj* (1. 1454), *chiaj* (1. 1418), *progaraj* (1. 1431),

parlaraj (1. 1502), *veiraj* (1. 1505) which rhymes with
metrai (1. 1506): *z* and *j* for final *i* are not attested as
far as it can be ascertained. It can be determined that
the pronunciation of this phoneme is /dʒ/ and it is
probably derived by the scribe by analogy to the initial
and intervocalic z/j described above.

From the preceding it is apparent that MS M. 819 was very probably
copied in the famous scriptorium of the Dukes of Mantua at the
end of the thirteenth century.

The complete text of the *Cort d'Amor* has been published only
once, by Léopold Constans, *Revue des Langues Romanes*, 20 (1888),
121-179, 209-220, 261-276, as Part III of "Les Manuscrits provençaux
de Cheltenham," abbreviated below as 'Constans.' The offprint of
this text which was corrected to a small degree by its editor is no
longer obtainable. Camille Chabaneau offered corrections to the text
published by Constans, in the *Revue des Langues Romanes*, 21
(January, 1882), 90-98, abbreviated below as 'Chabaneau.' Emil Levy
offered further corrections and revisions of the same text, benefitting
from the corrections added by Constans to the offprint, in the *Revue
des Langues Romanes*, 21 (May, 1882), 238-239, abbreviated below
as 'Levy.' [5]

C. A. F. Mahn, in his *Gedichte der Troubadours* (Berlin, 1856-
1873), II, no. 279, pp. 168-171, had previously published lines 1-182,
345-484, and 505-514 of the *Cort d'Amor*, and this text is abbreviated
below as 'Mahn.' K. Bartsch published exactly the same verses in his
Altprovenzalisches Lesebuch (Elberfeld: 1855), 34-38. Bartsch seems
unaware that 21 lines have been omitted between 1. 484 and 505, and
so prints them continuously. Line 484 is not even the end of a
sentence: *L'uels mi volon saillir del cor* is followed by *Tant vos haz
cellada l'amor*, which both Bartsch and Mahn omitted. Furthermore,
orthography in the Bartsch edition is radically different from that of
the manuscript, and it is apparent that for instructional purposes he
has simply attempted to standardize the original spelling. It seems,

---

[5] References to Emil Levy's *Petit Dictionnaire Provençal-Français* (2nd.
ed., Heidelberg: Carl Winter, 1923), are abbreviated below 'Levy PD'; references to his *Provenzalishes Supplement-Wörterbuch* (Leipzig: 1894), 8 vols.,
are abbreviated 'Levy SW'; references to Walter von Wartburg's *Französisches
Etymologisches Wörterbuch* (Bonn, Leipzig, Basel: 1928 to present), are abbreviated below 'FEW.'

therefore, that someone, either Bartsch or Mahn or a third unknown individual made the trip to England and copied lines 1-182, 345-484, and 505-514 from the manuscript. Both Bartsch and Mahn probably made use of this single copy for their respective publications which appeared within one year of each other, Mahn printing the original text unchanged, Bartsch printing a standardized text for student use. René Nelli and René Lavaud published lines 1159-1257 of the Constans text with a modern French translation in *Les Troubadours*, II, "L'Œuvre Poétique" (Bruges: Desclée de Brouwer, 1966), 236-243. Since this text is nothing more than a reprint of the Constans text it is not cited below.

In transcribing MS M. 819, I have attempted to reproduce the manuscript as faithfully as possible, making no corrections whatsoever. In many cases, the initial letter of a major division was left blank for the illuminator and I have inserted the restitution of these initials in brackets. Letters that have been deduced from abbreviations are italicized, and abbreviations that are unusual or misused are discussed in the notes accompanying the text. Similarly, the translation that accompanies the text is a literal one, departing from the Occitan only where a literal rendering would produce nonsense in English.

II. Date and Authorship of the Cort d'Amor

The *Cort d'Amor* occupies a unique position in Occitan literature for it is the earliest narrative love allegory in that language of which we have any record. Unfortunately the poem, which is preserved in fragments in only one manuscript, contains no historical references to events or individuals that might permit us to date its composition precisely. The fact that it exhibits no demonstrable influence by the *Roman de la Rose* of Guillaume de Lorris leads us to suppose that it was written earlier than 1235. References to the rose, or roses, occur in seven different verses of the *Cort d'Amor* (ll. 50, 56, 628, 959, 1262, 1601, and 1627), but in only one of these instances is the rose directly related to love:

> Qe prous dompna ab fresca color
> Es ruesa del vergiers d'Amor.
>
> (ll. 1260-1261)

In this case, however, it is clear that the poet is referring only to the lady's rosy, "amorous," apparently blushing complexion and intends no further significance. Furthermore, there is no direct, observable relationship between the personifications of virtues, vices, or aspects of love in the *Cort d'Amor* and the personifications of Guillaume's *Roman de la Rose*, for the personifications in the *Cort d'Amor* are each and every one drawn from the earlier Occitan tradition. Although it is impossible to prove that the author of the *Cort d'Amor* did not know (or could not know) the French poem, we can see quite plainly from even a cursory reading of the Occitan poem that there was probably very little influence of that type from the north.

In an equally negative way, it is also possible to note that the *Cort d'Amor* displays none of the cynical, slightly contemptuous satire so obvious in the later thirteenth century with the *Chastel d'Amors* discussed below, p. 64. More positively stated, the *Cort d'Amor* is still very close to the troubadour tradition of the twelfth century. In style and content our author resembles Raimon Vidal (ca. 1210-1215) more closely than he resembles Peire Guilhem (ca. 1250) in spite of the fact that the latter wrote allegory while the former did not. The specific relationship between the *novas* of these two authors and the *Cort d'Amor* is also examined below.

This close relationship to the troubadour Golden Age can be seen most strikingly in the personification of *Fin'Amor* herself. In the medieval Latin, northern French, and later Occitan poems the personification of Love is masculine, either as a direct personification of the word *amour* which is masculine in French, or more often as a version of Ovid's male Cupid, the god of love. Almost without exception, however, the troubadours referred to love, *fin'amor*, as "she" since the Occitan word is feminine: *Amors la dousa e la bona* (l. 30).

Significantly, the author of the *Cort d'Amor* had considerable difficulty remembering (or believing) that his heroine was in fact a woman. Ordinarily *Fin'Amor* is designated in the text by feminine pronouns (e.g., l. 351: *leis*), but she is designated at least ten times by masculine words as if she were a man: l. 48, *lo*; l. 353, *lo*; l. 354, *el*; l. 837, *lo*; l. 872, *el*; l. 879, *el*; l. 899, *el*; l. 903, *rei*; l. 1078, *el*; l. 1584, *el*. In one passage *Fin'Amor* is compared to a man:

> Enaissi con deu far lo seingner
> Qe tot lo mont ha a destreigner,

> Esgardet vas terra un petit,
> Con sabis on, ...
>
> (ll. 97-100)

Not surprisingly, other females receive the same treatment: in l. 369 *Corteszia* is referred to as *il*; and in l. 1132, *el* refers to the lady who looks in her mirror. The most striking example of this phenomenon is that of *Merce,* a woman who arrives at the court of Love as advocate for the abused lovers:

> E quan l'an vist*a* li baron
> No i a cel non sapcha bon.
> Mont polsa son caval lo flancs;
> Per un pauc qe non es stancs.
> *Aqest* trameto.l amador
> Per faire clam a Fin'Amor
> De las dompnas des cominals.
> Molt cuitas c'a tost le vasals.
> A tant es a cort desend*utz,*
> Tuit diçon: "Ben sia veng*utz.*"
> E *el* respon: "E Deu sal vos."
>
> (ll. 729-739)

Merce is a feminine noun in Old Occitan, and therefore the personification is feminine: "li baron l'an vist*a.*" She arrives on horseback, apparently riding her mount directly into the court, and at this point, our poet tells us that "he" (*Merce*) was sent by the lovers: "*Aqest* trameto.l amador." "He" dismounts to the court: "es a cort desend*utz,*" and "he" is welcomed by the vassals:

> "Ben sia veng*utz.*"

There are two potential explanations for these transexual identities. In the first place it is possible that either the author or the scribe — certainly the latter and possibly the former as well — were not native speakers of Occitan. We know the scribe was an Italian and that he often misspelled what he heard, and there is a remote possibility that the author was also a foreigner, one of those Italians who imitated the troubadours. His Occitan was obviously far superior to that of the scribe, but this does not remove the likelihood that he too was careless with pronouns.

On the other hand, it is possible that these "mistakes" are not really faults after all; they could have been logical consequences of the flow of the narrative. A rapid survey of the thirteen cases in question reveals that in context, nine of the ten masculine words referring to Fin'Amor appear in a context of "masculine" activity: in ll. 353-354 the ladies beseech Fin'Amor as their lord to save them from dishonor: "E preigan *lo* com lor seignor / Q'*el* las engart de desonor." In l. 837, Courtesy calls upon *Fin'Amor*, addressing her as one would a male lord: "La Cortesa d'Amor *lo* sona: / "Seinor, qar non portes corona?" In l. 872 the watchman proclaims that one has *joi* if Love bestows it: "Alquel han ioi cui *el* en dona." In l. 879 *Fin'Amor* offers a prayer to God, and it is stated in terms of a vassal addressing the suzerain: "*El* dis: 'Seinor Deu glorios.' " In ll. 898-899, the seneschal announces the wishes of *Fin'Amor*: "Qe.l ioglar sion escoutat / Q'*el* vol, ..." In l. 903, *Fin'Amor* is given the title of king: "Li joglar s'approchon del *rei*." In l. 1078, *Fin'Amor* assumes the additional male role of lover when Honor approaches: "*El* ac gran joi qan l'ac veszuda," and the matter of the treasury (another masculine domain) is brought up: "Q'*el* no i ten argent ni aur." It is only the first use of the masculine reference (ll. 47-48) which has no appreciable masculine context: "D'autra part Larguesza e Domneis / *Lo* meton en un leit d'orfres." The vast majority of the instances in which the feminine *Fin'Amors* is designated by a masculine word involve situations in which *Fin'Amor* acts in a predominantly masculine context. This has already been demonstrated in the case of *Merce*: she is a feminine abstraction when she is first seen by the barons, but her hasty arrival on horseback in the very midst of the court, her mission on the part of the lovers, and her greeting to the court are "masculine" activities in a "masculine" context, and as a result, the pronouns and adjectives referring to her are masculine. Similarly in the one passage where Lady *Corteszia* is signified by a masculine pronoun, she, too, is playing a male role: that of spokesman for her seigneur, the legal counsellor of *Fin'Amor*:

> [S] o dis Amors: "Bon conseil sai,
> Na Corteszia, q'eu vez lai,
> Voell qu'en fassa aqest iutgament,
> Qe sab per on monta e disent
> Amors, e qar sab ben q'*il* es
> Del mont la plus adreita res.
> *Il* lo fera be ses engan.
>
> (ll. 363-369)

Strangely, *Fin'Amor* here refers not only to *Corteszia* in masculine terms (l. 369) but also to Love (l. 367). *Corteszia,* too, is compared to a man:

> Cortesia pleigua son gan
> E doba se de iugar,
> Q'*om* cortes se fan pauch pregar
> Qant vei q'es luecs es avinents.
> Molt es grantz e preon sos sens.
> Pueis parlet com savis e pros.
>   (ll. 370-375)

There remain two more cases in which a feminine person is designated by a masculine word. In the first case, Laughter is obviously speaking of the lady:

> Enaisi plaing lo drutz e.l druda
> Es mil aitans morta e venduda
> Q'el non ausa ab omen parlar.
>   (ll. 962-964)

Most likely the scribe erroneously wrote *el* for *ilh.* In the second case, Honor is clearly speaking of the *jovencella*:

> E qant aqil colors li fail,
> Ez *el* se vei en son mirail,
> E connois qe trop s'es tarzada,
> Ill qier son don era pregada.
>   (ll. 1131-1134)

Apparently *el* here is also a scribal error for *ilh* since the *ill* of l. 1134 obviously refers to the same individual.

There is only one example in the text of a masculine person designated by a feminine word: "Qe qant *ill* a si dons conques" (l. 1655), and this too is apparently a scribal error similar to the one mentioned above.

From all of this it is possible to conclude that in the great majority of cases in the text of the *Cort d'Amor* in which a masculine word is used to designate a female person, the phenomenon is probably not a scribal error or grammatical mistake on the part of the author. Rather they represent a certain unconsciously changing attitude that could be indicative of the times: for decades the Occitan poets had regarded *Fin'Amor* as a woman, and a woman she remains in the *Cort d'Amor* but the nature of her position (seigneur and judge) and her activities (public address, coronation, the law court, possibly riding to war) either suggest or require in the mind of the poet certain attributes that he considers exclusively masculine. For this reason *Fin'Amor* and, on at least one occasion each, *Corteszia* and *Merce* are treated by the author as though they were male personifications. We have the opportunity to remark *Fin'Amor* here in transition from a female personification of an abstract idea to a male god representing the same idea. The *Fin'Amor* of the *Cort d'Amor* represents one step beyond Guiraut de Calanso's female *figura* and one step before Peire Guilhem's *dieus d'amors*. Accordingly I would suggest that the poem be dated after 1204 (Guiraut de Calanso), and before 1235 (Guillaume de Lorris) at the earliest, and before 1250 (Peire Guilhem) at the latest. The author of the *Cort d'Amor* was probably a contemporary of Raimon Vidal.

III. SOURCES OF THE CORT D'AMOR: LATIN PRECURSORS

It would be both redundant and presumptuous to attempt to review here the enormous quantity of material which could, however indirectly, serve as a "source" of the *Cort d'Amor*. [6] By the end of the twelfth century both the allegory and the *art d'aimer* were firmly established as elements of medieval literature, and in this respect the Occitan *Cort d'Amor* represents nothing new. Its uniqueness lies in

---

[6] For studies of origins and sources of medieval allegory cf. Ernest Langlois, *Origines et Sources du Roman de la Rose* (Paris: Ernest Thorin, 1891); William Allan Neilson, *The Origins and Sources of the Court of Love*, Harvard Studies and Notes in Philology and Literature, Vol. VI (Boston: Ginn and Company, 1899); Charles Oulmont, *Les Débats du Clerc et du Chevalier dans la littérature poétique du moyen âge. Etude historique et littéraire suivi de l'édition critique des textes* (Paris: Champion, 1911); Edmond Faral, *Sources latines des contes et romans courtois du Moyen Âge* (Paris: Champion, 1913); Clive Staples Lewis, *The Allegory of Love, a Study in Medieval Tradition* (Oxford: the Clarendon Press, 1936); Reto R. Bezzola, *Les Origines et la Formation de la Littérature courtoise en Occident* (Paris: 1944-1963); Peter Dronke, *Medieval Latin and the Rise of European Love Lyric* (Oxford: The Clarendon Press, 2nd. ed., 1968); Marc-René Jung, *Études sur le poème allégorique en France au Moyen Âge*, Romanica Helvetica, Vol. 82 (Berne: Editions Francke, 1971).

the fact that it is probably the first combination of allegory and *art d'aimer* to appear in an Old Occitan narrative poem.[7] Or rather, since the *Cort d'Amor* clearly did not spring fully formed from a vacuum, its immediate demonstrable sources are of a certain value both in comprehending elements of the poem itself, and in helping to color our concept of thirteenth century Occitan letters. With this understanding, those medieval Latin sources which indisputably contributed to the literary atmosphere of the thirteenth century and which undeniably influenced the composers of allegories and *arts d'aimer* in both the North and the South, in both French and Occitan, will be mentioned only briefly in this study if no direct relationship to the author of the *Cort d'Amor* can be demonstrated. Such medieval Latin poems as the *Romarcimontis concilium*[8] (early 12th century) and the *Altercatio Phyllis et Flora,*[9] both debates on the subject of love, probably had no direct influence on the author of the *Cort d'Amor.* It cannot be proven from his work that he knew either poem. On the other hand, it can be demonstrated from the text of his poem that among the classic Latin writers known to the Middle Ages, our author probably did know some of Ovid's poetry quite well, that in the medieval Latin tradition he might have known something of the treatise of Andreas Capellanus, and that he was familiar with several Latin fables.

Ovid

At least one of Ovid's lyric poems, *Amores* I, ii, contains four separate elements that reappear in the *Cort d'Amor*: the lover's sleepless night (ll. 1-5), the darts of love (ll. 6-8, 34), the fire of love (ll. 9-12, 46), and the personification of different elements in the lover's experience (ll. 31-38).

---

[7] The *novas* of Raimon Vidal de Besalú are probably earlier but they are neither allegories nor arts of love. The love allegory (ca. 1210) of Guiraut de Calanso is a lyric and does not involve an art of love as such. The *Chastel d'Amors*, both allegorical and didactic, exists only as a fragment, and the allegorical poem of Peire Guilhem (1234-1235) is only briefly didactic.

[8] Ed. G. Waitz in: *Zeitschrift für deutsches Altertum,* VII (1849), pp. 160-167.

[9] Ed. J. Grimm in: *Abhandlungen der Königlichen Akademie der Wissenschaften zu Berlin* (1843), pp. 218-229.

Where the description of lovers' behavior is concerned, the greater part of these passages in the *Cort d'Amor* are based squarely on the earlier troubadour tradition. However, there are some exceptions: the pallor of the lover, for example, is an Ovidian theme. [10] The lover's pale face, or the sudden loss of color in the complexion, is specifically cited four times in the *Cort d'Amor* (ll. 461-462, 1204-1207, 1463-1466, 1521-1523). The idea of a lover's pallor is obviously very closely related to the notion of love as a sickness, a fever, a dangerous flood of emotion, *lo mal d'amor* which robs the individual of strength and 'color,' which is the outward sign of strength. In Ovid this sickness, whether honest or feigned, represents weakness arising from long unfulfilled and often violent desire. In the troubadour lyrics, the pale complexion and the image of sickness tend to represent sincere suffering in the service of love. In the first example in the *Cort d'Amor,* the lover is presenting his case (apparently for the first time) to his lady and his sincerity is demonstrated to her by the fact that *mudet tres colors en una ora,* first black, then red, then white (l. 457). It is the emotional strain of declaring his love, the hope of acceptance and the fear of rejection that cause his apparent illness. In the second example, it is the lady who sees her complexion turn pale, or rather 'ugly,' *after* having fallen in love, and she makes it clear that her lover is the cause of it: "Aqest mal hai haiut per vos" (l. 1208), yet she does not state specifically what he has done to cause it. Her complaint remains rather vaguely *lo mal d'amor.* Once again in the third example, as in the first, the lover's loss of color, representing fear or pain, and the blush, representing embarrassment, are purely involuntary and therefore reliable indications of sincerity. In both the first and third examples the lover's words have indicated his feelings and the change in his complexion is cited as supporting evidence of his honesty. In the fourth example, the subject is again the lady and in this case she appears to be quite unaware that she is in love although her unconscious pallor has betrayed her emotions. At first glance, the messenger remarks, one would suppose that she was sick, but upon closer scrutiny it is clear that she does not have a fever. To those aware of such signs and able from experience to interpret them, it becomes immediately obvious that she too is suffering from *lo mal*

---

[10] *Ars Amatoria* I, ll. 723-730.

d'amor, even if she is unaware of it. [11] It is interesting to note that
the last two examples occur within the same intrigue and that the
messenger is quite certain of the propriety and ultimate success of
her errand because she is convinced, by their pallor, of the sincerity
of the two lovers. Pallor, for Ovid, represents a disguise cultivated
by the lover in order to appear overcome with desire. For the troubadours and the author of the *Cort d'Amor,* who could very well
have noted the original image in the *Ars Amatoria,* the loss of color
is either an involuntary response to the beloved or an involuntary
manifestation of suffering, in either case, *lo mal d'amor.*

The erotic dream is yet another Ovidian motif that the Troubadours incorporated into their lyrics. There are two examples in
Ovid's *Heroides*: Laodamia's dream of Protesilaus and Sappho's dream
of Phaon. [12] Such dreams are experienced by lovers in the *Cort
d'Amor.* In the first example from the Occitan poem (ll. 939-954),
the lover is the awakened dreamer, and in the second (ll. 1181-1190),
it is the lady, although it is unfortunate that in the lady's case the
nature of her dream was omitted by the scribe. The possibility of
censorship is not remote but given the general tone of the *Cort
d'Amor,* it is far more likely that these lines were accidentally forgotten. Still one cannot help wondering exactly what it was the lady
was thinking that caused *li dous sospir* to wake her! In any case, in
this text it is most probable that her dreams were more like the chaste
fantasies of the lover in ll. 941-945, or the lonely dreams of Ovid's
Laodamia, than the erotic dream of Sappho.

In other aspects of the lover's behavior, no longer involuntary, but
now quite conscious, Ovid counsels the cultivation of the lady's servants, in order that they might be kindly disposed toward the suitor
or lover and thus influence their mistress. [13] In a nearly identical
passage (ll. 551-557) the author of the *Cort d'Amor* expresses the
same idea. In the lines immediately following his advice concerning
the courting and bribing of the servants, Ovid takes up the problem
of the gifts to be sent to the lady. [14] Curiously, the author of the
Cort d'Amor continues his passage with the same advice, although

---

[11] For *lo mal d'amor* cf. *Roman d'Enéas,* ll. 7955-8000.
[12] *Heroides* XIII, ll. 107-111 and XV, ll. 123-136.
[13] *Ars Amatoria* II, ll. 251-260.
[14] *Ibid.,* ll. 261-270.

the nature of the gifts differs: Ovid's gifts of birds, fruit and nuts are replaced in the medieval text by feudal emblems, sleeves, necklaces and rings, all of which were more normally bestowed by ladies upon their knightly admirers as love tokens to be worn into combat and tournaments. It seems obvious that these two instructions to the lover are not necessarily related, and the fact that both Ovid and the author of the Cort d'Amor take up the same two pieces of advice in the same order demonstrates more than coincidence.

Here it seems likely that our author had the text of the *Ars Amatoria* at least, either before his eyes or committed to memory. This is all the more probable because nowhere else in troubadour poetry do we find such advice. Although the troubadours and their ladies relied heavily on messengers (or *jongleurs*) in order to deliver their letters and songs, the messenger was usually a trusted friend or servant of the sender and under no circumstances was it ever a question of bribing the lady's servants. Furthermore, the troubadours were not ordinarily concerned with gifts except as tokens of love, never as a means of winning love, and as a general rule, the gifts were bestowed by the lady, not by the suitor who was normally limited to the performance of services. [15]

In the same vein but far more significantly Ovid gives specific advice in favor of the use of force in love. [16] Astonishingly enough, and contrary to all troubadour teaching, the author of the *Cort d'Amor* takes an identical position (ll. 576-584). It is perhaps ironic that this brutal advice is given by Lady Cortezia, but it is quite plain that such an attitude was almost universally rejected by the troubadours. There is only one extant poem in which the use of force is defended and that position, oddly, is taken by a lady, one of the *trobairitz* known only as Lady H., in a *tenso* with the troubadour Rofin. [17] Just as Lady H. and her defense of force are unique in the *corpus* of troubadour poetry, so, in the same way, lines 576-584 seem

---

[15] Cf. *Les Poésies du troubadour Raimon de Miraval*, ed. L. T. Topsfield (Paris: A. G. Nizet, 1971), p. 267, xxxii, "Cel que no vol auzir chanssos," ll. 9-13: "De la bella, don sui cochos, / Desir lo tenir e.l baiszar, / E.l jazer e.l plus conquistar, / Et après, mangas e cordas, / E del plus qe.il clames merces."

[16] *Ars Amatoria* I, ll. 663-666.

[17] Jules Véran, *Les Poétesses provençales du Moyen Âge et de nos jours* (Paris: Aristide Quillet, 1946), pp. 101-104.

unique in the *Cort d'Amor* and antithetical to the rest of the poem. One of the general themes of the *Cort d'Amor*, with the exception of these nine lines, is the submission of the lover to the lady's will, in order that he might merit her love, and in lines 525-538, the physical violation of the lady is expressly forbidden by *Cortezia*. She specifies in no uncertain terms that the lover may not ask the lady to go to bed with him — and here sexual consummation is implied — without debasing their love. Should such a thing happen, he will become vile and miserable and cease to behave like a knight and a gentleman. But, *Cortezia* continues, this does not mean that the *jazer*, the sensual meeting in bed (often with both individuals naked, probably the original intention of Lady H.'s domna: "E vol qu's quecs jur et pliva / Enanz que.ls voil ab si colgar / Que plus mas tener e baisar / No.lh faran," ll. 5-8), has been forbidden. The two keys to *Cortezia*'s discourse are *respeig*, respect (l. 533), and "li dara son bel don" (l. 534). Out of respect for her lover, his devotion, his service, and above all his obedience (i.e., his respect for her), she will give him her beautiful 'gift,' which is not necessarily her body in a sexual union, but is more likely the right to contemplate her naked body, or perhaps a kiss or an embrace ("l'aura entre sos bratz," l. 535), or in cases of ultimate reward, the right to spend the night ascetically in her bed. The important point, however, is the fact that the lady freely bestows her 'gift'; it is not wrested from her by force. The conclusion to this passage is absolutely unequivocal: "Aiso queron li drutz leial; / Qui pus en demanda fai mal" (ll. 537-538). An unsolvable problem arises, however, from the fact that it is Lady *Cortezia* who delivers both speeches, lines 525-538 forbidding violation and lines 576-584 encouraging it, both of them within the context of the same address.

Finally, it is relevant that this last and most curious evidence of Ovidian influence quite closely follows two previous examples: lines 551-557 on bribery, and lines 543-590 on gifts, and in fact the entire 47 lines from line 543 to line 590 have a distinctly Ovidian flavor that is quite separate from the general tone of the rest of the poem. In these lines *Cortezia* also advises the poor lover to pretend that he is rich "ab un petit de bel garnir" (l. 545), and the angry lover to avoid his lady so long as he is irritated and his manners are abrupt. She counsels the lover to listen to praise of his lady's husband and to remark in a self-serving way that the jealous husband can't be all that bad "qar dieus volc alte qu'es a voz" (l. 574). Everything in this passage conveys the Ovidian idea of pursuit with the lover as hunter and the lady as prey while the rest of the poem stresses instead the concepts of merit, value and humility, with both lover and lady striving for perfection in keeping their covenant once it has been made.

This is the only passage in the entire *Cort d'Amor* that strikes such a discordant note, and there are three possible explanations that come to mind. It may be a later insertion by another author, possibly by a scribe, who was more familiar with Ovid, or perhaps the original poet acknowledging the popularity of Ovid, might have included it in his text in order to broaden the appeal of his poem. On the other hand, perhaps we, as modern readers, are misunderstanding what the poet means to signify by "s'ill se suffre a forsar / Prenda son ioi ses demorar." Here the noun describing the act is *joi,* one of the key words in the troubadour ethic which signifies 'inspiration, enthusiasm, the game that requires heart and soul and body and mind' and which never signifies anything else. The poet did not use the words *gaug* or *jauzimen* which ordinarily signify 'joy' or 'enjoyment,' hence, 'plea-sure,' and therefore it may be that what takes place here is not, after all, the violation or rape that it first appears to be, but rather the *jazer* which is alluded to elsewhere in the text. It is the phrase "un petit de forsa" that is misleading since modern readers tend to equate the use of force with rape, particularly in a context such as this passage provides. I would suggest, however, that these lines should be read with both the Ovidian and the troubadour traditions in mind: the *joi* that is taken is not sexual consummation, but the rigors of the *jazer,* after which the suitor is accepted, not as a lover in the modern sense of the word, but as a trusted and intimate companion. The force that is used is not the violence we ordinarily connect with the crime of rape, but the insistence, the reiterated requests, the verbal pressures, the kisses and embraces that are typical of the troubadour-suitor and which do ultimately add up to a kind of force. It is pos-sible that our poet has taken the obvious Ovidian theme of force and adapted it, along with several other Ovidian themes, to the troubadour ethic.

Andreas Capellanus

The only other Latin work besides that of Ovid which had a demonstrable relationship to the *Cort d'Amor* is the medieval Latin love treatise of Andreas Capellanus, *De arte honesti amandi,* or *De Amore* as it is also known, written late in the twelfth century at the court of Troyes. By the thirteenth century, Andreas' work was well known, and the first French translation dates from the first half of the thirteenth century and comes from the neighborhood of Verona. The sole surviving manuscript of the translation of Douart la Vache was completed in 1290. [18] If the author of the *Cort d'Amor* knew the *Art of Love,* however, it is most likely that he knew the Latin text since the Occitan poem is probably earlier than most of the French translations.

It must be noted from the outset that Andreas was a Frenchman who did not have the advantage of being raised in the courtly atmosphere of Occitania. In Northern France, even at the court of Troyes under Marie of Champagne, the great-granddaughter of the first troubadour, the courtly tradition was an imported concept. Consequently Andreas' treatise represents a sort of compendium of love material, courtly or not, and it includes a good deal of non-courtly Ovid. It is entirely possible that Andreas and the author of the *Cort d'Amor* arrived at similar motifs independently by drawing on the same traditions. However there are enough points of coincidence to warrant a comparison.

It is primarily in Book I, Chapter VI, the fifth dialogue in which a nobleman speaks with a noblewoman, that similarities abound. The man, in attempting to convince the lady to accept him as a suitor, assures her that only those women who have enlisted in the classic 'army' of Love, "quae amoris noscuntur aggregari militae," [19] are worthy of praise in all the world's courts, and this reference is clearly drawn from Ovid's "militat omnis amans et habet sua castra Cupido." [20] However, the woman in her counter-argument, uses the more strictly medieval image of the court of Love, and here the literal sense of court is that of the place of judgment, or law court, which the lady in her hesitation compares to Hell. [21] The person who falls

---

[18] Andreas Capellanus, *The Art of Courtly Love,* translated with notes and introduction by John Jay Parry (New York: Ungar, 3rd. printing, 1970), p. 21.

[19] Andreas Capellanus, *Regii Francorum, De Amore, libri tres,* ed. E. Trojel (Munich: Eidos Verlag, reprint, 1964), Book I, VI, fifth dialogue, p. 86.

[20] *Amores* I, ix.

[21] *De Amore,* pp. 86-87.

in love does so easily and desires to remain so because love is pleasant. But love is simultaneously most unpleasant, for at all moments the lover risks displeasing or offending the beloved, risks accusation, examination, judgment, and condemnation, even rejection. The court or palace of Love may at any moment be transformed into a court of law with Love sitting in judgment. The lover has not the equal and opposite power of falling out of love, and so having once entered Love's court, he is powerless to escape Love's judgment and the pains of love, equal to those of Hell.

The *Cort d'Amor* is precisely this same court. Since no title is given in the manuscript, the Occitan poem has been arbitrarily assigned the title *Cort d'Amor* because that is the word used in the poem to describe the gathering of *Amor* and her barons: "Tota la cort estet en paz" (l. 126); "A tant es [Merce] a cort desendutz" (l. 737); "Tan rica cort no er iamais" (l. 858); "Sapchatz qe.l cortz en val mais" (l. 1075); "Eu no.m soj entremessa / Ad aqesta cortz de parlar" (ll. 1335-1336). The court is also referred to as *parlament*: "Qe cant Amors ten parlament, / No.s taing haza galiament" (ll. 27-28): "Aqi s'asis a parlament / Amors ..." (ll. 95-96; "E vi Merce venir corrent / Qe volg esser el parlament" (ll. 727-728). The legal, judicial nature of the court, as opposed to the legislative connotation of *parlament*, is emphasized by the fact that two major judgments are decided during the course of the day, one by Love herself, concerning the covetous (ll. 781-834), and the other by *Cortezia* at the request of *Fin'Amor*, concerning the proper nature of love (ll. 377-408). The judgment of *Cortezia* is not only pronounced but is written into a chart, signed by Love, sealed with her ring, and carefully stored away (ll. 409-420), perhaps in order to give it an air not only of legality but also of permanence.

Andreas' god of love pronounced judgments, too, but the court of love in *De Amore* is a place of punishment as well as a place of judgment. [22] Although the judgments of *Fin'Amor* and the god of love are different in nature, they are similar in style, and it is worthwhile to note that in both poems the sentences pronounced by the judge are judgments against women and do not include male transgressors.

The judgment theme is heavily reinforced in Andreas' second Book, Chapter VII, in which "various decisions in love cases" are

---

[22] *Ibid.*, pp. 76-77.

reported. Here twenty-one different examples of love quarrels requiring arbitration are cited, and in each case the judge pronouncing the court's decision is a woman or group of women:

> Countess Mary of Champagne (cases I, III, IV, V, XIV, XVI, XXI)
>
> Lady Ermengarde of Narbonne (cases VIII, IX, XI, XV)
>
> Queen Eleanor (cases II, VI, VII)
>
> Adele of Champagne, queen of France (cases XVII, XIX, XX)
>
> a court of ladies in Gascony (case (XVIII)

It is this series of judgments that more closely resembles the judgment of *Cortezia* and *Fin'Amor*. The judgments reported by Andreas involve specific cases which require specific decisions, although they may serve as general precedents in later cases. In case XVII, for example, Queen Adele refers to an earlier decision by the Countess of Champagne against love between husband and wife. In the same way, the first eleven judgments pronounced by *Fin'Amors* often refer to specific cases and are clearly intended to set precedents. More to the point, however, the woman as arbitrator and judge in matters of love is a literary tradition summarized in these pages by Andreas and obviously continued by the *Cort d'Amor*.

More concretely however, Andreas gives a rather detailed description of the palace of Love which is symbolically distinct from the workings of the court, just as the palace of *Fin'Amor* is separate from her *parlament*, the first referring to the static location, the second to the function of her court. In Andreas' text, the palace is first mentioned by the man. [23] The woman admits that allegorically this description is too obscure for her. Her suitor explains the allegory of the gates and continues with a description of his personal encounter with the god of love and his own impressions of the garden of *amoenitas* where the god and his queen live. [24] The castle [25] of the god of

---

[23] *Ibid.*, p. 73.

[24] *Ibid.*

[25] Concerning the allegory of the edifice, cf. O. Dammann, *Die Allegorische Canzone des Guiraut de Calanso "A lieis cui am de cor e de saber" und ihre Deutung*, Diss. (Breslau, 1891), pp. 11-29, and Roberta D. Cornelius, *The*

love stands in the middle of the world, *in medio mundi*, and *Fin'Amor*, too, has her castle near the center of the known world on Mount Parnassus. The god's throne is located under a tree in the center of a meadow, "in prima igitur et interiori parte in medio loci," and *Fin'Amor* has built her castle in the center (on the top?) of the mountain, "Ze.l mei loc ac un castel" (1. 71). [26] Both castles are surrounded by gardens or orchards, and both gardens have a marvellous fountain. [27] The fire of love is found in the vicinity of the palace in both cases. For Andreas, the fiery ray comes from the East and is obviously related to the sun. In the *Cort d'Amor* the fire of love (ll. 52-54, 853-855) is an equally symbolic, unrealistic flame. Both the god of love and *Fin'Amor* are surrounded by beautiful blissful lovers, and both the god of love and *Fin'Amor* have jongleurs and music in their palaces which is, of course, quite typical of medieval nobles. Finally, both individuals are referred to as the "King who rules the world." [28] It is important, however, to remember that Andreas Capellanus is describing the god of love, a masculine deity who represents Love, while the author of the *Cort d'Amor* is describing Love herself, "Amor la dousa et la bona" (1. 30). Andreas god is first seen wearing his crown, and *Fin'Amor* is crowned early in the sequence of events (ll. 835-866). Both have power and dominion, even habits and manners comparable to that of earthly kings, but they remain supernatural rulers of the world, "second only to Christ," and they are not in themselves mortal rulers of terrestrial kingdoms. The Latin text remains closer in this respect to the Ovidian conception of Cupid, while the Occitan personification springs from the troubadour tradition of the female *Fin'Amor*. It is apparent, however, that the

---

Figurative Castle, a Study in the Medieval Allegory of the Edifice with Especial Reference to Religious Writings, Diss. (Bryn Mawr, 1930), *passim.*

[26] Angus Fletcher, in his study: *Allegory, The Theory of a Symbolic Mode* (Ithaca, New York: Cornell University Press, 1964), p. 210, remarked that "There are, for example, sacred places which are free of contagion.... These uncontaminated places can be of several kinds, their main claim to sacred value residing in their supposed centrality to a given universe."

[27] D. W. Robertson, Jr. in his *A Preface to Chaucer, Studies in Medieval Perspectives* (Princeton, New Jersey: Princeton University Press, 1962), p. 386, explained that "There are significant gardens in works of all kinds — in saints' legends, in ribald comedies like the *Miles Gloriosus*, in fabliaux, in romances, and so on. And most of them reflect in one way or another, the gardens of the Bible...."

[28] *De Amore*, p. 77; in the *Cort d'Amor*, ll. 95-98, 837-842.

Cort d'Amor and certain passages of Andreas' *De Amore* bear a certain fairly extensive resemblance to each other, which implies, if not direct contact, at least a common tradition.

Other Latin sources

There is one minor Latin source (or possibly two) used by the Occitan author in the composition of his poem: the fable of the ant and the lion (ll. 107-116) and the fable of the stag at the fountain (ll. 1663-1669). The first, although it is attributed in the text to a certain *Iohanitz,* has proved impossible to trace. Léopold Hervieux in his compendium of Latin fabulists [29] includes the fables of a thirteenth century fabulist known as Johannes de Capua, who in 1280 translated some Indian fables into Latin. [30] Unfortunately the list of his fables does not include the story of an ant and a lion. However, one of the fables related by Johannes in his second chapter, that of the lion and the bull, bears some resemblance to the theme of the fable of the lion and the ant cited by *Fin'Amor*: false denunciations lead to the separation of friends. In this fable the lion has taken the bull, Senesba, as his favorite, elevating him in the court and conferring the highest dignities upon him. Soon, however, deceived by the traitor Dimna's clever accusations, the lion believed Senesba guilty of treason and had him executed, only to regret it deeply afterwards. The similarity in the theme and the similarity in the names of the fabulists, Iohanitz-Johannes, argue that perhaps this is the source of the fable, and that it was only incompletely remembered by the author of the *Cort d'Amor.* This, nonetheless, remains conjecture, since the date of the *Directorium* of Johannes is 1280, which is certainly too late for the *Cort d'Amor,* and thus Iohanitz remains impossible to identify at this point.

Hervieux lists another fabulist, Johannis de Schepeya, [31] among whose stories one does find the well-known Aesopic fable of the stag at the fountain, but the translator, an English bishop, died in 1360, which is much too late for the *Cort d'Amor.* This fable is certainly

---

[29] Léopold Hervieux, *Les Fabulistes latins depuis le siècle d'Auguste jusqu'à la fin du Moyen Age,* 5 vols. (Paris: 1883, 2nd edition, 1893-1899; 2nd. edition Burt Franklin reprint, n.d.).

[30] *Ibid.,* V, pp. 1-167.

[31] *Ibid.,* IV, pp. 417-450.

Greek in origin, and not Indian as the first may be, and can be found
in numerous other collections of fables including the *Isopet* of Char-
tres, no. 30, and *Isopet* II of Paris, no. 32. [32] However, it remains
impossible to know whether or not the author of the *Cort d'Amor*
encountered these fables in Latin, or in one of the Romance languages
or whether he read them himself or simply heard them recited. The
latter is entirely possible since the troubadour Guilhem de Montanhagol, a troubadour of the first half of the thirteenth century, devotes
one strophe of a lyric poem to this same fable. [33]

Taking into account the relatively high correlation between the
themes and motifs of the *Cort d'Amor* and those found in the love
treatises of Ovid and Andreas Capellanus, as well as a certain fami-
liarity with fables that appeared first in Western Europe in Latin
versions, it is quite probable that the author of the *Cort d'Amor* was
a cleric, or that he had had formal, probably clerical, training and
could read Latin. It has long been evident, even from only a super-
ficial reading of the troubadour biographies preserved in the *vidas,*
that many of the troubadours were well educated and probably read
Latin. [34] We must imagine that Ovid, and later Andreas Capellanus,
were read in Latin by at least some of the troubadours, possibly by
our author as well, and that they were as passionately discussed and
at least as well known as the Church Fathers, if not better.

IV. Sources of the Cort d'Amor: Old French Influences

A more complicated problem is presented by the Old French
sources of the *Cort d'Amor*. Whether our author knew French or
French poetry at first hand is difficult to judge with any degree

---

[32] Julia Bastin, *Recueil Général des Isopets,* SATF (Paris: Champion,
1929-1930), 2 vols.

[33] *Les Poésies de Guilhem de Montanhagol, troubadour provençal du
XIIIe siècle,* ed. P. T. Ricketts (Toronto: Pontifical Institute of Mediaeval
Studies, 1964), pp. 93-98, ix, "Non estarai, per ome qe.m casti," strophe v,
ll. 37-45.

[34] *Les Biographies des Troubadours, Textes provençaux des XIIIe et
XIVe siècles.* eds. J. Boutière and A.-H. Schutz, édition refondue par Jean
Boutière (Paris: Nizet, 1964). Cf. in particular the *vidas* of Guiraut de Bor-
neilh, Arnaut de Mareuil, Uc Brunet, Gui d'Uisel, Daude de Pradas, Uc de
Saint Circ, Peire d'Alvernha, the Monk of Montaudon, Folquet de Marseille,
and Peire Cardenal.

of certainty. It would not, in any event, be impossible since in the latter half of the twelfth century Marseille was the port of embarkation used by those Frenchmen participating in the crusades in the Holy Land, and they and their armies had necessarily to cross large portions of Occitania in order to reach that port. It is more likely, though, that Occitan seigneurs, soldiers and singers encountered French literature far from France, in the Holy Land itself, during the various crusades in which they too took part. It is not in the least unusual to find in the troubadour *vidas* and *razos*, that one or another poet took up the cross and passed *outra mar*. [35] There, the Occitan crusaders must have come into close contact with the French songs and romances of the time although this contact must have been more often oral than written.

Furthermore, we learn from the *razos* that French jongleurs did perform in the South:

> En aqest temps vengeron dos joglars de
> Franza en la cort del marqes [of Montferrat]. . . . [36]

These jongleurs played a *stampida* on the viola, and Raimbaut de Vaqueiras was persuaded to compose in Occitan a *stampida* based on their French melody. It is very likely, given the Southern cultivation of the virtue of largess, that these two were not the only performers to travel south.

On the other hand, troubadours were, naturally and by profession, a travelling sort, accustomed *anar per cortz*, and it is not surprising to find them in French courts. When Alienor of Aquitaine moved north to join first one husband (French) and then the other (Angevin), she moved substantial portions of her court with her, and opened the way for increased literary communication between Occitania and France. Very likely Bernart de Ventadorn visited France in her retinue, and could have even visited Troyes while Chrétien and the chaplain Andreas were living there. There is, therefore, a considerable likelihood that Occitan poets knew French poetry rather well.

Where Old French literature is concerned, as in the Latin tradition, numerous works contributed to the development of the love treatises and allegories, and together these works contributed to the

---

[35] *Ibid.*, pp. 185, 311, 465.
[36] *Ibid.*, p. 465.

general literary atmosphere of early thirteenth century France with which our author, as a learned man, was probably quite familiar. Among these works are the various versions of the love debate, elaborations on the story of Floire and Blanchefleur [37] from the twelfth century; a discussion between two lovers overheard by a narrator, "Le donnei des amants" [38] from the same period; *Li Fablel dou Dieu d'Amour* [39] a short time later; "Comment l'amant doit donner," [40] a fragment from a lost art of love from the early thirteenth century; the *Lai de l'Oiselet* [41] from the same period in which a little bird lists the rules of love; and "Dou vrai chiment d'amours," [42] an early thirteenth century art of love, one of the sources of the love allegory *De Venus la Déesse d'amour*. [43] Each of these poems, either allegory or art of love, more often both, has certain elements in common with the *Cort d'Amor*: the garden of love with springtime greenery and flowers, often with a fountain, the personification of love as god or goddess, a discussion of the nature of true love, a judgment delivered in a specific case, and often certain elements of magic or the marvellous. Nonetheless, it is impossible to demonstrate that any one of these poems was specifically known to the author of the *Cort d'Amor*. It cannot be proven that he knew them and yet it is undeniable that he certainly knew poems very like them from which he borrowed these motifs.

Similarly, as Marc-René Jung pointed out, [44] the quasi-allegorical passages in the great romances inspired by the Greek and Latin classics, and composed and circulated in the late twelfth century, the monologue in dialogue form, and the allegorical personification of mythological figure, served to prepare the literary atmosphere for the *Roman de la Rose*. [45]

---

[37] Charles Oulmont, *Les Débats du Clerc et du Chevalier, op. cit.* Cf. also *Le Jugement d'amour ou Florance et Blanchefleur*, ed. M. Delbouille (Paris: 1937).

[38] Ed. G. Paris, in: *Romania*, 25 (1885), pp. 497-541.

[39] Ed. A. Jubinal (Paris: 1834), and I. C. Lecompte, in: *Modern Philology*, 8 (1910-1911), pp. 63-86.

[40] J. Morawski, "Fragment d'un art d'aimer perdu," *Romania*, 48 (1922), pp. 431-436.

[41] Ed. G. Paris, in: *Légendes du Moyen Âge* (Paris: 1912), pp. 274-291.

[42] Ed. A. Langfors, in: *Romania*, 45 (1918-1919), pp. 205-219.

[43] Ed. W. Foerster (Bonn: 1880).

[44] *Etudes sur le poème allégorique*, pp. 170-191.

[45] *Ibid.*, pp. 171-172.

Jung also points out that Chrétien de Troyes, during this same period or only a short time after, uses the same sort of monologue-dialogue in which Love is personified. *Li Deus d'Amors* himself appears in Yvain (l. 5371), but Jung notes that "partout, ailleurs, Amors est du féminin, même si elle (ou: il) se comporte comme un chevalier errant (ll. 1382, 6035, 6041)." [46] Thus the personification of Love, parallel but nonetheless distinct from the classical concept of Cupid, is established early in the medieval tradition of the romance, ca. 1160, at least as early as any extant lyric in a Romance language. In the romance, Love may be either male or female, either a personified "force," a "power," an "active abstraction," or the god (or goddess) of Love, a character able to take part and influence events.

Besides these works, which are probably only very indirect sources, the Old French material falls naturally into two more categories: those works that the author mentions but knew apparently only by reputation, and those works he probably knew well and may have read. The first category includes those works whose characters are mentioned by the author as examples of a specific type or situation, but which apparently had no other influence on his work. It is still possible in these cases that the Occitan author had read them and knew them very well, but this simply cannot be proven by reference to the *Cort d'Amor*. This category remains therefore a list of those works that are merely mentioned, directly or indirectly, and from which nothing else is borrowed, literary influence being impossible to demonstrate. The latter category includes those works whose influence can be demonstrated by comparison of themes, metaphors, phrases, style, etc., and which are truly sources of the *Cort d'Amor*.

There are in our poem several examples of Old French works that could be classified in the first category, the first two examples occuring together early in the text. The lady assures her lover thus:

> S'ieu ren vaill, so es per vos,
> Q'anch Galvains ni Sordamors,
> Ni anch Floris ni Blanchaflors,
> Ni l'amors Ysolt ni Tristan,
> Contra nos dos non valg un gan.
>
> (ll. 314-319)

---

[46] *Ibid.*, p. 185.

It will be demonstrated below that the Old French romance of *Floire et Blanchefleur* may have influenced the author of the *Cort d'Amor* considerably and that he probably knew it quite well. It is the reference to the other couples that probably falls into our first category, and it is the first of these couples, Galvains and Soredamors, that is rather disturbing. The lady, listing three of the most famous pairs of faithful lovers in medieval lore in order to compare them unfavorably to her lover and herself, has included a brother and sister! Soredamors is the sister of Sir Gauvain in Chrétien de Troyes' Arthurian romance *Cligès* (1176). In reality the love affairs in that story are first that of Soredamors and Alexander and later that of their son Cligès and Fénice. That this story was well known in Occitania in the middle of the thirteenth century is demonstrated by references to it in the slightly later poems *Jaufre* [47] and *Flamenca,* [48] but it is most unlikely that our author had any first hand acquaintance with it, since a direct knowledge of the story of Soredamors would automatically prohibit her name from being linked in a love context with that of Gauvain, her brother. It is not likely that our author simply knew another (perhaps Southern) version of this story since Chrétien appears to have invented this particular sister of Gauvain himself. [49]

Like Soredamors and Gauvain, but far less shocking, it is evident that Tristan and Ysolt as well are cited only as a well known example of a famous couple, for there is nothing in the *Cort d'Amor* to indicate borrowing from or influence by this Celtic romance. Rather it seems from the numerous references by the troubadours to Tristan and Yseult [50] that they are simply a motif common throughout the lyric tradition of the troubadours and that the motif has been transferred into the Occitan narrative tradition by way of the Occitan lyric. It is entirely possible that our author knew the story indirectly, that he had heard some version of it recited, or that he had read it himself, but it is evident from his Occitan text that he did not allow it to influence his own composition.

---

[47] Lines 7609-7612.

[48] Lines 677-678.

[49] Cf. Madelaine Blaess, "Arthur's sisters," *International Arthurian Society Bibliographical Bulletin,* 8 (1956), pp. 69-77.

[50] Cf. F.-G.-M. Raynouard, *Choix des poésies originales des troubadours* (Paris: Didot, 1817), II, pp. 312-316.

In precisely the same way, Aia and Landric, the presumed heroine and lover of an Occitan *chanson de geste* which is now lost, are cited as an example of perfect lovers. The lady is urged by her messenger "Amatz lo mais c'Aia Landric" (1. 1518), and at least three troubadours have mentioned this couple in exactly the same context. [51] It is therefore quite possible that this couple also entered Occitan *novas* as a motif by way of the lyric, and that it entered the lyric by way of the *chanson de geste*! This particular reference is part of the Old Occitan tradition rather than Old French and, unfortunately, the original poem being lost, it is impossible to trace with any precision. Numerous interesting hypotheses have been proposed on this subject but until the present they remain unsubstantiated by any text.

The last of the direct references in the *Cort d'Amor* concerns Marcoul and Salomon (ll. 988-999), characters from a twelfth century collection of proverbs: *Les Dits de Marcoul et de Salomon*. It has been pointed out that Salomon represents the moralist and Marcoul the parodist, [52] but Constans noted that here the roles are reversed, "et l'attaque est attribuée à Marcoul (Marcon)." [53] It is possible, however, that this passage is not necessarily intended to be construed in that manner, for here the part played by Marcon is not viewed as clever and amusing; the satiric parodist who resolves the enigmas of Salomon and proposes others is not applauded. The righteous lover has no choice but to play the part of Salomon (the wise moralist) since the gossips insist on playing the part of Marcon (the licentious satirist). In Occitania, at least, the reader or audience approved and identified with Salomon, while in France they apparently approved and identified with Marcoul, hence what appears to Constans as a reversal of the roles. Nevertheless, the general scarcity of proverbs in the *Cort d'Amor* leads one to believe that, once again, the reference in question is simply a well known and popular literary motif.

Floire et Blanchefleur

The romance of Floire and Blanchefleur, on the other hand, is not only cited in the *Cort d'Amor* (ll. 316-319), but also in the lyrics

---

[51] Cf. Translation Note to l. 1518, pp. 220-221 below.

[52] *Histoire de la littérature française*, 23 (1895), pp. 688-689.

[53] L. Constans, "Les manuscrits provençaux de Cheltenham," *Romania*, 20 (1888), p. 215, note I.

of at least five troubadours of the golden age,[54] and in the romance of
Jaufre.[55] It is entirely possible that the story of Floire and Blanchefleur was so well known by the thirteenth century that all memories
of the French version were forgotten, and that it circulated orally in
Occitan, and not in Old French. Nonetheless, the French version is
the only one that has survived, and it is still possible to trace certain
similarities between it and the *Cort d'Amor*.

There are, first of all, two small, nearly insignificant details: the
author of the *Cort d'Amor* writes of "viij.xx. que donas qe pulsellas"
(1. 23) exactly as the author of *Floire et Blanchefleur* writes: "En
ma tour avec mes puceles, / Ou il en a sept vinz de beles, / A honeur
servir la feisoie."

This viij.xx. is the earliest attestation of the system of counting
by twenties to be found in the South,[56] and it could easily have been
borrowed from the story of *Floire et Blanchefleur*. In a similar way,
the Occitan author seems to have borrowed the notion of 'pretty as
a picture' ("Bella borsa, bella centure / Com s'era tot fait en pein-
ture, ll. 677-678), from ll. 2650-2651 and ll. 2668-2669 of *Floire et
Blanchefleur*:

> Les narilles avoit mielz fetes
> Que s'il fussent as mains portretes.

> De cors est ele tant bien fete
> Con s'ele fust as mains portretes.

Furthermore, the poet's description of Babylon, an exotic, oriental,
and slightly unreal city, resembles our author's account of *Fin'Amor*'s
castle on Mount Parnassus. As in Andreas' *Amoenitas,* and the *Cort
d'Amor,* the emir's castle is located in the center of the city:

> El mileu de ceste cité
> A une tor d'antiquité.[57]

The walls of *Fin'Amor*'s castle and the walls surrounding the emir's
garden are of gold and azur:

---

[54] Raynouard, *Choix,* II, pp. 304-305: the Countess of Die, Arnaut de
Mareuil, Folquet de Romans, Aimeri de Belenoi, and Gaucelm Faidit.
[55] Lines 7599-7604.
[56] *FEW,* XIV, pp. 444-445.
[57] *Floire et Blanchefleur,* ll. 1623-1624.

> Qe non ha una peira e.l mur
> Non luisza con d'aur o d'azur.
>
> (ll. 73-74)
>
> De toutes parz est clos a mur
> Tout paint a or et a azur. [58]

This similarity could be explained perhaps by the artist's search for a word denoting a color or precious stone that rhymes with *mur*: *azur*. Still the gardens themselves bear certain resemblances to each other. Each garden contains fantastic birds: the Occitan birds mingle with flowers and instruments and sing all the songs there are in the world (ll. 67-70, 860-862, 1062-1064), while the song of the French birds is so sweet that it charms wild beasts and makes men dream of love (ll. 1750-1765). In addition, both gardens contain marvellous trees and flowers: *Fin'Amor*'s flowers are her loyal subjects, strewn on her path (ll. 42-50), perfuming her bed (ll. 55-58), decorating her crown (ll. 91-94), and in the excess of extreme joy produced by her coronation, they even detach themselves from their earth-bound stems and roots in order to become mobile and to leap toward her face (ll. 847-852). Rather ambiguously, all the flowers in the world "do what they can to honor her." Rarely do we think of flowers 'doing' anything besides growing, blooming, and dying, and it could be that that is exactly what the author means: the very existence of the flowers is in honor of *Fin'Amor*. Yet it is impossible to ignore those flowers that leapt for joy and the trees that ran to meet their lady and to bow before her at her coronation, for they truly are in the realm of the marvellous. More practically, the wealth of Love is measured in flowers: they are the *joias q'hom no vent* (ll. 1581-1587), which are not kept for money, but only for delight and pleasure and which are the proper currency of Love, who keeps them in her treasury. Since flowers are abundant nearly everywhere, the whole world becomes the treasury of Love.

In *Floire et Blanchefleur* the trees, flowers, and particularly the spices in the emir's garden are marvellous mainly by their quantity and variety (ll. 1780-1793), but the emir's garden also contains the very exotic *arbre d'amours* (ll. 1804-1819). It is this tree which, through enchantment, will help the emir choose his next bride by allowing one of its flowers to fall upon the most beautiful maiden

---

[58] *Ibid.*, ll. 1748-1749.

(ll. 1836-1851). There is little indication, however, that *Fin'Amor*'s running, bowing trees and leaping flowers are in any way directly inspired by the emir's *arbre d'amours,* unless, perhaps, the Occitan author was encouraged by it to give his imagination free rein.

The magic fountains in the two poems are slightly more similar. *Fin'Amor*'s fountain is especially exotic for it is caught in a golden shell, flows and ceases according to mysterious laws, and has a most magical and salutory effect on any man who drinks from it (ll. 83-90, 843-846). It does not seem to affect women, whereas the emir's fountain decidedly reacts only to women, or rather to maidens, separating the virgins from the others by changing the color of its waters (ll. 1800-1803, 1820-1833).

Finally, both gardens are compared to Paradise. *Fin'Amor* is surrounded by the apple trees of the Biblical Paradise (ll. 91-92), and she orders the chart containing her judgment, once it has been signed and sealed, placed in her vaults located in the Earthly Paradise (l. 416). The Earthly Paradise then, would be located in the vicinity of Mount Parnassus (ll. 40-41), in Greece, north of Delphi. In this case, our author is either ignorant of the geography of the eastern Mediterranean, which is unlikely since the crusades in the Holy Land had familiarized a good number of western Europeans with that area, or he is indulging in a bit of poetic licence. It was assumed throughout the Christian Middle Ages that the Earthly Paradise, the Garden of Eden, was located in the Holy Land itself, although, of course, its specific location was lost. Our medieval author avoids the blasphemy of actually placing *Fin'Amor*'s court and garden in the Biblical Eden by transporting them to Greece. His choice of Mount Parnassus as the site is a logical one because that mountain has always been a magic place, the home of various deities, sacred first to Dionysius, with shrines to the Corycian nymphs and Pan, later to Apollo. Under the Roman poets it was the home of the Muses, and the role of *Fin'Amor* as inspirer of poets could easily lead to an identification between her and the Muses, and then to a natural assumption that she lived on Mount Parnassus in the Muses' traditional home. Ovid's Venus lived on Mount Parnassus as well, and consequently it is the appropriate home of *Fin'Amor*.

The identification of the *vergier d'amour* with the Biblical Earthly Paradise developed in a slightly different way. Charles Oulmont in

his study of the *Débats du Clerc et du Chevalier,*[59] explained how
the concepts of the Garden of Eden in *Genesis,* home of the first
couple, the garden in the *Song of Songs,* scene of the lover's meeting
and their hymn to love, and the depiction of the celestial Jerusalem
in *Revelations,* appealed to the imagination of the Middle Ages, and
how medieval poets combined elements of each in order to arrive
finally at the landscape of the profane but still mysterious garden
of Love.

In *Floire et Blanchefleur,* because the location of the garden and
the castle is the city of Babylon, east of Jerusalem in the Mesopota-
mian Valley, the author may be correct without the risk of blasphemy
(ll. 1766-1771). He does not state that the emir's garden is Paradise,
only that one of the rivers of Paradise, the Euphrates, runs through
it. With this allusion he implies that the emir's garden resembles
Eden by sheer proximity, and by the fact that it is watered by one
of Eden's rivers. This identification with the Biblical Paradise is encouraged by the poet's assertion that the emir's garden contains all
possible varieties of fruit, flowers, trees, birds, and spices (ll. 1792-
1799). This may not be Paradise, but anyone who entered the garden
would believe that it was!

The concept of a lover's paradise, a garden of Love, is a natural
enough development, and the Occitan poet did not have to read or
hear a French poem in order to discover it. However, outside of
the *alba,* the troubadours do not insist on the *vergier d'amour,* and the
author does mention Floris and Blancaflor in his own poem. It is
therefore very possible that the author of the *Cort d'Amor* really did
know the story of *Floire et Blanchefleur* in a version very like the
one that has survived in Old French, and that he was inspired by
it in certain instances. Once again, as with the influence of Chrétien
de Troyes, all the evidence is more or less circumstantial, although
in this case there is a good deal more of it, and none of the evidence
is specific enough to warrant a conclusive assertion that *Floire et
Blanchefleur* is a direct source of the *Cort d'Amor.* Rather we must
assume that our author could have known all of these works in one
version or another, that he probably did, and that he may have drawn
on all of them for his inspiration, modifying whatever he borrowed
and changing it to suit his own poetic vision.

---

[59] pp. 6-12.

V. OCCITAN LYRIC SOURCES

By far the largest number of direct sources of the *Cort d'Amor* are to be found in the troubadour poetry of the twelfth and early thirteenth centuries. There will be no attempt here to explore the origins of the troubadour lyric, for there is little doubt that the Occitan lyrics themselves were the sources from which our author drew much of his inspiration, and it is most probable that he was himself unaware of the specific sources of the motifs he borrowed. The Occitan lyrics consisted of songs whose topic or subject was very often, though not necessarily, love. The troubadours had a tendency, however, to inject the philosophy and the vocabulary of their love ethic into all of their poetry, even their satires and their political songs. [60] Since the subject of a love song is normally the sense of joy or suffering which the poet wishes to communicate either to his beloved or to the world at large, together with his reasons for feeling as he does, almost all troubadour poetry is in some sense didactic, and nearly all love songs are to a certain extent, arts of love: "Do as I have done and rejoice," or "Do not do as I have done and thereby avoid misery." Although the troubadours themselves, from beginning to end, were, in a typically medieval way, continually probing, analyzing, and defining the realm of *Fin'Amor*, of necessity each poet viewed it with a different and highly personal attitude, and this accounts for the wide diversity of depictions. Rarely is the poetry of two troubadours indistinguishable, one from the other. Some troubadours, like Marcabru, lean more heavily toward the moralistic and didactic vein, while others, like Bernart de Ventadorn, tend toward the pure song of joy or suffering, and the examination of private emotions. By the first quarter of the thirteenth century, perhaps in conjunction with the rise of scholasticism, perhaps as a result of the invasion of their territory by the crusading French and the subsequent threat to their institutions, troubadour poetry assumed an even more didactic tone, lamenting the passing of the golden years of

---

[60] Cf. *Poésies complètes du troubadour Peire Cardenal (1180-1278)*, ed. René Lavaud (Toulouse: Privat, 1957), pp. 62-68, "Ben volgra, si Dieus o volgues," ll. 31-40. For additional political songs, see also the poetry of Bertran de Born, *Poésies complètes de Bertran de Born,* ed. A. Thomas (Toulouse: Privat, 1888).

cortezia and poetry, and teaching the precepts of *Fin'Amor* to those for whom they were foreign concepts. This didactic tendency reached a culminating point with Guilhem de Montanhagol, where, in a frequently quoted passage, [61] he forbids sexual indulgence and defends love as a source of chastity. [62] As a result, the troubadour poetry as a whole forms a most substantial art of love, which is surprisingly consistent, with only a very small number of nonconformists. [63] This process, by which troubadour poetry becomes more and more defensive and didactic, will continue until the fourteenth century when Matfré Ermengaut will publish his *Breviari d'Amor*, a compendium of all the troubadour motifs and themes, an art of love *par excellence*. [64]

In addition to art of love, troubadour poetry frequently involves personification of abstract ideas to such an extent that it continually verges on allegory. Jean Pépin has noted that allegory is fundamentally a function of language which, by its very defects, is allegorical. [65] Ironically, the innately allegorical medium of language is used to construct an allegorical tale in which the tale itself represents something else.

One of the first, and also one of the simplest intentional allegories to appear in literature through the conscious use of the ambiguity and versatility of language is the personification of abstract ideas. Marc-René Jung notes that "l'origine des personnifications est double; elle se trouve ou dans la langue même, ou alors dans la tradition littéraire. C'est un fait linguistique que l'abstraction a tendance à se rendre indépendante du sujet parlant, à s'animer." [66] He links this tendency to the lyric poem: "La poésie lyrique, enfin, est pleine d'abstractions personnifiées, peu variées, cependant; elle est en outre empreinte de formules traditionnelles et de situations topiques qui

---

[61] Cf. Joseph Anglade, *Histoire sommaire de la littérature méridionale au moyen âge (des origines à la fin du XVe siècle)*, (Paris: Editions de Boccard, 1921), p. 91.

[62] *Ed. cit.*, p. 122, xii, "Ar ab lo coinde pascor," ll. 11-20.

[63] Among the very few nonconformists we would have to place Lady H., cited above, who defended the use of force in love.

[64] *Le Breviari d'Amour de Matfré Ermengau*, ed. G. Azais, 2 vols. (Paris: 1862).

[65] *Mythe et allégorie. Les origines grecques et les contestations judéo-chrétiennes* (Aubier: Editions Montaigne, 1958), p. 47.

[66] *Etudes sur le poème allégorique*, p. 21.

reflètent un haut degré d'abstraction. Le climat de généralité dans lequel baignent les poèmes allégoriques est déjà tout entier dans la poésie lyrique." [67] This use of personification is most vividly illustrated in the lyric *Psychomachia* of Peire Cardenal:

> Falsedatz e desmezura
> An batailla empreza
> Ab vertat e ab drechura
> E vens la falseza.
> E deslialtatz si jura
> Contra lialeza,
> E avaretatz s'atura
> Encontra largueza;
> Feunia vens amor
> E malvestatz valor,
> E peccatz cassa sanctor
> E baratz simpleza. [68]

Peire Cardenal, of course, is a troubadour of the thirteenth century, probably even a contemporary of the author of the *Cort d'Amor,* but allegorical personifications appear in the poetry of even the earliest troubadours. [69] In a poem by Marcabru, for example, the allegory of the battle between personified vices and virtues, another replica of the *Psychomachia* of Prudentius, melts into the metaphor of Prowess, a mighty bird that has been destroyed, of which only beak and claw and wing remain, and from this metaphor develops a wish that these remnants be preserved by the defenders for "from a small sapling, a mighty branch will grow if it is given proper care." [70] Although the first two strophes do introduce an acceptable allegory in a traditional form, the third strophe reduces it all to a bundle of mixed metaphors, thus suggesting that, in composition, troubadour poetry probably follows the thematic development of the great oral epics, [71] and not the

---

[67] *Ibid.,* p. 19.

[68] *Ed. cit.,* p. 78, xvii, "Falsedatz e desmezura," ll. 1-12.

[69] Cf. Charles Camproux, "Faray un vers *tot* covinen," *Mélanges de langue et de littérature du moyen âge et de la renaissance offerts à Jean Frappier* (Geneva: Droz, 1970), I, pp. 159-176. Professor Camproux explores the allegory of the two "dames-chevaux" in this poem by Guilhem IX.

[70] *Poésies complètes du troubadour Marcabru,* ed. J.-M. L. Dejeanne (Toulouse: Privat, 1909), XI "Belh m'es quan la rana chanta," ll. 9-32.

[71] Albert B. Lord, *The Singer of Tales* (Cambridge, Massachusetts: Harvard University Press, 1960).

orderly development of related metaphorical images typical of the more
modern concept of a lyric poem. The little allegory in the two strophes by Marcabru was lightly abandoned when an unrelated image
in a similar, related theme came to the poet's mind. These partial,
usually undeveloped allegories abound in troubadour lyric poetry.

The personification of *fin'amor* and certain aspects of it as well
as the personification of concepts opposed to it, which we find also
in the *Cort d'Amor,* spring from the Occitan language and the troubadour lyric tradition. Admittedly some of the troubadour poets tend
more often in the direction of personification and allegory than others.
Of the twenty-five lyric poems of Arnaut de Mareuil, [72] twenty-one
poems contain one or more personifications with a total of nineteen
different personifications: *Amors, Merces, Chauzimens, Ensenhamens,
Pretz, Cortezia, Honor, Jois, Orguelh, Car Tener, Humilitatz, Razos,
Jovens, Solatz, Gaiesa, Gailhardia, Paratges, Franqueza,* and *Natura.*
Love herself is personified in twenty different poems by Arnaut. Ten
of Daude de Pradas' seventeen lyric poems [73] involve thirteen different
personifications: *Natura, Amor, Merce, Razos, Humilitatz, Bels Jois
Novels, Pretz, Valors, Bel Desir, Beltat, Joven, Fals Conselh,* and *Mals
Aips.* Most frequently of course, it is again Love who is the favorite
personification for she appears in seven poems. The poem by Peire
Cardenal cited above contains seventeen personifications in the first
strophe alone: *Falsedatz, Desmezura, Vertat, Drechura, Falseza, Des-
lialtatz, Lialeza, Avaretatz, Largueza, Feunia, Amor, Malvestatz, Valor, Peccatz, Sanctor, Baratz,* and *Simpleza.*

Of the twelve "barons" cited in the *Cort d'Amor,* it has been
possible to locate nine in the works of earlier troubadours. *Joi, Solatz,
Corteszia* and *Pretz* appear in the lyrics of Arnaut de Mareuil as we
have already noted. *Bon'Esperansa* appears as *Bon'Esper* in a poem
by Daude de Pradas, [74] while *Largueza* is mentioned in the poem by
Marcabru cited above, and, as we have seen, by Peire Cardenal.
Domneis appears in the seventh poem by Peire d'Alverhna, [75] and

---

[72] *Les Poésies lyriques du troubadour Arnaut de Mareuil,* ed. R. C. Johnston (Paris: Droz, 1935). The poems by Arnaut which do not involve personifications are, in Johnston's edition: V, IX, X, XVII.

[73] *Poésies de Daude de Pradas,* ed. A.-H. Schutz (Toulouse: Privat, 1953).

[74] *Ed. cit.,* "En un sonet gai e leugier," ll. 5-10.

[75] *Peire d'Alvernha, Liriche,* ed. Alberto del Monte (Turin: Loescher-
Chiantore, 1955), VII, "Deiosta.ls breus jorns," l. 48.

Peirol introduces *Dousa Compania* and *Drudaria*. [76] Only *Ardiment*, *Paors*, and *Celamens* have been so far impossible to locate as personifications, in spite of the fact that references to them abound.

Of the seven "peers" and the seven "enemies," all but the *Bailessa d'Amor*, *Malparliers*, *Putaria*, and *Fals Semblantz* have been verified. Mercy, Honor, Valor, and Youth appear in Arnaut de Mareuil's lyrics, and Sense is perhaps presented by Daude de Pradas as *Razos*. *Merce* and the enemies *Vilania* and *Orguoill* are mentioned by Peirol, [77] while *Malvestat* is cited above by both Peire Cardenal and Marcabru. Clearly the characters of the *Cort d'Amor* are not descendants of Latin mythology, [78] nor are they visitors from France. They are instead natives of Occitania.

Including these troubadours who supplied our author with personifications, there are numerous other Occitan poets who inspired him in other ways. In fact, there are forty troubadours all told, whose phrases, motifs, or ideas reappear fairly intact in the *Cort d'Amor*:

I. North: Poitou, Limousin, Périgord.

1. Guilhem IX, Poitou, ll. 533, 549-557.
2. Bernart de Ventadorn, Limousin, ll. 275-276, 317.
3. Gaucelm Faidit, Limousin, ll. 316, 494-495, 998.
4. Guiraut de Calanso, Limousin, ll. 525-526.
5. Arnaut de Mareuil, Périgord, ll. 316, 317, 451-452, 667-688, 791-798, 905, 939-940, 942-953, 1109, 1307, 1518, 1551-1554.
6. Arnaut Daniel, Périgord, ll. 27-28, 52, 71, 907.
7. Bertran de Born, Périgord, l. 317.
8. Guilhem de la Tor, Périgord, ll. 902, 1292-1297, 1469-1474.

II. East: Auvergne, Velay, Vienne, Provence, Italy.

1. Peire d'Auvergne, ll. 640-642.
2. Peire Rogier, Auvergne, ll. 293-296, 427, 1182-1184.
3. The Monk of Montaudon, Auvergne, l. 592.
4. Na Castelloza, Auvergne, ll. 791-798.
5. Peirol, Auvergne, l. 998.

---

[76] C.A.F. Mahn, *Die Werke der Troubadours*, 4 vols. (Paris: 1846-1853), II, pp. 12-14, x, "Camjat ai mon consirer," ll. 12-15.

[77] *Ibid.*, ll. 52-54.

[78] Cf. both Jean Pepin, *op. cit.*, and C. S. Lewis, *op. cit.*, for the mythological origins of allegory.

6. Pons de Capdoilh, Velay, l. 317.
7. Guilhem de St. Didier, Velay, ll. 51-54, 473-475.
8. Folquet de Romans, Vienne, l. 316.
9. Raimbaut d'Aurenga, Provence, ll. 317, 637-638, 988-989, 1292-1297.
10. The Countess of Dia, Provence, l. 316.
11. Folquet de Marseilla, Provence, ll. 494-495, 791-798, 1448-1452, 1521-1525.
12. Guilhem de Montanhagol, Provence, ll. 1469-1474, 1663-1669.
13. Paulet de Marseilla, Provence, l. 1518.
14. Sordel, Italy, ll. 1448-1452.
15. Lanfranco Cigala, Italy, l. 959.
16. Bertolomeo Zorzi, Italy, l. 317.
17. Bonfacio Calvo, Italy, l. 457.

III. South West: Bordelais, Gascony, Catalonia, Roussillon.

1. Aimeric de Belenoi, Bordelais, l. 316.
2. Cercamon, Gascony, ll. 1182-1184.
3. Marcabru, Gascony, ll. 91-92, 97-98, 189, 395-400.
4. Bernart Marti, probably Gascony, ll. 906, 907.
5. Guilhem de Cabestanh, Roussillon, ll. 931, 1227-1229, 1448-1452.

IV. Central: Toulousain, Quercy, Languedoc, Albigeois, Rouergue, Gevaudan.

1. Peire Raimon de Toloza, Toulousain, ll. 293-296, 1292-1297, 1448-1452, 1518.
2. Uc de St.-Circ, Quercy, ll. 403-404.
3. Azalais de Porcaraigues, Languedoc, ll. 1168-1180.
4. Peire Vidal, Albigeois, ll. 791-798, 998, 1660-1661.
5. Aimeric de Peguilhan, Albigeois, l. 1524.
6. Raimon de Miraval, Albigeois, ll. 959, 1016-1017.
7. Uc Brunet, Rouergue, ll. 1448-1452.
8. Daude de Pradas, Rouergue, ll. 53-54, 317, 403-404, 484-485, 494-495, 1128-1139.
9. Perdigo, Gevaudan, ll. 1196-1203, 1521-1525.

V. Unidentifiable:

1. Dame H., ll. 575-584.

The specific contributions of each of these troubadours are cited below in the *Notes to the Translation*. The verses in the *Cort d'Amor* that they inspired are given above, and the corresponding lines from the troubadour lyrics will be found in the *Notes* cited under these verse numbers.

It would be repetitive to review here each of the specific lyric sources of the *Cort d'Amor,* but several very interesting statistics that emerge from this table bear mention. Nearly 10 % of the lines (162 out of 1721) can be directly traced to these forty troubadours. Eighteen of them contributed more than one idea to our author, and two, Daude de Pradas and Arnaut de Mareuil, were very influential: six motifs from Daude de Pradas and twelve from Arnaut de Mareuil reappear in the *Cort d'Amor.* These troubadours, whose lyrics can be considered direct sources of our poem, include some of the earliest poets: Guilhem IX, Cercamon, Marcabru, and Bernart de Ventadorn, as well as thirteenth century contemporaries: Uc de Saint-Circ, Guilhem de Montanhagol, and Guiraut de Calanso. Although these forty troubadours are not limited to natives of any single area, and do represent almost all of Occitania, there is an unusually high proportion of Italians: Bertolomeo Zorzi, Bonifacio Calvo, Sordello, and Lanfranco Cigala. This is perhaps explained by the comparative lateness of the *Cort d'Amor,* for with the Albigensian crusade many of the troubadours *faidits* fled to Italy. At least four of the *trobairitz,* the lady troubadours, are represented: the Countess of Dia, Azalais de Porcaraigues, Na Castelloza, and the Lady known only as Dame H. One very famous troubadour who is absent from this list is Guiraut de Borneilh, the "Master" of the troubadours who was closely identified with the *trobar clus,* the complex and hermetic development of the lyric.

The table and this study necessarily overlook the more general troubadour sources which do not appear in the *Cort d'Amor* in observable form. For example, the influence of Peire Cardenal, who lived nearly one hundred years (1180-1272) and composed at least 96 poems, must have been tremendous, but we have no demonstrable evidence of his influence on the author of the *Cort d'Amor.*

Guiraut de Calanso

Among the extant troubadour lyrics, only two are allegories complete in themselves, and both of these are products of the thirteenth century. Peire Cardenal's allegorical fable of the rain that fell on a city and turned insane all those upon whom it fell,[79] is dated nearer the middle of the thirteenth century, between 1250 and 1265,[80] and so it probably was not known to our author when the *Cort d'Amor* was composed. No trace of it can be found in our poem.

The other very famous allegory by Guiraut de Calanso, "A lieis cui am de cor e de saber," is dated at the latest 1204,[81] and our author probably did know of it. This poem has, unfortunately, become obscure to those readers who do not breathe a "courtly" atmosphere. As early as the late thirteenth century, only eighty years later, Guiraut Riquier required 947 verses in order to explain, more or less unsuccessfully, the subtleties of these fifty-four lines.

The relationships between Guiraut's allegory and the *Cort d'Amor* are numerous and explicit, and an examination of details may serve to clarify both poems. In the first place and typical of troubadour poetry, or rather of the Old Occitan language, *amor* is feminine; Guiraut's personification is a woman (l. 25, *ela*), just as she is in the *Cort d'Amor*. Guiraut calls her *el menor tertz d'amor* (l. 4), 'the lesser third of love,' and this definition has provoked some speculation. It is the sixth strophe of Guiraut's poem that helps to define *el menor tertz d'amor*:

> Al segon tertz taing franquez'e merces
> Car sobeiras es de tant gran rictat
> Que sobre totz eissaussa son regnat.

The second third is the spiritual, unselfish love that can exist between men and women. The last third rules more than heaven for it is the *raison d'être* of the entire world. The *menor tertz* is probably not the crude carnal love that Guiraut Riquier thought it was, but rather the first step in the sequence, leading next to the spiritual love which truly unites men and women, and thence to the divine love that reunites men with God, and this is not in itself immoral although it can easily be perverted, as the troubadours say, into *fals'amor*. It

---

[79] *Ed. cit.*, p. 530, LXXX, "Una ciutatz fo, no sai cals."

[80] *Ibid.*, p. 534.

[81] Otto Damman, *Die Allegorische Canzone, op. cit.*, p. 9. H. R. Jauss, "Entstehung and Strukturwandel der allegorischen Dichtung," Part 5 "Die Minneallegorie als esoteriche Form einer neuen *ars amandi*," *Grundriss der romanischen Literaturen des Mittelalters* (Heidelberg: Carl Winter, 1968), VI/I, p. 230, dates this poem between 1196 and 1202.

can just as easily, however, lead to the second third, for the lady represents desire, not the lust of sexual love, but the chaste desire through which the lover is perfected (*melhurar*).

In the *Cort d'Amor*, Love is *Fin'Amor*, not only Desire, Guiraut's first third, but also Spiritual Love, his second third, for in the longer poem she represents both the aspiration toward perfect love and its attainment. In the series of speeches delivered by *Fin'Amor* to her twelve barons early in the poem, the general topic of each discourse is one or another of the rules for the management and governing of desire. Before actually entering the castle, however, the entire court will hear the judgment of *Cortezia* (ll. 377-408), who defines *Fin'Amor* as quadripartite, consisting of good faith, loyalty, moderation, and intelligence. These four elements could correspond to the *quatre gras mout les* mentioned by Guiraut de Calanso (l. 29), but for the fact that the four qualities cited by *Cortezia* are not means of ascension or degrees of progress, but a simple definition of love. Our author was not, however, ignorant of Guiraut's four degrees (*fenhedor, precador, entendedor, drut*), for *Fin'Amor* herself announces that *Drudaria* and *Pres* (*pretz*, merit), hold the keys to the castle, the realm of perfect love (ll. 76, 325-344). Since they are the "keys," those lovers who have attained these conditions will be welcomed royally, with no difficulty in gaining access to the castle itself, the state of perfect love. *Drudaria* and *Pretz*, the keys to the castle, function also as her watchmen and guards, who prevent the unworthy from entering. The worthy are those to whom their ladies grant *merce*. *Merce* is a complicated notion, [82] but most commonly it refers to the granting of the lover's request, which, if he is a *fin amador*, will not be dishonorable to the lady in any way. For *Fin'Amor*, therefore, *Drudaria* and *Pretz* are the keys to the castle, the fourth degree, the last step.

In the *Cort d'Amor*, it is after *Cortezia*'s very lengthy discourse concerning dress, deportment, and more abstract aspects of *Fin'Amor*, that *Merce* arrives, makes a request of *Fin'Amor*, and receives the

---

[82] Cf., for example, Jean P. Th. Deroy, "Merce ou *la quinta linea Veneris*," VIe Congrès International de Langue et Littérature d'Oc et d'Etudes Franco-Provençales, II, *Langue et Littérature du Moyen Âge* (Montpellier, September, 1970), pp. 309-328. Deroy identifies *merce* specifically with the *quarta linea* of the ancients: "cette *merce* mûrement réfléchie est accordée en récompense d'un long service d'amour qui rehausse l'éclat de la *valor* de la dame." p. 324.

judgment she seeks against women who love for money, a topic not
suitably discussed within the castle of *Fin'Amor,* the realm of pure
love. The coronation of *Fin'Amor* follows and then the cortege enters
the palace accompanied by various marvellous events heralding a new
era, or a new status for the lover (ll. 853-858).

The rest of the *Cort d'Amor* concerns the maintenance and perfection of *Fin'Amor,* or pure love, which is a subtle blend of desire
and *drudaria,* a combination of Guiraut de Calanso's first and second
thirds of love. In this portion of the poem, roughly the second half
of the surviving lines, the topics of the discussions revolve around
the dangers, especially the gossips, that threaten the established pair
of spiritual lovers, and the advice of Honor, Valor, the Bailiff of
Love, Prowess, and Sense. As if to emphasize the more positive aspect
of life within the castle walls, as opposed to that of the aspirants
outside, "el barri [. . .] que ten del mon plus de l'una meitat" according to Guiraut, there is even a lovers' dance and a ritual exchange
of kisses and flowers.

In more physical terms, Guiraut's figura lives in a *palays* (l. 25),
while *Fin'Amor* inhabits a *castel* (l. 71), and it is there that each
holds her court. The building described by Guiraut has five entrances
as opposed, for example, to the four entrances at the four cardinal
points of the compass in the castle of love described by Andreas
Capellanus. Once again, as with the thirds of love, and the four
steps, there has been much speculation on the significance of the five
doors, but most probably, the *cinc portals* are the two eyes, the two
ears, and the mouth: the vision of the lady and the inspiration of
her beauty, her words of gratitude and praise, and the kiss she bestows
in order to seal the relationship.

The five portals as such do not appear in the *Cort d'Amor*; however, the themes of sight, hearing and speaking, and the kiss recur
consistently. In a long passage, the lover speaks repeatedly of the
difficulties he experienced because his lady did not *see* in the Soph-
oclean sense that the miserable man she saw before her eyes was
dying for love of her (ll. 479-483). His eyes are leaping from his
face with the supreme effort of concealing his overwhelming love
(ll. 484-485). When he discourteously suggests that she would be
more sympathetic to his cause if she only felt a portion of his agony,
he immediately retracts this unworthy wish and utters his hope that
she never be forced to see her reflection in her mirror turn pale

from suffering (ll. 489-492). And finally, he blames his condition on his own treacherous eyes that betrayed him by loving the lady more than their owner: they were so attracted to her beauty that they received the wound from which he is presently suffering (ll. 493-496). According to the lover, his eyes argue in self-defense that great good will come of it because the beautiful person they have shown him was never without humility, and he will ultimately receive great good from her (ll. 497-500). Later, another lover refers to the traditional arrow from the eyes of the beautiful woman which wounded his heart and kindled desire (ll. 1447-1452). Finally, *Cortezia* herself confirms that the lady's eyes do indeed have a certain power (ll. 609-610).

Love, in her speech to Discretion, remarks that it is also very important that the lady hear good things about her suitor, that he speak courteously to all with that in mind (ll. 281-284). Similarly, *Cortezia* points out that friendship grows from hearing good things, from a good reputation (ll. 563-564, 626-627). Very often in the troubadour lyric and in the *Cort d'Amor*, speaking and hearing are combined with the kiss for special recognition in the lovers' interview. The word and the deed are combined, *far e dir plazer d'amor* (ll. 521-524, 305-308). The role of sight, hearing (i.e., graceful and courtly discourse) and the kiss in the progress and development of love, is an identifiable theme in the *Cort d'Amor*, and it is possible to infer from this that the author might accept Guiraut's premise that once having passed the point of kindling desire with the eyes, it is easier to obtain an audience with the lady and ultimately a kiss. Having passed the first two doors, it is easier to pass the other three.

Certain other elements of Guiraut's poem are drawn from Ovid. In fact, this poem is the first troubadour lyric to depict a Goddess of Love so nearly identical to the Latin Cupid: blind, invisible, winged, naked, shooting arrows of steel, lead, and gold. In other respects Love resembles the *Fin'Amor* of the troubadours and the *Cort d'Amor* quite closely. Both wear crowns and give judgments, indeed they rule the world after the manner of earthly kings, although neither is concerned with titles or material wealth. Each personification does battle in order to defend her interests.

Evidently the figure described in fifty-one lines of Guiraut de Calanso's poem could not be developed as completely as the *Fin'Amor* described in the longer text, and she is certainly enigmatic, representing as she does, a combination of the Latin and Occitan traditions.

Fin'Amor, by contrast, is described in considerably more words, but it is more concrete, less symbolic information that is conveyed, generally outlining her daily activities, and reporting her speeches. Compared to Guiraut's goddess, *Fin'Amor* is a more human figure who holds court, addresses her *parlament,* moves about in a normal way, and even devoutly offers prayers of thanksgiving to God, her own seigneur. She is surrounded by marvels, and such things happen in her name, but she herself is scarcely marvellous: she is an Occitan seigneur, not a Latin goddess. Nothing approaching an actual description of her physical person is given at any point in the *Cort d'Amor* although praise of feminine physical beauty was a popular motif in the troubadour poetry. As a result, Guiraut's basically pagan personification remains entirely allegorical in nature while the *Cort d'Amor* tends more explicitly away from allegory toward the more practical art of love. By drawing on the tremendous amount of poetry that was literally floating in the air around him in the form of popular songs, our author had only to take one additional step and gather it all together into one more large compendium in order to produce the allegorical art of love that we call the *Cort d'Amor.*

VI. Sources of the Cort d'Amor: Occitan narrative

It is not without significance that the earliest Occitan narrative masterpiece, *Boecis,* [83] describes a lady of marvellous power and rank who dispenses judgment and justice, punishing the unjust and rewarding the faithful both on earth and afterward, in both the name and the place of God. More than a century later, *Fin'Amor* will perform precisely the same function, following the precedent set by Lady Philosophy. Although Philosophy was in fact a Latin lady transported from the Latin tradition into Occitan, there are within the Occitan narrative tradition itself numerous references to myriad powerful ladies and a great deal of poetic material that will be incorporated later into the *Cort d'Amor.*

---

[83] *Boecis, Poème sur Boèce (Fragment), le plus ancien texte littéraire occitan,* eds. René Lavaud and Georges Machicot (Toulouse: Institut d'Etudes Occitanes, 1950), and *Der Altprovenzalische "Boeci,"* ed. Christoph Schwarze (Munster, 1963).

Troubadour narrative poetry proper originated early in the Occitan tradition with the *ensenhamens,* didactic narratives in octosyllabic lines addressed by the troubadour to his jongleur in order to teach him his business. The earliest of these, "Cabra juglar," a poem of 146 lines composed approximately 1160 by Guiraut de Cabreira, [84] is little more than a list of famous epics and romances, ancient as well as medieval, that were indispensable to the repertoire of any successful jongleur. By the thirteenth century, however, the scope of the *ensenhamen* had been expanded to include other topics, and Guiraut de Calanso warns his jongleur that he will have to know something of love. [85] In his poem Guiraut refers to the basically Ovidian description which he related in the second, third, and fourth strophes of his famous lyric poem. The didactic nature of the *ensenhamen* itself as a genre, and the fact that Guiraut felt he must instruct his jongleur in the nature and attributes of Love, clearly indicate that a new dimension had been added to the demands made upon a jongleur by his audience. Earlier jongleurs needed only to know the tales that were then circulating and which did not involve anything specifically related to Love as a character. Guiraut's jongleur, on the other hand, needed in addition to the old sagas and romances a working definition of *Fin'Amor*. It is very likely that Guiraut was only saying in effect: "You must know the song that I myself have composed regarding Love," but apparently the jongleur of the thirteenth century was expected by the troubadour who hired him, or by the audience who heard him, to have, in his repertoire, allegorical songs that taught or celebrated the mysterious personification of Love. Guiraut's advice to his jongleur reflects in a limited way the slightly altered tastes of the early thirteenth century poets and also presumably the tastes of their audiences, and in this respect his poem helps to define the atmosphere in which the *Cort d'Amor* was created and probably recited. If certain allegorical elements of either poem are obscure to the modern reader, they were very probably not obscure to the contemporary audiences.

Approximately contemporaneous with the *ensenhamen,* troubadours were also writing other forms of short narrative poetry including the

---

[84] K. Bartsch, *Denkmaler der provenzalischen Litteratur* (Stuttgart: Bibliothek des Litterarischen Vereins XXXIX, 1856), pp. 88-94.

[85] *Ibid.,* pp. 94-101, "Fadet joglar," ll. 202-225.

love letter or *salut d'amor*. [86] Pierre Bec, insisting that its distinguish-
ing characteristic is not the salutation but its epistolary nature, goes
on to note that in fact, the usual metrical form is quite consistent
with that of the novella, the Occitan *novas*, with only rare exceptions
appearing in the metrical form of a song. [87] Eighteen *saluts d'amor*,
all dating from the twelfth century, have been preserved. Of these,
five can be attributed to Arnaut de Mareuil, the earliest known author
of these letters, leading Mr. Bec to suppose that "il paraît d'autre
part probable qu'Arnaud a été, sinon l'inventeur, du moins le maître
incontestable du genre, et c'est sur lui que les autres auteurs ont dû
plus ou moins s'aligner." [88] Not surprisingly the author of the *Cort
d'Amor* also found an imitable model in Arnaut's love letters and
three passages of considerable length from the *Cort d'Amor* can be
traced directly to one of his *saluts*.

First, the description of the ideal lady given by *Cortezia* (ll. 667-
692) corresponds rather closely to Arnaut's *descriptio puellae* in
the first *salut*. [89] The traditional progress of the description, from the
top of her head to her feet or the hem of her dress is established
here. Although our author follows Arnaut's references to her forehead,
nose, mouth, teeth, chin, neck, hands, figure, and even concludes by
also mentioning her gentle habits of speech, he inexplicably omits
Arnaut's references to her hair, eyes, and breast, all traditional objects
of praise in the troubadour lyric. More importantly perhaps, our
author adds eight lines concerning the lady's dress and her white
linen. This might be only an adaptation of Arnaut's preoccupation
with the lady's white skin which is mentioned six times in this short
passage, but it is also very likely that it represents changing fashions.

In the second place, we find in the *Cort d'Amor* the motif of the
lover's dream (ll. 942-953), and it very closely resembles Arnaut's
account of the lover's dream. [90] Each lover falls asleep, dreams that
he (or his heart) is reunited with his lady, experiences the bliss, *lo*

---

[86] Cf. A. Parducci, "La 'lettera d'amore' nell'antico provenzale," *Studi
Medievali*, nuova serie, XV (1942), pp. 69-110, and Paul Meyer, *Le Salut
d'amour dans la littérature provençale et française* (Paris: 1867).

[87] *Les Saluts d'amour du troubadour Arnaut de Mareuil, Textes publiés
avec une introduction, une traduction et les notes par Pierre Bec* (Toulouse:
Privat, 1961).

[88] *Ibid.*, p. 30.

[89] *Ibid.*, pp. 71-91, "Dona, genser qe no sai dir."

[90] *Ibid.*, ll. 140-152.

grans zoi, of his lady's favors, and then awakens to his great sorrow. Arnaut would give up the lordship of Reims if he could only remain in that state of dream and so avoid the languishing caused by unsatisfied desire in the waking state. The lover in the *Cort d'Amor* marvels that he is not driven out of his senses by the unbearable sorrow he, too, feels upon awakening and discovering that he cannot find his lady nearby.

Thirdly, our author follows Arnaut in citing a list of famous lovers whose happiness, however great, could not have been equal to that of the present couple (ll. 315-318). Again our author has adapted his model to suit his own purposes. Arnaut cited only the ladies while the later poet listed the couples; Arnaut's list included Greek heroines in addition to Blanchefleur and Iseult, while our author retained the latter, rejected the former, and added the strange couple Soredamors and Gawain. We know already from the discussion above that our author could have discovered the comparison to Tristan and Iseult from any of several different troubadours, and to Floire and Blanchefleur from at least three, that is, of course, if it did not occur to him spontaneously. It is likely though that having borrowed both the *descriptio puellae* and the dream motifs from Arnaut's first love letter, our author probably found his inspiration for the list of lovers in the same poem.

Not long after Arnaut wrote his love letters, probably at some point during the upheavals of the Albigensian crusade, jongleurs began to consider it necessary to introduce certain songs with a few preliminary remarks concerning the life of the poet and the subject of his song. Presumably the authors and their particular styles were not so well known nor as immediately recognizable as they once had been, hence the need for an introduction, and in this way the prose *vidas* and *razos* of the early thirteenth century were created. [91] Although the *vida* or biography of the poet tended to give origins, facts of birth and family, and life history in a fairly straightforward manner, several of the *vidas* based apparently on information drawn from the songs, verge on the fantastic and have all the attributes of a story sufficient in itself. [92]

---

[91] *Biographies des Troubadours, op. cit.*

[92] Cf., for example, the *vida* of Guilhem de Cabestanh, *ibid.*, pp. 530-555, and the *razo* to Peire Vidal's "De chantar m'era laissatz," *ibid.*, pp. 368-369.

By the beginning of the thirteenth century, these shorter narrative forms, the *ensenhamen*, the *salut*, the *vidas*, and the *razos* had been expanded in length and detail until they reached the status of a "new" genre, the *novas* or novella. The specific origins of the genre are still subject to much speculation, although it does seem to have evolved naturally, i.e., it is not an artificial form arbitrarily invented by any single individual, as the sonnet is generally believed to be. Rather the *novas* seem to have developed from some of the same sources as the French *fabliau*: primarily popular story-telling. Although his poem conforms to the formal definition of the *novas*: a narrative poem in octosyllabic couplets, written in the vernacular language and relating the events of a courtly adventure, the author of the *Cort d'Amor* called his poem a "romance" (ll. 9-11). In Old Occitan *romans* refers simply to the vernacular language and, by extension, to anything written in the vernacular. Raimon Vidal uses the word in a more specific generic sense in his poetical treatise *Razos de Trobar*: "La parladura francesca val mais... a far *romanz*, retronsas et pasturellas." [93] Later the author of *Flamenca* uses the word similarly: "Vai sus Alis... / Pren lo *romanz* de Blancaflor. / Alis se leva tost e cor / Vas una taula on estava / Cel romans" (ll. 4477-4480). [94] It is most likely that the *Cort d'Amor* was written after the *Razos de Trobar*, which appeared very early in the thirteenth century, and probably before Flamenca, written between 1240 and 1250. *Romanz*, in referring to the *Cort d'Amor*, therefore, has here its ordinary meaning of narrative poem written in the vernacular language. This general description in no way excludes the more precise definition of the *novas* which also applies to the *Cort d'Amor*. To be exact, the *Cort d'Amor* is, like the *Novas del Heretic*, an example of the *novas rimadas*, the longer poetical narrative in octosyllables which treats a philosophical subject. The text of the *Cort d'Amor* comprises 1721 verses, but it is incomplete at the end, and there is nothing in the text or the manuscript to indicate the original length of the poem. The topic, insofar as we can tell from the lines that remain, could certainly be classified as both courtly and philosophical.

---

[93] Cited in E. Levy, *Supplement-Wörterbuch*, VII, 373b-374a.

[94] *Ibid.*, cf. also *FEW*, X, 453b and 455b, and especially P. Voelker, "Die Bedeutungs entwicklung des Wortes *Roman*," *Zeitschrift für romanische Philologie*, X (1886), pp. 485-525.

The novas of Raimon Vidal

Raimon Vidal de Besalú, a Catalan troubadour, wrote three *novas* in addition to his poetical treatise, which are generally recognized as the first of this genre to appear in Gallo-Romance, and they represent the very early stages of its development. The earliest of the three is probably "Abrils issi'e mays intrava," [95] a *novas* of the *ensenhamen* tradition which must be dated before 1213 since Peire II of Aragon is mentioned as still living. From this it can be deduced that this *novas* could have been written no earlier than 1196, the first year of his reign, nor any later than his death in 1213 in the battle of Muret against the French. This *novas* is the longest of the three, consisting of 1773 verses, of which eight lines and sixteen fragments are lost. The theme or subject is developed in two parts: the first laments the decline of poetry, hospitality, and the courtly tradition, and the second narrates certain aspects of the good old days in an attempt to teach a younger man the ways of the courtly life as it used to be and ought to be lived.

Instead of conforming to the *novas* as we have defined it, "Abrils issi" represents a developmental stage of the genre, combining both the *ensenhamen* and vaguely biographical elements of the *vidas*. In this *novas* Raimon's tendency to quote frequently from the works of other troubadours serves two functions: 1. it lends authoritative support to the subject under discussion, 2. it serves to develop and amplify his themes. In his earlier *Razos de Trobar*, citations from the troubadours serve the first purpose; in his later *novas* "So fo e.l temps" they serve the second. In "Abrils issia" they fill both functions. Here he quotes the older troubadours in order to prove both the nobility of times past and the decadence of the present generation. Unfortunately this tendency lends an air of pedantry, although it is entirely consistent with the subject of the poem: the instruction of a jongleur, an *ensenhamen*.

---

[95] "Abrils issi'e mays intrava," ed. Wilhelm Bohs, *Romanische Forschungen*, 15 (1904), pp. 216-296; with a Spanish translation in: Ramón Milá y Fontanals, *De los Trobadores en España* (Barcelona, 1861, 2nd. ed., 1889), pp. 295-312; and *Raimon Vidal. Poetry and Prose*, II, "Abril issia," ed. W. H. Field, Studies in the Romance Languages and Literatures (Chapel Hill, North Carolina: University of North Carolina Press, 1971).

Far more subtly, the author of the *Cort d'Amor* utilizes the same device although he is not instructing a jongleur in his art or the history of his profession, but rather a group of ladies, "viij.xx. que donas qe pulsellas." After the lecture on the nature of love delivered by *Fin'Amor* herself in the form of eleven short speeches addressed to the twelve barons, the ladies listened attentively, but required further elaboration on the specifics of love (ll. 345-353, 359-362). It is *Cortezia* who delivers the *ensenhamen* in response to this request, and there follow numerous lectures on the subject of Love which are addressed to the court at large, with the exception of that pronounced by the Governess of Love who addressed her speech directly to the unmarried maidens in the audience (ll. 1157-1160). She describes the ritual of the *jazer*, initiating, so to speak, the young ladies into the mysteries of the naked embrace.

The didactic nature of the *Cort d'Amor* correlates quite closely in this respect with the pedantry of Raimon Vidal's "Abrils issia." Both *novas* are intended for the edification of the young. Where Raimon quotes the authority of the earlier troubadours, naming them in the poem, the author of the *Cort d'Amor* simply borrowed verses and images from their songs, apparently assuming, probably correctly, that the sources would be recognized. Certainly the more obvious ones like the parable of the thief borrowed from Perdigon (ll. 1196-1203), and the fable of the stag borrowed from Montanhagol (ll. 1663-1668), were immediately recognized and appreciated. It is quite possible that a certain significant part of the pleasure taken in this poem by a contemporary audience lay precisely in this recognition and identification of themes and motifs from popular songs. The *Cort d'Amor*, then, represents in some aspects a development of the *ensenhamen* as it can be traced from Guiraut de Cabreira through Guiraut de Calanso and Raimon Vidal.

The second of Raimon's three *novas*, "So fo e.l temps c'om era iays," [96] is often given the title *Judici d'Amor* because that is its general theme: like the *Cort d'Amor* it describes a court of love, although the judge is not *Fin'Amor* but a mortal man, Uc de Mata-

---

[96] Eds. C.A.F. Mahn, *Gedichte der Troubadours*, 4 vols. (Berlin, 1862), II, cccxli, pp. 23-37, from a single manuscript; Max Cornicelius, Diss. (Berlin, 1888); and a fragment by Milá y Fontanals, *De los Trobadores*, pp. 289-293.

plana. This *novas* is not as long as the first, having only 1397 lines and no lost or fragmentary verses. It is not datable although it is quite likely that it was written within the lifetime of Sir Uc de Mataplana who plays the role of judge and who died in 1213 of wounds he received in battle near Toulouse, serving under Peire II, against Simon de Montfort. This would tentatively date this *novas* at approximately the same time as the first. There are six manuscripts or fragments of this poem extant, and to a certain degree, this testifies to the popularity of the piece. The *novas* resembles a debate in which two or more different points of view are argued, much like the traditional Occitan *tensos* and *partimens*, hence the title *Judici d'Amor*.

This *novas* has considerably more literary merit than the first if only for the depiction of Uc de Mataplana who appears here as a relatively more complex character than any of the others in this *novas* or the earlier one. He is obviously aware of the delicacy of his position and his reputation, and yet he hesitates to consider the case presented to him by the jongleur. Whether this hesitation arises from modesty or rather from previous experience with such problems, the character of Sir Uc is an appealing and impressive one. He may have served as a model for the depiction of *Fin'Amor* who, in the *Cort d'Amor*, resembles nothing so much as a medieval baron like Sir Uc, and he is certainly intended, and succeeds, as a model of the perfect courtly knight and an able judge in courtly affairs. The picture of his court is delicately drawn. The guests playing dice and chess on carpets of four different colors, the curiosity of the guests when the jongleur arrives, are small scenes which are very effectively and elegantly described. Similarly, although far less realistically, and with good reason, the activities of the court of *Fin'Amor* are described.

Once again, on a much larger scale, Raimon makes use of citations from the works of other troubadours, including Raimbaut de Vaqueiras, Bertran de Born, Folquet de Marseille, Uc Brunet, Gaucelm Faidit, Bernart de Ventadorn, Raimon de Miraval, and even an anonymous poet.

Finally, since this *novas* seems to have been very popular, at least more popular than the other two, to judge from the number of manuscripts, one must assume that this topic was in considerable vogue at the time it was written or not long thereafter, and so it deserves some attention. It revolves around a judgment quite similar to those that concluded the Old French *débats du clerc et de chevalier*, in which a person of authority, the god of love, Love herself, or a baron known for gentleness and courtly wisdom, presides over the case and renders judgment. In the *Cort d'Amor* there are at least two such formal judgments, one rendered by *Fin'Amor*, the other by her baron, *Cortezia*. The case itself normally springs from a debate or to use the Occitan term, a *tenso*, which means a dispute or quarrel involving "tension" as opposed to the *partimens*, an artificial debate in which points of view are arbitrarily chosen and defended regardless of personal convictions. *Tenso* eventually came to designate also that type of poetry which dealt with a dispute or quarrel. The fact that the *tenso* often required certain mental gymnastics in order to follow the more or less philosophical argument, together with the fact that the subject of the quarrel described by Raimon is a problem of courtly behavior, so complex that it requires an impartial judgment delivered by a third party, may explain its great popularity.

The similarities between Raimon's *novas* and the *Cort d'Amor* suggest that our author was either directly inspired by Raimon's *novas*, or that the two narratives were written more or less simultaneously in response to a widespread and growing public interest in the literature of trial and judgment by the courtly code. The *Cort d'Amor* is identical to Raimon's *novas* in this respect. In the judgment pronounced by *Fin'Amor* (ll. 821-834), the *tenso* or case being considered is a dispute between the true lovers and those women who love for money, and *Merce* has been sent by the lovers to bring the case before *Fin'Amor*, in order that she may dispense justice. In the instance of the judgment delivered by *Cortezia* (ll. 377-408), it is not a specific case that is examined, but rather the definition of *Fin'Amor* and so the judgment takes the form of a decree. On a less formal level, the first eleven speeches of *Fin'Amor* outline what we may assume are previous judgments made at the court of Love, and each of the subsequent speeches made by her barons clarify some point in the "courtly" code.

The third and last of Raimon's *novas*, "Unas novas vos vuelh comtar," [97] is the shortest, consisting of only 450 lines, all of which are complete. As with the others, this *novas* is not datable except

---

[97] Eds. C. Appel, in: *Provenzalische Chrestomathie*, 6th ed. (Leipzig, 1930), pp. 193-197; I. Cluzel, *L'École des Jaloux (Castia-gilos): fabliau du XIIIe siècle par le troubadour catalan Raimon Vidal de Bezalú* (Paris: Les amis de la langue d'oc, 1958).

insofar as it was probably written after the death of Anfos VIII of Castile (1199), since the author in his first ten lines speaks of him in the past tense. It was King Anfos who, according to Raimon Vidal, gave the *novas* the title *Castia-gilos* by which it is commonly known, and which was later used to designate all pieces concerning the punishment of the jealous husband. Although the *Cort d'Amor* bears no relationship in theme or plot to the *Castia-gilos,* the motif of the jealous husband recurs on numerous occasions. First the watchman proclaims:

> Ar es lo luochs e la saiszos
> Qu'ieu haz endormitz los gilos.
> (ll. 81-82)

Cortezia, in three different passages recommends that the jealous individual be regarded with contempt (ll. 565-568, 706-708, 710-724), and *Plazers,* the seneschal, states that the jealous husbands will no longer threaten courtly lovers (ll. 990-994). Jealousy, generally recognized as a serious fault on the part of the husband, and the violence that usually accompanies it, provided the troubadours with much poetic material that appeared frequently in all their literature from the lyric to the *vidas, razos,* and *novas.* The considerable emphasis on jealousy, to the exclusion of other vices rejected by the courtly code, such as pride, is a slightly later development and very typical of the thirteenth century, culminating in the greatest *Castia-gilos* of all, *Flamenca.* In this tradition, both the *novas* of Raimon Vidal and the *Cort d'Amor* represent the middle stages.

Chronologically speaking, it was possible for the author of the *Cort d'Amor* to have had the advantage of knowing all three of the *novas* of Raimon Vidal de Besalú. It could have been the very existence of these *novas,* that is, the appearance of the "new" genre and its popularity, that led our author to choose this form. It is also likely that, in composing his compendium, he was inspired by Raimon's fondness for quoting earlier troubadours. The didactic nature of the *Cort d'Amor* can be traced to the tradition of the *ensenhamen,* to which Raimon's "Abrils issi" belongs, and the subject is an imitation of Raimon's *Judici d'Amor.* The dramatic effect of dialogue was very possibly impressed upon our author by the *Castia-gilos,* and it is certainly this poem and its popularity that encouraged him to incorporate the motif of jealousy. The primary difference between the *novas* of Raimon Vidal and the *romanz* of the *Cort d'Amor* is the allegorical nature of the latter.

Other narrative allegories

The earliest purely allegorical narrative love poem composed in Old Occitan is impossible to designate. There are only three which have survived: the *Cort d'Amor*, an allegorical *novas* by Peire Guillem, [98] and fragments of an allegory based on a *Chastel d'Amors*. [99] Both the *Chastel d'Amors* and the *novas* are later than the *Cort d'Amor*, although not so much later that they do not belong to the same period and the same "atmosphere." The *novas* of Peire Guillem (who could be Peire Guilhem de Tolosa), can be dated between June, 1252 and July, 1253 since Thibaut I of Navarre (d. 1253) and Alphonse X of Castille (r. 1252-1284) are mentioned as still living. [100] The *Chastel d'Amors* is not datable in any precise terms, but one of its early editors, Antoine Thomas, considers it a later work than the *Cort d'Amor*, and dates it closer to the middle of the thirteenth century. "L'auteur du *Chastel d'Amors* est inconnu, toute conjecture à ce sujet manquerait absolument de base. Tout ce qu'on peut dire, c'est qu'il vivait et composait probablement au treizième siècle plutôt vers le milieu que vers la fin." [101] Thomas notes that the *Cort d'Amor* is an earlier poem, and may have served as an inspiration to the author of the *Chastel d'Amors*: "Un auteur anonyme, à peu près contemporain de Calanson, nous a laissé un long poème allégorique connu sous le nom de *Cour d'Amour*: on y trouve une courte description du *castel* d'Amour. La chanson de Guiraud de Calanson et la *Cour d'Amour*, tels sont vraisemblablement les modèles dont s'est inspiré l'auteur du *Chastel d'Amors*." [102]

We can assume that Guiraut's allegorical lyric, the *Cort d'Amor*, Peire Guilhem's *novas*, and the *Chastel d'Amors* were produced in

---

[98] Editions of this poem, "Lai on cobra sos dregz estats," can be found in: Raynouard, *Lexique Roman* (Paris: 1838), I, pp. 405-411; Mahn, *Werke*, I, pp. 241-250; and K. Bartsch, *Chrestomathie Provençale*, 6th ed. (Marburg: 1904), cols. 291-296.

[99] Ed. A. Thomas, *Annales du Midi*, I (1889), pp. 181-196. R. Lavaud and R. Nelli have reprinted Thomas' text in *Les Troubadours* (Bruges: Desclée de Brouwer, 1965), II, pp. 242-257.

[100] Jung, *Études sur le poème allégorique*, p. 161.

[101] *Ed. cit.*, p. 186.

[102] *Ibid.*, p. 187.

roughly that order within approximately 50 years of each other between 1210 and 1260, and that they represent a new development
in Occitan poetry: allegory fully developed and complete in itself,
as opposed to the common practice of allegorical amplification of a
specific point. In attempting to explain the appearance of the entirely allegorical poem at this time, Antoine Thomas theorized that:
"L'amour a mis la chanson sur les lèvres des premiers troubadours;
la chanson, à son tour, a mis un amour plus ou moins réel dans le
cœur ou dans la tête de ceux qui sont venus après eux. Dès que
l'amour est devenu le thème banal de toute poésie, à l'expression
simple, et par cela même poétique, de sentiments sincères, telle qu'on
la trouve chez un Bernard de Ventadour, succèdent bientôt de singu-
liers raffinements. On s'ingénie de plus en plus à définir, et à peindre
l'amour, à mesure évidemment qu'on le sent moins. On la personnifie,
par un souvenir de l'antiquité, et ce premier pas fait, on se lance à
bride abattu dans la voie de l'allégorie. De là, une littérature d'un
caractère tout artificiel qui se développe dans le midi de la France à
la fin du douzième siècle." [103] Thomas is correct in seeing the literary
phenomena of the thirteenth century as a consequence of the pre-
ceeding era. The four allegories in question do not represent a totally
new poetic event. Their poetic form, with the obvious exception of
Guiraut's lyric, is that of the standard troubadour narrative poetry
which appeared in the middle of the twelfth century with the *salut
d'amor* and the *ensenhamens*: octosyllabic lines in rhyming couplets.
This form was retained, and simply lengthened to produce the *novas*
and *romans* of the thirteenth century. Thomas is inexact, however,
when he dismisses personification of vices, virtues, ideals, and concepts as a "souvenir of antiquity," since it is quite apparent from
the troubadour poetry of the twelfth century that personification is
a normal function of the troubadour language. Thirteenth century
authors found personification aplenty in their native Occitan poetry
and had no need of ancient memories in order to dredge it up again.
It is likely, though, that the rise of scholasticism at this time, with
its emphasis on ancient or Biblical authority and the allegorical expli-
cation of primarily Biblical texts, particularly the work of St. Augus-

---

[103] *Ibid.*

tine, [104] contributed to the taste for allegory, thus permitting development of the allegory latent in nearly all troubadour poetry.

It is also simplistic and perhaps too romantic to believe with Antoine Thomas that "love inspired the songs on the lips of the first troubadours," since it is generally agreed at present that the troubadour love song has very complex origins including Latin liturgy, Spanish-Arabic poetry, and certain elements of folkloric song and dance. According to at least one scholar, it was more likely politics than love that inspired the first known troubadour, Guilhem IX. [105] Even less acceptable is Thomas' statement that "the love song inspired a more or less real love in the head or heart of their successors." In opposition to the supposed sincerity of a Bernart de Ventadorn whom Thomas cites, we have a Marcabru, certainly a troubadour of equal standing and contemporary to Bernart, who declared that he had *never felt* the joy of Love:

> Amor no vueill ni dezir,
> Tan sap d'engan ab mentir;
> Per aiso vas lo vueill dir
> C'anc d'Amor no.m puec jauzir. [106]

If we dare speak of inspiration at all in this context, it is plain from the tone of most of Marcabru's poems that he was not inspired in the least by love, but on the contrary, by the abuses of love that he apparently perceived in the society around him. In the context of medieval poetics as a whole, [107] it is probable that sincerity had very little immediate relationship to the creation of poetry, aside from the obvious fact that the troubadours certainly were deeply committed in most cases to the concepts and ideals of *fin'amor*. As a result, it was probably not the "banality of the love theme" that drove poets in desperation to allegory. It was rather a desire for refined and extensive definition of a concept that was becoming increasingly misunderstood that led them to adopt the popular allegorical form as a means.

---

[104] Cf. D. W. Robertson, Jr., *A Preface to Chaucer*, p. 229.

[105] Charles Camproux, *Le Joy d'Amor des Troubadours, jeu et joie d'amour* (Montpellier: Causse et Castelnau, 1965), p. 125.

[106] *Ed. cit.*, pp. 28-30, VII, "Ans que.l terminis verdei," ll. 9-12.

[107] Paul Zumthor, *Langue et techniques poétiques à l'époque romane* (XIe-XIIIe siècles) (Paris: Klincksieck, 1963), *passim*.

Similarly it is problematic to conjecture that the later troubadours intensified and developed the depiction of Love in inverse proportion to the strength of their actual sentiments, and to conclude that the thirteenth century love allegory is, as a result, "a literature of a completely artificial nature" is unjustified. This last, however, is a common assessment of medieval allegorical poems. Marc-René Jung remarked that "les médiévistes de naguère ont tous été victimes de ce préjugé qui faisait de l'allégorie un procédé froid et mécanique," [108] and he cited the attitudes of Ernest Langlois, Gaston Paris, and Ch.-V. Langlois in this same vein. A. Jeanroy, referring to the personifications of abstractions that constantly appear in troubadour poetry, complained that "ces êtres simplifiés ne sont naturellement capables que d'une sorte d'action, qui ne peut être mieux exprimée que par le verbe de même racine que le substantif qui les désigne: *Humilitatz* doit *humiliar*, *Orgolh* doit *orgolhar*, et ainsi de suite. On ne voit pas du tout ce que la pensée peut gagner à ces tautologies, et on voit fort bien, à moins qu'on ne soit charmé du rabâchage, ce que l'expression y perd." [109] More recently Charles Camproux remarked in reference to the political upheavals and military campaigns of that period that "les transformations en train de s'accomplir avec violence n'empêchaient apparemment pas de jouir des meilleurs comme des pires traditions. D'ailleurs cette allégorie [that of Peire Guilhem] est un signe des temps: l'artificiel finira par prendre le pas sur la poussée vitale." [110]

In this same context Jung noted that:

> Les manuels d'histoire de la littérature codifient cette attitude en rangeant les poèmes allégoriques sous l'étiquette de la littérature didactique. A les lire, on a l'impression qu'il existe un genre didactique, qui peut (malheureusement) prendre la forme allégorique. C'est le contraire qui est vrai: la forme allégorique devenant la forme dominante, la littérature didactique (tout comme la littérature amoureuse, politique, ou dramatique) subit l'influence de cette forme. Et encore faudrait-il distinguer entre l'enseignement débité par une personnification, et le poème allégorique où l'enseignement res-

---

[108] *Études sur le poème allégorique*, p. 10.
[109] *La Poésie lyrique des troubadours*, II, p. 122.
[110] *Histoire de la Littérature Occitane*, 2nd. ed. (Paris: Payot, 1971), p. 52.

sort du jeu dialectique et complémentaire de différentes personnifications. [111]

Jung also pointed out that no medieval theoreticians considered the
allegorical poem *per se*: "Dans l'ensemble, les œuvres en langue vulgaire ne doivent rien aux théories de l'allégorie, car celles-ci négligent
l'aspect de la création littéraire. Les théoriciens s'occupent de deux
types d'allégorie, de l'allégorie-ornement et de l'allégorie-exégèse." [112]
    For the three allegories at hand: the *Cort d'Amor*, Peire Guillem's
novas, and the *Chastel d'Amors*, neither of these cases is relevant. All
three are entirely allegorical poems in which ornament and exegesis,
if they appear at all, are secondary. "Les théories sur l'allégorie pas-
sent complètement sous silence le *poème allégorique*. Les poétiques
et les *accessus* ne s'occupent pas non plus de ce genre littéraire. Et
pourtant il a existé." [113] One could object to Jung's classification of
the allegorical poem as a genre since allegory is generally recognized
at present as a mode, but it is clear that the description of the medieval allegorical poem was, for all intents and purposes, left to the
reader.
    In the modern era there have been numerous attempts to define
and describe allegory in general and medieval allegory in particular, [114]
but D. W. Robertson Jr., in his *Preface to Chaucer*, provides a simple
and workable definition which permits us to examine the *Cort d'Amor*:
rejecting the notion that 'symbol' refers to things and that 'allegory'
refers to actions, Robertson states that "allegory is simply the device
of saying one thing to mean another, and its ulterior meaning may
rest on things or on actions, or on both together." [115]
    Thus, the Occitan love allegory in the thirteenth century is not
a "new" genre, for it represents no forms or ideas new to the Occitan
literary tradition. It represents instead a new combination of many
older genres, themes, and motifs, not the least of which were fur-
nished by the troubadour lyrics and the Occitan novas: the authors

---

[111] *Études sur le poème allégorique*, p. 10.
[112] *Ibid.*, p. 11.
[113] *Ibid.*, p. 18.
[114] Cf. A. Fletcher, *Allegory, the Theory of a Symbolic Mode, op. cit.*;
E. Honig, *Dark Conceit, the Making of Allegory* (London: 1959); and
Rosemond Tuve, *Allegorical Imagery, Some Medieval Books and their Posterity* (Princeton, New Jersey: Princeton University Press, 1966).
[115] *Op. cit.*, p. 300.

of the allegories poured the concepts and styles of the former into the structure provided by the latter. The *novas* of Peire Guilhem and the *Cort d'Amor* are the only such allegories that have been preserved, since the allegorical lyric of Guiraut de Calanso at the beginning of the century, and the *Chastel d'Amors,* after 1250, represent transitional stages: the birth and the decline of narrative love allegory.

VII. LITERARY VALUE OF THE CORT D'AMOR

The narrative of the *Cort d'Amor,* as the title implies, revolves around the activities of the court of *Fin'Amor.* This lady is extremely difficult to describe in specific terms. The author gives her the epithet "la dousa et la bona," tells us that she lives on Mount Parnassus in her marvellous castle surrounded by her barons and the world's lovers, and all we know further is that she rules the world (ll. 95-99, 839-840), and that her wealth is that of the entire world (ll. 1590-1594). This is the extent of the specific, direct information we are given concerning her, and it is disappointing that our author does not once provide a physical description of her. In fact, he seems to avoid physical portraits of the characters he presents with the brief exceptions of Honor, Valor, and the Bailiff of Love who are dressed alike (ll. 1071-1073), and Youth whose appearance is described in the last lines.

It is clear from the beginning that the poet intends for his poem to be primarily didactic in nature. Those who desire the flower and the courtesy of love, and care for nothing else, but prefer to remain with *joi,* must pay careful attention to this romance (ll. 1-16). It is equally clear that the lessons will be given by the speeches and conversations of various personifications:

> Ora zuzatz coment araszona
> Sa gent, Amors la dousa e la bona.
> Mas premieramens vos dirai
> Sos conpainons, ni hon estaz
> Ab cui faz acordament
> D'Amor lo lial zutgament.
> (ll. 29-34)

The notion of judgment and the agreement of *Fin'Amors* and her barons are introduced early, and they will serve as the foundation upon which the edifice of the narrative and the allegory will rest. The twelve barons are introduced in lines 42-47 and in line 76, in precisely the same order in which they will be addressed by *Fin'Amors* in her eleven speeches: *Jois, Solaz, Ardiment, Corteszia, Bon'Esperansa, Paors, Larguesza, Domneis, Celamens, Dousa Conpania, Drudaria,* and *Pretz*. In essence, each "baron" is defined by the illustrations of *Fin'Amor*'s discourses; the suzerain tells her vassals what their duties and responsibilities are. On the assumption that they were irreconcilable, Marc-René Jung wondered that both *Ardimens* and *Paors* were found together at the court of *Fin'Amors,* and he resolved the conflict by concluding that fear was necessary for the suitor while boldness was required only of women: "Craintes pour le soupirant, hardiesse pour la femme, telle est la répartition que propose notre auteur." [116] Unfortunately the resolution is not that simple because certain verses in the address to Boldness do indeed concern the lover:

> E cel que de re non s'esfreda
> Sitot, s'a petit de moneda,
> S'adoba ades de ben servir.
>
> (ll. 169-171)

> E per vos vai a parlament
> Drutz a si dons ardiment.
> En amor, non val re paors;
> Ardimentz es la claus d'amors.
>
> (ll. 177-180)

Fin'Amor never implies that Boldness is exclusively the province of the woman. On the contrary, she specifically states twice that the lover will occasionally have need of boldness in the pursuit of perfection. Fear, on the other hand, is apparently assumed to be a natural attribute of women, for in her address to that baron, *Fin'Amor* dramatizes only the fear of the lover, and in her earlier address to Boldness, the fear of the woman was taken for granted:

> Que vos fatz toszeta ardida
> Q'a paors neis d'aucel qant crida.
>
> (ll. 159-160)

---

[116] *Études sur le poème allégorique,* p. 150.

Furthermore, Laughter makes it quite clear in his speech that the
lady is indeed expected to be afraid of certain things:

> Enaisi plaing lo drut e.l druta
> Es mil aitans morta e venduda
> Q'el [h] non ausa ab omen parlar
> Ni gen vestir ni gen causar,
> Ni s'ausa deportar ni rire,
> Qe non haia paor d'aucire.
>
> (ll. 962-967)

Jung's facile resolution of the problem is insufficient. Both fear
and boldness are clearly intended by the author to signify aspects of
the behavior of both lover and lady. One really need not wonder
"comment Ardimen et Paors, qui sont tous deux de la compagnie,
peuvent s'entendre," for each serves a similar purpose in attaining
the desired end, and by examining this purpose as it relates to the
end, the unity of the poem becomes clearer. The end for which both
lover and lady are struggling is definitely not the physical possession
of the other, for in that case boldness and fear would be irreconcilable, and equal measure of each would in fact result in a static condition. Encouraged by boldness but held back by fear, both lover and
lady would find themselves rooted to the ground unable to advance
or retreat. Instead of the physical possession of the beloved, which
Jung apparently believes Fin'Amors represents: "Il est intéressant de
noter que le personnage portant le nom de Fin'Amors, ne représente
pas ce que la critique moderne entend par fin'amors. ... La conception de l'amour, telle qu'elle se manifeste dans la première partie de
la Cour d'Amour, correspond moins à la fin'amors de la poésie lyrique
qu'à l'amour courtois des romans," [117] the goal that the Cort d'Amor
in fact teaches is: "novella amor / D'una domna de gran valor,"
(ll. 21-22) the cultivation and attainment of a state or condition of
fin'amor. In this case, Fear and Boldness work together in alternately,
not simultaneously, restraining and encouraging both the lover and
lady as they strive for perfection. It is the seneschal of Love himself,
Sir Pleasure, who states this principle:

---

[117] Ibid., p. 155.

Mas ieu dic qe re non enbria
Qe mos seihner es poderos
Qe ia luszengiers ni gelos
Ne ceran dan a drut cortes.
Ans lur pro mas be lur pes
Qar en luoc fan tan gran paor,
Q'el non parlara auien lor,
E si con l'aurs e.l fluec s'escura,
Aqesita paor los meillura
Q'il si gara de fol parlar
E fai ab sen tot son afar.

(ll. 991-1001)

Fear, then, has a purifying effect, like fire, in that it inspires moderation: *fai ab sen tot son afar*. Boldness reassures the lovers that the goal is worth achieving and ultimately within reach, while Fear warns them of the dangers of excess. Together, Fear and Boldness are not in the least irreconcilable but rather, as the two sides of the coin define the penny, so Fear and Boldness define moderation, *meszura*.

From this brief digression it becomes clear that all twelve of *Fin'Amor*'s barons function more or less in this way. Each one represents one element in the struggle to achieve *Fin'Amor*, each represents one of the channels through which desire must flow before it can be successfully converted — sublimated if you will — into *Fin'Amor*.

From this it is obvious that each of the twelve barons was very carefully chosen by the author in order to represent the "vassals" of *Fin'Amor*, the members of her immediate household, the permanent residents of her castle, her lieutenants, and finally, the component parts of the idea of *Fin'Amor*, most specifically the way that desire must be transformed in order to attain merit and valor. Their number is twelve for significant reasons: *Fin'Amor* relates to her twelve barons, just as Charlemagne related to the twelve peers of France, and as Christ related to the twelve apostles. The comparison is not intended to be blasphemous, for it represents only a parallel on a lower level of the hierarchy of ideas. Charlemagne represents one sort of perfection, that of the warrior king, *Fin'Amor* represents another type of perfection on a slightly higher level, that of a social ethic, while Christ represents the highest level of human moral perfection. One may suppose that the twelve peers of France represent different aspects of the soldier-knight: "Roland est preux et Olivier est sage," that the twelve apostles represent different aspects of human morality including even the traitor and the doubter along with the faithful, and that the twelve barons of *Fin'Amor* therefore represent different aspects of the ethical behavior defined by the term *fin'amor*. As suggested above, not one of these personifications was invented by our author. Instead of creating characters to fit his allegory, our poet simply gathered together personifications that were already famous and clearly understood from the poems of the earlier troubadours.

The 244 verses comprising the eleven speeches delivered to the twelve barons by their seigneur can thus be considered a definition of *Fin'Amor*. These, together with the first 100 introductory verses, in which the season, location, landscape, and characters are presented to the listener, set the didactic tone of the poem. The next 63 verses (345-408) maintain the sober instructional style of the sermon. When Love had finished her prepared speeches, the ladies requested further information concerning the nature of love, and *Fin'Amors* required Dame Courtesy to pronounce the judgment in which she defines love succinctly in 32 lines (ll. 377-408). At this point the first semblance of action to appear in the poem takes place: the judgment pronounced by Courtesy is written in a chart, signed, sealed, and carefully stored away (ll. 409-420). After this, however, the author returns to his original didactic style and permits Courtesy to embark on a very long discourse (ll. 421-724). It is almost certain that this discourse has been distorted in the manuscript, for in ll. 709-710 it is *Corteszia* who responds to this speech by *Corteszia*: "[C]orteszia ditz: 'Dompn pros, / D'aiso m'acort eu ben ab vos.'" Any resolution of this problem must remain conjectural, but there is one point in this very long speech where, as a result of faulty transition, we could logically suspect a scribal omission of several lines, possibly including the introduction of another speaker. In verses 652-656, *Cortesia* solemnly pronounced the doom of the lady who had been deceived:

> E dompna puis engans i es
> Ni pot esser d'engan represa,
> Jamais non pot esser cortesa,
> Ni pus com pot estain durar,
> Non pot iamais son prez cobrar.
>
> (ll. 652-656)

But verses 657-708 incongruously take up the physical description of the lady:

> E ill cabeill ssion coindament
> Estretz ab fil d'aur on d'argent, etc.
>
> (ll. 657-658)

It is quite possible that at this juncture the scribe (or the reader dictating to the scribe) omitted several lines, and that another speaker of whom we are unaware has introduced another topic. It is impossible to know who this speaker might be, but there are several likely candidates, since neither *Solasz* nor *Dousa Compania* speaks elsewhere in the poem and the subject of the lady's beauty would be suitable to either of the concepts they represent.

Immediately after *Corteszia*'s response to this speech, *Merce* arrives in much haste in order to present before the court the case of the aggrieved lovers against those ladies who loved for money (ll. 727-780). *Fin'Amor* herself delivers the judgment in this case:

> Aquellas qi qeron soldadas
> Er getat de ma companna.
>
> (ll. 824-825)

With this judgment terminating on l. 834, the first major division of the extant *Cort d'Amors* is concluded, for in these 834 lines is depicted the law court of Love, and in the lines that follow, the coronation and royal court of Love will be portrayed. Although the didactic tone will be continued to a certain extent, the number of new characters introduced and the amount of dramatic activity described will increase considerably. It is in the last half, for example, that the humbler castle folk will be introduced: the jongleurs *Ris* and *Deportz* in l. 884; their sister *Na Coindia* in l. 886; *Plazers*, the seneschal in l. 898; and the courtiers *Cor, Deszir, Dous Esgar,* and *Baiszar* in ll. 1568 and 1570. The *Baillessa d'Amor* will arrive in l. 1068 with *Honor* and *Valor*, and we are led to believe that although the *Baillessa* could be one of *Fin'Amor*'s own vassals, she does not live at the castle of Love, and as the bailiff she probably represents external social restrictions on Love. Nor are *Honor* and *Valor*, like *Merce* who arrived earlier, permanent residents of the castle, but rather they are peers of *Fin'Amor*, powerful seigneurs in their own right. We are told that *Merce* arrived "Qe volg esser el parlament" (l. 728), and we can assume that she had undertaken to deliver the request of the lovers of her own volition in order to relieve their suffering, which would be in keeping with her nature, and that she was not commanded by *Fin'Amor* to appear. Likewise *Honor, Valor* and the *Bailessa d'Amor* "son vengudas ad auzir los chan" (l. 1070). To the list of peers we must also add *Proessa,* who first speaks in verse 1334, *Sens* who first speaks in verse 1647, and *Joven* who is introduced in the very last fragment, verse 1718. It is evident from their activities and their remarks that these seven are not, like the first twelve, vassals of *Fin'Amor,* but autonomous seigneurs of equal rank, who are her companions, advisers, and friends: "Qant ellas entron e.l palais / Sapchatz qe.l cort en val mais" (ll. 1074-1075). Our poet is careful to demonstrate, by their late arrival after the sermons, by their manner, and by their speech, that they do not necessarily belong to the realm of *Fin'Amor,* that they control realms of their own, and that they are present at the court only because they wish to be. Sense, for example, gives Love his opinions freely and freely offers his services in war:

> Eu vos hai dig mon vejaire
> E vos fai oimais vostre afaire
> E qant comandares: "Montatz!"
> Eu serai dels premiers armatz.
> (ll. 1692-1695)

This is certainly not the speech of a vassal to his suzerain but rather that of one comrade-in-arms to another. On the other hand, *Fin'Amor* declares herself the vassal of *Honor*:

> Mos cors prenc de vos e mos fieus,
> E qar eu soi sener d'amor,
> Hai causit lo pus ric seinhor.
> (ll. 1124-1126)

This exchange between *Fin'Amors* and *Honor* is, at first glance, most bizarre. *Fin'Amor* couches her speech in the language of love and assumes the male role of lover in her greeting:

> Vos mi tenes en tal liam,
> Con pus m'aucisses, no m'en clam.
> (ll. 1089-1090)

Vostra dousa amors m'esperona.
Pos bella es, siatz me bona.

(ll. 1093-1094)

Regardon, pus son cor no.us cela,
Le vostre sers qe tant vos ama.

(ll. 1100-1101)

Ja mos cors non haura repaus
Tro qe.m digas coment sera
S'ill vostre bel cors m'amera,
Q'ieu soi vostre hom en tota guisza,
Qe Fin'Amor e.l cor m'astiza
Un fuec don m'es suaus la flama,
Qe del vostre bel cors m'aflama.

(ll. 1106-1112)

Although this fairly long speech is entirely unexpected, it does provide a very important definition of *Fin'Amor,* not, as previously, in terms of her own various aspects, but this time in terms of her relationship to another virtue. In this case we are afforded a most significant insight into the specific relationship between Love and Honor, and it is clear that *Fin'Amor* approaches her guest with utmost humility and formality, with moderate speech and eager desire, with both fear and boldness, in short, with all the aspects outlined earlier in her court of law. Once again, as noted earlier, the feminine Love assumes a masculine role, for the context requires that she approach Honor as the lover must approach the lady, as the aspirant must approach the ideal. Most curiously, however, *Fin'Amor* states that *fin'amor* has inspired a flame in her heart and that Honor's beautiful body inflames her further. We can only conclude that, like the gods and goddesses of the Greek pantheon, *Fin'Amor* is also subject to the concept she represents. We find Aphrodite forever falling in love with some beautiful youth, Cupid pricking himself with one of his own arrows at seeing Psyche, and similarly *Fin'Amor* falls in love with Honor.

Even more curious, however, is Honor's response to *Fin'amor*'s greeting, for she introduces for the first and only time, in the *Cort d'Amor,* the *carpe diem* theme:

[A] jlors respon ela: "Soi ben vostra,
Q'ieu non soi ges aqil qe mostra

Orguell mentre q'es iovencella
Qi a la color fresca e novella
E qant aqil colors li fail,
Ez el se vei en son mirail,
E conois qe trop s'es tarzada
Ill qier so don era pregada.

(ll. 1127-1134)

Inexplicable as it may seem, the author had good reason to put this speech on the lips of Honor, for she is the only one who could logically advocate the commitment of the young woman to love and still remain beyond reproach. She is, after all, Honor, and if she supports the games and rituals of *Fin'Amor,* it can only be because they are honorable beyond suspicion. She does, nevertheless, give sage words of warning against certain follies, primarily the use of artificial color on the face, and she is particularly anxious that ladies learn to speak carefully:

Dompna non deu parlar mas gent
E suau e causidament,
E deu tant gent sos mots assire
Qe totz hom son solaz desire,
Qe las pauraulas qe son fors,
Demostran los talens del cors,
Per qe non deu dire folor,
Dompna qe s'enten en valor.

(ll. 1147-1154)

All seven, Mercy, Honor, Valor, the Bailiff of Love, Prowess, Sense, and Youth, are virtues and they relate to *Fin'Amor* as equals, as "Peers." René Nelli remarked that:

L'idée vraiment féconde de l'érotique du XIII° siècle, c'est que l'amour est toujours plus que l'amour: s'il tient, en effet, une place si importante dans la conscience des hommes et des femmes c'est qu'il leur apparaissait comme lié à des vertus qu'ils considéraient comme plus précieuses encore que lui. Sans ce mystérieux *amor* qui pouvait, à leur gré, se changer en *joi* ou se perdre en jouissance, ils savaient qu'il n'y avait point de *jovens,* point de générosité, de Prix, de Valeur; point de Merci, point de Charité. [118]

---

[118] *L'Erotique des Troubadours* (Toulouse: Privat, 1963), p. 5.

It is significant that the virtues related to *Fin'Amor* in the *Cort d'Amor* are seven in number. They are apparently intended to be indirectly parallel to the seven Christian virtues: Prudence, Temperance, Fortitude, Justice, Faith, Hope, and Charity, and they stand in opposition to the seven vices of *Fals'Amor*: *Villania* (Vilany, l. 12), *Malvestat* (Wickedness, l. 19), *Putaria* (Prostitution, l. 19), *Cobezesa* (Covetousness, l. 740), *Orguei* (Pride, l. 742), *Falz Semblantz* (Hypocrisy, l. 1676), and *Malparlers* (Slander, l. 1678). These, in turn, are indirectly parallel to the seven deadly Christian sins: Envy, Avarice, Lust, Sloth, Gluttony, Anger, and Pride. Ultimately, this interpretation remains problematical, since it is impossible to know how much of the text has been lost, and how many more personifications are yet to be introduced. For this reason, the numerical symbols of the poem cannot be legitimately explored further.

In the second part of the *Cort d'Amor*, the formal aspects of the law court, which prevailed in the first half, are abandoned. After the coronation of *Fin'Amor* (ll. 835-966), the company enters the Palace of Love, thus signifying physically that the rule of *Fin'Amor* had been consecrated, and now the realm is proclaimed by the herald:

> Cobezesa es morta e aunida,
> E havem Orguel abattut
> Ara si guardon li cornut
> Qe mon senior porta corona.
> Alquel han ioi cui el en dona,
> E totz om es malauros
> Que non s'acompania ab vos.
> Noi havem fag lo iugament
> D'Amor: fols es qui non l'aprent.
>
> (ll. 868-876)

From this point on, the court of *Fin'Amor* resembles not a court of law, but rather a royal household. The banquet begins with a prayer in which *Fin'Amor* offers her thanks to God, her suzerain (ll. 879-882). The jongleurs arrive with music and dancing, which is so infectious that lovers and ladies leap from their seats in order to dance, but *Fin'Amor* orders her seneschal to reseat them so that the jongleurs may be heard. Laughter, the first jongleur, delivers a lecture of 72 lines (ll. 905-977) castigating the gossips and slanderers, the *lausengiers*. Amusement then speaks, less emphatically, against deceiving the lady (ll. 1006-1040), and finally, Dame Grace, their sister, describes

the responsibilities of the lady, once she has accepted her suitor
(ll. 1041-1067). Immediately afterward, Honor, Valor, and the Bailiff
of Love arrive and, after they are welcomed by Love, each speaks
according to her nature (ll. 1127-1331). Lady Prowess next gives
warning against the foolish, presumptuous lovers, and then, by way
of illustration of the opposing virtue, she relates a lengthy anecdote
in which a messenger takes it upon herself to reveal to both lady and
suitor the desires of the other, since the two concerned are too hes-
itant and cautious to bring up the subject.

After this speech the lovers resume their interrupted dance, jewels
are exchanged as tokens of Love, flowers are strewn about, and the
courtiers Heart, Desire, Sweet Regard, Pleasure, and Kissing and
the baron *Domneis* join the dancers. Before long, however, the tumult
becomes too much for the other barons to bear and, because they
remember that not all lovers are happy, they request that the fes-
tivities be ended. Through the seneschal, *Fin'Amor* orders an end to
the dancing, and Pleasure warns the lovers of the threat of Pride:

> ...... Za Dieus non veia,
> Cortesa gens, qi vos gerreia!
> Qe re non de hom tant onrar
> Com bona dompna a fin amar,
> Mais per aqest mieu blonde cap,
> Be.m peszara s'orguels non sap,
> E.l garsona la que.l mante,
> Lo poder qe ha contra me,
> Qe za non er longa sazons
> Qe l'en veran mil gonfanons
> Que volrian en un gran soil
> De clamar [v]eser ab un oil,
> Q'ieu non voell soffrir la clamor
> Qe fan dompnas e amador.
> E si vos, seinhor, m'o laissatz
> Non er pus suffert en patz.
> (ll. 1631-1646)

I have reproduced the entire speech given by Pleasure because it is
this passage and the speech of Sense which immediately follows that
have led several scholars to believe that, in the rest of the poem which
has been lost, *Fin'Amor,* her barons, and peers, go to war against
Pride. In the next passage, Sense responds to the seneschal's speech
with satisfaction:

> [S]ens estet en un farestol
> E plaz li molt qar Amors vol
> Gerreiar per tener dreitura.
> El pensa qe sos fieus pejura.
> E al dig: "Anseis qe movatz,
> Ad aqest besoing me sonatz."
> (ll. 1647-1652)

He goes on to castigate not Pride but "li fol drut feinedor" and he concludes:

> Amors, si aiso non venjatz,
> Totz es vostre prez abaissatz.
> (ll. 1716-1717)

After this speech by Sense, Youth is introduced (ll. 1718-1721), but the rest of the poem is missing. Strangely enough, Marc-René Jung also noted on page 154 of his study that "ensuite, Jovens, blond et couronné de fleurs de lis, prend la parole," but on page 155 he inexplicably forgot that Youth had appeared: "On chercherait en vain dans la suite de *Fin'Amors*, des personnages-notions aussi importants que *Mezura* ou *Joven*."

While Constans felt that as a result of l. 1651 (1659 in Constans' edition), *Anseis qe movatz*, only a few lines were missing, Prof. Jung believes that the speeches of Pleasure and Sense represent a call to arms, a preparation for battle against *Orguelh*, and, in short, a courtly *Psychomachia* in which the virtues of *Fin'Amor* combat the vices of *Fals'Amor*:

> Or ces paroles sont prononcées par Sens, juste après l'appel aux armes d'Amors. Nous ne croyons pas qu'elles annoncent la fin du poème; elles ne sont qu'un moment de retardement avant la prise des armes. Sens veut encore placer son discours avant que les barons partent en campagne. On peut donc supposer que la partie finale devait raconter la guerre d'Amour et de ses barons contre Orgueil. Malheureusement, il ne nous reste que l'appel à la guerre. Cette dernière partie du poème (si elle a jamais existé) se situerait dans la tradition de l'allegorie morale, où les Vertus affrontent les Vices. Du côté d'Orgueil, on aurait sans doute rencontré Convoitise et Malparlier, déjà cités, mais l'auteur y aurait probablement ajouté d'autres personnifications. [119]

---

[119] *Etudes sur le poème allégorique*, pp. 154-155.

In the first place, as we have seen, Prof. Jung has overlooked the appearance of Youth after the speech by Sense. It is very probable that Youth, like every other peer introduced up to this point, would have had something to say, and it is equally possible that there were other peers not yet presented, perhaps even *Mezura* whose absence Prof. Jung notes, or perhaps barons named in the earlier verses, who might also have had something to say on the subject of war. This of course remains conjecture, but even so, we cannot ignore the appearance of Youth, and therefore, Jung's suggestion that Sense wanted to speak his mind before the barons left for the campaign would probably apply at least to Youth, if not also to other individuals. The departure for war, if such indeed is the case, could not have been as precipitous as Jung suggests. An early as ll. 776-780, Mercy called for vengeance on the false ladies:

> De lor avetz torts e pecatz,
> E fares mal vostra fasenda
> Si de vos non han bella esmenda.
> E c'om digua q'a bon signor
> Han servit, membre.us de lor.

Fin'Amor responded to this "call to arms" by pronouncing a judgment against "aqellas qui qeron soldadas" (l. 824), but, significantly, she did not go to war in order to avenge the suffering of the lovers. On the other hand, as we have already seen, the death of Covetousness and the defeat of Pride were announced earlier at the coronation: "Cobezesa es morta e aunida, / E havem Orguel abatut." It is granted that Pride will always rise again, but that it should threaten so soon after its alleged defeat, in fact the same day, reflects very negatively upon the strength of *Fin'Amor*. Instead, I would suggest that the reference to Pride in the speech by the seneschal represents a threat to the noisy lovers, essentially: "If you continue in this manner of behavior, you will fall victim to pride, and pride is ultimately an enemy of pleasure (*lo poder qe ha contra me*). Therefore I ask you to exercise moderation and be quiet (*Q'ieu non voell soffrir la clamor*)." This speech is in no way a call to arms. Rather it is a warning: "If you continue in this way, it will not be long before you will see a thousand banners marching against you." In the following speech, Sense merely continues the metaphor of battle, although he applies the image not to the pride of the noisy lovers, but to the foolish presumptuous lover and the gossips who also threaten the well-being of true lovers. Like Mercy, Sense only *wishes* that *Fin'Amor* go to war and he so counsels. It is plain from a careful reading of the text that *Fin'Amor* herself has indicated no intention of declaring war. Sense very clearly demands to know why in fact Love has *not* declared war:

> Per qe.lz ne castias, bel Seinher?
> Qe laisson e.l fol brut e.l feiner?
> (ll. 1686-1687)

While the possibility that the *Cort d'Amor* ends in war cannot be entirely excluded, it is apparent that such a conjecture remains extremely hypothetical. The appearance of Youth at the end of the fragment, the basically pacific character of *Fin'Amor*, and the nature of the speeches by Pleasure and Sense together with the futility of the earlier request for vengeance delivered by *Merce*, leave only a remote possibility that the *Cort d'Amor* ends in war.

It seems far more likely that the *Cort d'Amor* ends as it begins, with the daily business of a medieval seigneur. The activities of the Occitan Lady, the powerful 'King' *Fin'Amor*, form what little plot structure there is in the poem, as we have it, and these activities fall into two basic categories: those didactic formal events (speeches, discourses, pleadings, judgments, the signing and sealing of charts) that pertain to the court of law, and those less solemn activities (feasts, dancing, coronation, story-telling) that pertain to the routine of a noble household.

The first 834 lines teach the aspiring lovers what *Fin'Amor* is and how to go about approaching it, what to embrace and what to avoid. Almost all of this information is formally preached by *Fin'Amor* and *Cortezia*. In the last 887 lines, these precepts are illustrated by a numerous cast of characters, who reveal different aspects of the courtly life in different tableaux. The first half of the poem deals generally with the regulation and control of desire, while the second half deals with the maintenance and defense of *drudaria*. In other words, the first 834 lines depict the legal court during which the *parlament* is passive, and the last 887 lines depict the royal court in which the *parlament* is active. In this respect, the *Cort d'Amor* is parallel to medieval religious festivals, which often began with sermons and ended with theatre.

It is interesting to note that this relationship between the "halves" of the extant *Cort d'Amor* is supported stylistically by the poet's use of direct discourse, specifically his tendency to allow his characters to quote someone else in their speeches. For example, the first half is primarily static with 501 verses of 834 in direct quotation of only three figures: *Fin'Amor* (217 verses), *Cortezia* (246 verses), or *Merce* (38 verses). Oddly, *Cortezia* has slightly more to say than *Fin'Amor* on the general theme of desire and its proper control. Within these direct discourses, the lover is quoted directly in 79 verses, the lady is quoted directly in 53 verses, the wise are quoted in 10 verses, the wife in 4, the false woman in 2, the good woman in 2, the husband in one, and the barons of the court in one, for a total of 152 lines of "double" direct quotation. In three lines, the lover quoted by *Fin'Amor* quotes himself presenting an example of "triple" direct quotation (ll. 801-803).

The last 886 lines, which deal with the concept of *drudaria*, are slightly more descriptive and a good deal more dramatic, since the cast of speaking characters increases considerably from 3 to 14. *Cortezia* speaks only 3 lines, and *Fin'Amor* only 47, of which 4 verses make up her prayer. Prowess has the largest speaking part with 226 verses, and in her speech she quotes the messenger for 139 lines. The messenger in turn quotes the lover for 19 lines (ll. 1444-1462), and the lady (hypothetically) for 2 lines (ll. 1500-1501). In this same speech Prowess also quotes the lady in response to the messenger for 14 lines (ll. 1475-1484). In the rest of the poem Sense is quoted directly by the author for 66 lines; Pleasure, the seneschal, in 45; Amusement, the jongleur, in 35; the Governess in 28; Dame Grace in 27; Domneis in 14; Valor in 13; the watchman in 9; and the lovers present at the court are quoted directly in 3 verses for a total of 516 lines of direct quotation. The number of verses quoted directly are nearly equal in both halves: 501 in the first 835 lines, 516 in the last 866 lines, although this conclusion must remain provisional since the rest of the poem is lost.

It is from the quotations within the quotations that the sense of drama in the second half derives. Within direct quotations the lover is quoted by someone else in 138 verses. He in turn quotes the serf for three lines of "triple" direct quotation. The lady is quoted by someone else in 99 lines in addition to which she quotes first herself for 6 lines (ll. 1187-1192), and then the thief for 2 lines (ll. 1198-

1199). "They" are also quoted by someone else in 7 verses. Including the complicated anecdote related by Prowess, the "double" quotations total 377 verses, and the "triple" quotations total 36 verses, an increase of 225 and 23 verses respectively over similar types of quotations in the first half. This use of the direct style gives the second half of the *Cort d'Amor* a most vivid dramatic flavor which, like a tale within a tale, is highly entertaining and realistic. Noting this anecdotal style within the larger framework of the allegorical narrative, specifically in the discourses of the Bailiff, Valor, and especially in that of Prowess, Prof. Jung remarked that these passages are in fact "un véritable morceau de bravoure, pour un jongleur habile." [120]

Stylistically then, the *Cort d'Amor* shows the same division we have already noted thematically. The first half of the *Cort d'Amor* is the static, sermonic, art of love, in which the manipulation and control of Desire are taught in the court of law. The second half of the poem is principally the dramatic love allegory, in which the elements of Drudaria are illustrated by the activities of the royal court.

The problem of the nature of the medieval "courts of love," the *cours d'amour* described by Jean de Notredame [121] in the sixteenth century, a problem that so perplexed Provençal scholars like Raynouard, Fauriel, and Anglade, is somewhat clarified by our poem. The problem, in essence, is whether there existed in the Middle Ages actual courts of love, tribunals with advocates, judges, and a certain theoretical jurisdiction, to which litigants could bring their disputes and where they would find honest, learned arbitration. While F.-H.-M. Raynouard assumed that the love courts were a reality, [122] Fauriel argued only that they *could* have existed, [123] and even as recently as 1921, Anglade equivocated on the subject. [124] Gaston Paris, on the other hand, stated that in the Middle Ages "on ne trouve *court d'amour* (ou d'Amours) que dans le sens de 'cour du dieu (ou de la déesse) d'Amour,' ce qui n'est pas du tout la même chose, cour, au

---

[120] *Ibid.*, p. 154.

[121] *Vies des plus célèbres et anciens poètes provençaux* (1575).

[122] *Choix*, I, p. lxxxv.

[123] C. Fauriel, "André le Chapelain, auteur d'un traité de l'amour," *Histoire Littéraire de la France*, 21 (1895 facsimile reproduction), p. 237.

[124] J. Anglade, *Histoire sommaire*, p. 26.

sens où les modernes prennent le mot dans 'cour d'amour,' signifiant
'cour de justice, tribunal.' " [125] Paris agreed with Frédéric Diez in
seeing in these alleged courts nothing more than intellectual social
games like the *tenso*, the *jeux d'esprit* in which different views are
defended and in which arbitration is normally required, like the *jeux
parties*, the *jocs d'amor* of ll. 293-294 of the *Court d'Amor*. Gaston
Paris asked: " . . . qui ne voit que nous avons là, comme ailleurs, de
purs jeux d'esprit, des espèces aussi imaginaires qui ont fait le bonheur
à différentes époques, des sophistes, des rhéteurs, des scolastiques, et
des casuistes?" [126] The single most obvious argument against the existence of these courts is the fact that they could have had very little
authority and so by virtue of their uselessness in practical terms, their
existence is doubtful. The very fact that the names of the parties
involved were kept secret, as in the case of Raimon Vidal's *Judici
d'Amor*, or were brought to court as a group action, as in the case
of the aggrieved lovers in the *Cort d'Amor*, prevents any authority
from executing the sentence passed by the judge. Any decisions made
in such courts, including the judgments of both *Cortezia* and
Fin'Amors in the *Cort d'Amor*, even though they are signed, sealed,
and locked away in vaults, must remain on the level of theory, for
they are impossible to enforce. Gaston Paris admitted, however, that
these decisions were not without some effect:

> Que ces décisions, étant donné le singulier état d'esprit que
> nous fait connaître la littérature courtoise du XIIe siècle, aient
> pu exercer parfois une influence sur les idées, sur les senti-
> ments, portant sur les actions de tel ou tel chevalier, de
> telle ou telle dame, c'est ce que je me garderais bien de
> contester; mais elles en ont exercé comme la philosophie à
> la mode, les romans et les poésies du jour, le ton changeant
> des conversations mondaines, exercent dans tous les temps. [127]

The implication for our poem, then, is that no one, even in theory
considered the decisions rendered by *Cortezia* and *Fin'Amor* as laws
to be obeyed. The public that read or heard the *Cort d'Amor* was
instead gratified, even entertained to find that the social and behavioral

---

[125] G. Paris, "Le cours d'amour au moyen âge," *Journal des Savants*,
1888, p. 666, note I.
[126] *Ibid.*, p. 728.
[127] *Ibid.*, pp. 733-734.

customs they practiced were here solemnly proclaimed by a no less august figure than *Fin'Amor*, the peer of all the other less exciting virtues recommended to them by the Church. As Gaston Paris pointed out, the problems discussed and the lessons taught in these "courts" were intended not so much for the education of lovers, who have no need for instructions and no concern for rules, but for the information of the curious, the ignorant, and the aspiring: for the uninitiated. [128] In the *débats du clerc et du chevalier* and in Andreas Capellanus' *De Arte Honesti Amandi*, Book V, the authoritative figure is the god of love. In the troubadour *tensos* and *partimens* the judge is a wise person who is known for his or her courtesy, like Raimon Vidal's Uc de Mataplana in the *Judici d'Amor*. In Andreas Capellanus' Book II, the authority is a high-born lady or a court of ladies, and in the *Cort d'Amor* the judgments are pronounced by *Corteszia* and *Fin'Amor*. Like the courts of love suggested in the *débats du clerc et du chevalier*, in Andreas Capellanus' treatise, in the troubadour *tensos* and *partimens,* and in Raimon Vidal's *Judici d'Amor,* the court of love depicted in our poem represents a fantasy based on the intellectual amusement derived from the debate, and projected into an entire allegorical structure. Although in the case of the *Cort d'Amor* this structure includes many details extraneous to the debate itself (castle, barons, coronation, etc.), the allegory remains true to the fundamental principles of debate: the definition and demonstration of opposing positions, and ultimately, a resolution in favor of one or the other argument. [129] As a result, the didactic and the allegorical serve the parallel purpose of teaching and illustrating. We must conclude that the courts of love existed first in literature, and that any actual dramatizations of these courts was inspired by the literature and not the reverse. The *Cort d'Amor* is one of the more sophisticated examples of these intellectual games that has survived in Occitan literature.

In spite of the lack of authoritative documentation for dating the composition of the *Cort d'Amor,* and the fragmented nature of the manuscript itself, we can nevertheless safely assume that it is the first narrative love allegory in Old Occitan. The complex and sophisticated level of expression observable in the 1721 lines which have been

---

[128] *Ibid.,* p. 728.

[129] We must assume that in the missing verses of the *Cort d'Amor,* the final resolution is in favor of *Fin'Amor.*

preserved, indicate that the author was a learned man, probably able to read Latin, and apparently familiar with Old French literature. It is clear, however, that the sources of the poem are overwhelmingly Occitan. Genre, themes, style, allegory, motifs, and concepts, all were inspired by the troubadour tradition of the twelfth and early thirteenth centuries, and as a result, the *Cort d'Amor* is significant as a compendium of the ethic of *fin'amor*, and encyclopedia of love. The Occitan love allegory, especially the *Cort d'Amor*, illustrates not an artificial literature signifying decay, but a culmination and summary of the Golden Age of the troubadours and their concept of love.

★ ★ ★

Explanatory notes to the translation and variants to the original may be found in two lists at the end of the texts. An asterisk signals the inclusion of information in the lists.

SELECTED BIBLIOGRAPHY

I. THE *CORT D'AMOR*

A. TEXT

Manuscript M. 819 of the Pierpont Morgan Library in New York, formerly Phillipps 8335 in the library of Sir Thomas Phillipps in Cheltenham, England, also known as Chansonnier N, folios 31r. through 46v.

B. EDITIONS

Bartsch, K., *Altprovenzalisches Lesebuch*. Elberfeld, 1855, pp. 34-38.

Mahn, C. A. F., *Gedichte der Troubadours*, II. Berlin, 1856, no. 279, pp. 168-171.

Constans, L., "Les Manuscrits provençaux de Cheltenham," *Revue des Langues Romanes*, 20 (1888), pp. 121-179, 209-220, 261-276.

Nelli, R., and Lavaud, R., *Les Troubadours*, II. Bruges, 1966, pp. 236-243.

II. OCCITAN POETRY

A. TROUBADOUR LYRICS

Aimeric de Belenoi, *Poésies du troubadour Aimeric de Belenoi*, ed. M. Dumitrescu. Paris, 1935.

Arnaut Catalan, *Le Poesie del Trovatore Arnaut Catalan*, ed. F. Blasi. Florence, 1937.

Arnaut Daniel, *Canzoni*, ed. G. Toja. Florence, 1960.

Arnaut de Mareuil, *Les Poésies lyriques du troubadour Arnaut de Mareuil*, ed. R. C. Johnston. Paris, 1935.

Bernart Marti, *Les Chansons de Bernart Marti*, ed. E. Hoepffner. Paris, 1929.

Bernart de Ventadorn, *Bernart von Ventadorn: seine Lieder mit Einleitung und Glossar*, ed. C. Appel. Halle, 1915.
Bernard de Ventadour, troubadour du XIIe siècle: chansons d'amour, ed. M. Lazar. Paris, 1966.
The Songs of Bernart de Ventadorn, ed. S. Nichols. Chapel Hill, 1962.

Bertran d'Alamanon, *Le Troubadour Bertran d'Alamanon*, ed. J.-J. Salverda de Grave. Toulouse, 1902.

Bertran de Born, *Poésies complètes de Bertran de Born*, ed. A. Thomas. Toulouse, 1888.

Bonifacio Calvo, *The Poems of Bonifacio Calvo,* ed. W. D. Horan. Paris, 1966.

Cercamon, *Les Poésies de Cercamon,* ed. A. Jeanroy. Paris, 1922.

Daude de Pradas, *Poésies de Daude de Pradas,* ed. A.-H. Schutz. Toulouse, 1953.

Folquet de Marseille, *Le Troubadour Folquet de Marseille,* ed. S. Stronski. Cracow, 1910.

Gaucelm Faidit, *Les Poémes de Gaucelm Faidit,* ed. J. Mouzat. Paris, 1965.

Guilhem IX, *Les Chansons de Guillaume IX, duc d'Aquitaine,* ed. A. Jeanroy. Paris, 1927.

Guilhem Ademar, *Poésies du troubadour Guilhem Ademar,* ed. K. Almquist. Upsala, 1951.

Guilhem de Montanhagol, *Les Poésies de Guilhem de Montanhagol, troubadour provençal du XIIIᵉ siècle,* ed. P. T. Ricketts. Toronto, 1964.

Guilhem Peire de Cazals, *Guilhem Peire de Cazals, troubadour du XIIIᵉ siècle,* ed. J. Mouzat. Paris, 1954.

Guilhem de la Tor, *Le poesie di Guilhem de la Tor,* ed. F. Blasi. Florence, 1934.

Guiraut de Bornelh, *Sämtliche Lieder des Trobadors Giraut de Bornelh,* ed. A. Kolsen. 2 vols., Halle, 1910, 1935.

Jaufre Rudel, *Les Chansons de Jaufre Rudel,* ed. A. Jeanroy. 2nd. ed., Paris, 1924.

Lanfranco Cigala, *Liriche per Lanfranco Cigalo,* ed. G. Toja. Florence, 1952.

Marcabru, *Poésies complètes du troubadour Marcabru,* ed. J.-M. L. Dejeanne. Toulouse, 1909.

Monge de Montaudon, *Der Mönch von Montaudon,* ed. E. Philippson. Halle, 1873.

Peire d'Alvernhe, *Peire d'Alvernha, Liriche,* ed. A. del Monte. Turin, 1955.

Peire Cardenal, *Poésies complètes du troubadour Peire Cardenal (1180-1278),* ed. R. Lavaud. Toulouse, 1957.

Peire Raimon de Tolosa, *Le poesie di Peire Raimon de Tolosa,* ed. A. Cavaliere. Florence, 1935.

Peire Vidal, *Les Poésies de Peire Vidal,* ed. J. Anglade. Paris, 1923.
   Peire Vidal, Poesie, ed. D'A. S. Avalle. Milan and Naples, 1960.

Peirol, *Peirol, Troubadour d'Auvergne,* ed. S. C. Aston. Cambridge, 1953.

Perdigon, *Les Chansons de Perdigon,* ed. H. J. Chaytor. Paris, 1926.

Raimbaut d'Aurenga, *The Life and Works of the Troubadour Raimbaut d'Orange,* ed. W. J. Pattison. Minneapolis, 1952.

Raimbaut de Vaqueiras, *The Poems of Raimbaut de Vaqueiras,* ed. J. Linskill. The Hague, 1964.

Raimon de Miraval, *Les Poésies du troubadour Raimon de Miraval,* ed. L. T. Topsfield. Paris, 1971.

B. TROUBADOUR NARRATIVES

Anonymous, *Boécis, le plus ancien texte littéraire occitan,* eds. R. Lavaud and G. Machicot. Toulouse, 1950.
   Der altprovenzalische 'Boeci,' ed. C. Schwarze. Münster-Westfallen, 1963.
   ———, *La Chanson de la Croisade Albigeoise,* ed. E. Martin-Chabot. Paris, 1957.
   ———, *Chastel d'Amors,* ed. A. Thomas, *Annales du Midi,* 1 (1889), pp. 181-196.

Anonymous, *Deux Manuscrits provençaux du XIVe siècle*, eds. J.-B. Noulet and C. Chabaneau. Paris, 1888.
——, *The Romance of Flamenca, a Provençal Poem of the Thirteenth Century*, ed. M. E. Porter, trans. M. J. Hubert. Princeton, 1962.
Arnaut de Mareuil, *Les Saluts d'amour du troubadour Arnaud de Mareuil*, ed. P. Bec. Toulouse, 1961.
Daude de Pradas, *The Romance of Daude de Pradas on the Four Cardinal Virtues*, ed. A. Stickney. Florence, 1879.
The Romance of Daude de Pradas called Dels Auzels Cassadors, ed. A.-H. Schutz. Columbus, 1945.
Matfre Ermengau, *Le Breviari d'Amour de Matfre Ermengau*, ed. G. Azais. 2 vols., Paris, 1862.
Raimon Vidal, "Abrils issi'e mays intrava," ed. W. Bohs, *Romanische Forschungen*, 15 (1904), pp. 216-296.
"Castia-gilos," *L'Ecole des Jaloux*, ed. I. Cluzel. Paris, 1958.
"So fo e.l temps c'om era iays," ed. Max Cornicelius. Diss., Berlin, 1888.

C. ANTHOLOGIES

Anglade, J., *Anthologie des troubadours*. Paris, 1927; re-edited, 1953.
Appel, C., *Provenzalische Chrestomathie*. 3rd. ed., Leipzig, 1907.
Audiau, J. and Lavaud, R., *Nouvelle anthologie des trouvadours*. Paris, 1928.
Bartsch, K., and Koschwitz, E., *Chrestomathie provençale*. 6th. ed., Marburg, 1904.
——, *Altprovenzalische Lesebuch*, Elberfeld, 1855.
——, *Denkmäler der Provenzalischen Litteratur*. Stuttgart, 1856.
Bec, P., *Petite anthologie de la lyrique occitane du moyen âge*. Avignon, 1954.
Berry, A., *Florilège des troubadours*. Paris, 1930.
——, *Anthologie de la poésie occitane*. Paris, 1961.
Cluzel, I., *Les Troubadours catalans des XIIe et XIIIe siècles*. Paris, 1954.
Jeanroy, A., *Jongleurs et troubadours gascons du XIIe et XIIIe siècles*. Paris, 1957.
Mahn, C. A. F., *Die Werke der Troubadours in provenzalische Sprache nach den Handschriften der Pariser Nationalbibliothek*. 4 vols., Paris, 1846-1853.
——, *Gedichte der Troubadours*. 4 vols., Berlin, 1856-1873.
Milá y Fontanals, R., *Los trobadores en España*. Reprint, Barcelona, 1966.
Nelli, R., and Lavaud, R., *Les Troubadours*. 2 vols., Bruges, 1960-1966.
Raynouard, F.-G.-M., *Choix des poésies des troubadours*. 6 vols., Paris, 1816.
Véran, J., *Les Poétesses provençales du moyen âge et de nos jours*. Paris, 1946.

III. OLD FRENCH POETRY

Anonymous, "Comment l'amant doit donner," ed. J. Morawski, *Romania*, 48 (1922), pp. 431-436.
——, *De Venus la déesse d'amour*, ed. W. Foerster. Bonn, 1880.
——, "Dou vrai chiment d'amours," ed. A. Langfors, *Romania*, 45 (1918-1919), pp. 203-219.
——, *Du Dieu d'Amour*, ed. A. Jubinal. Paris, 1834.

Anonymous, *Eneas*, ed. J.-J. Salverda de Grave. Halle, 1891.
———, *Floire et Blanchefleur*, ed. M. Pelan. Paris, 1937.
———, *La Clef d'Amors*, ed. A. Doutrepont. Halle, 1890.
———, "Lai de l'oiselet," ed. G. Paris, *Légendes du Moyen Âge*. Paris, 1912.
———, "Le donnei des amants," ed. G. Paris, *Romania*, 25 (1896), pp. 497-541.
———, *Les Débats du clerc et du chevalier*, ed. Ch. Oulmont. Paris, 1911.
Chrétien de Troyes, *Cligès*, ed. A. Micha. Paris, 1968.

IV. LATIN POETRY

A. TEXTS

Andreas Capellanus, *The Art of Courtly Love*, ed. and trans. John Jay Parry. New York, 1959.
Anonymous, "Altercatio Phyllis et Flora," ed. J. Grimm, *Abhandlungen der Königlichen Akademie der Wissenschaften zu Berlin*, 1843, pp. 218-229.
Anonymous, "Concile de Remirmont, *Romarcimontis Concilium*," ed. G. Waitz, *Zeitschrift für deutsches Altertum*, 7 (1849), pp. 160-167.
———, *Les Fabulistes latins depuis le siècle d'Auguste jusqu'à la fin du moyen âge*, ed. L. Hervieux. 5 vols., 2nd. ed., Paris, 1893-1899.
———, *Recueil général des Isopets*, ed. J. Bastin. 2 vols., Paris, 1929-1930.
Ovid, *The Art of Love and other Poems*, trans. J. H. Mozley. Cambridge, Massachusetts, 1962.
———, *Heroides and Amores*, trans. Grant Showerman. Cambridge, Massachusetts, 1963.

B. STUDIES: OVID IN THE MIDDLE AGES

Bartsch, K., *Albrecht von Halberstadt und Ovid im Mittelalter*. Reprint, Amsterdam, 1965.
Dronke, P., *Medieval Latin and the Rise of European Love-Lyric*. 2 vols., 2nd. ed., Oxford, 1968.
Munari, F., *Ovid im Mittelalter*. Zurich and Stuttgart, 1960.
Paris, G., "Chrétien Legouais et autres traducteurs ou imitateurs d'Ovide," *Histoire Littéraire de France*, 29 (1885), pp. 455-525.
Scheludko, D., "Ovid und die Troubadours," *Zeitschrift für romanische Philologie*, 54 (1934), pp. 129-174.
Viarre, S., *La Survie d'Ovide dans la littérature scientifique des XIIe et XIIIe siècles*. Poitiers, 1966.

V. OTHER STUDIES

Anglade, J., *Histoire sommaire de la littérature méridionale au moyen âge (des origines à la fin du XVe siècle)*. Paris, 1921.
———, *Le Troubadour Guiraut Riquier. Étude sur la décadence de l'ancienne poésie provençale*. Paris, 1905.
Bezzola, R. R., *Les Origines et la formation de la littérature courtoise en Occident (500-1200)*. 5 vols., Paris, 1944-1963.
Blaess, M., "Arthur's Sisters," *International Arthurian Society Bibliographical Bulletin*, 8 (1956), pp. 69-77.
Camproux, Ch., *Le Joy d'Amor des troubadours. Jeu et joie d'amour*. Montpellier, 1965.

Camproux, Ch., *The Joi of Love of the Troubadours*, trans. L. Jones (unpublished).

——, *Histoire de la littérature occitane*. 2nd. ed., Paris, 1971.

Cornelius, R. D., *The Figurative Castle. A Study in the Mediaeval Allegory of the Edifice with Especial Reference to Religious Writings*. Bryn Mawr, 1930.

Dammann, O., *Die Allegorische Canzone des Guiraut de Calanso "A lieis cui am de cor e de saber" und ihre Deutung*. Diss. Breslau, 1891.

Deroy, J. P. Th., "Merce ou la quinta linea Veneris," VIème Congrès International de Langue et Littérature d'Oc et d'Etudes Franco — Provençales, II, *Langue et Littérature du Moyen Âge*. Montpellier, September, 1970, pp. 309-328.

Diez, F., *Leben und Werke der Troubadours*. Leipzig, 1882.

Douais, Mgsr., *Documents pour servir à l'histoire de l'Inquisition dans le Languedoc*. Paris, 1900.

Faral, E., *Sources latines des contes et romans courtois du moyen âge*. Paris, 1913.

——, *Les Arts poétiques du XIIᵉ et XIIIᵉ siècles. Recherches et documents sur la technique littéraire au moyen âge*. Paris, 1924.

Fletcher, A., *Allegory, the Theory of a Symbolic Mode*. Ithaca, 1964.

Flutre, F., *Table des noms propres avec toutes leur variantes figurant dans les romans du moyen âge*. Paris, 1955.

Grente, G., ed. *Dictionnaire des Lettres Françaises*, I, *Le Moyen Âge*. Paris, 1964.

Guiraud, J., *Histoire de l'Inquisition au moyen âge*, II, *L'Inquisition au XIIIᵉ siècle en France, en Espagne, et en Italie*. Paris, 1938.

Haskins, Ch. H., *The Renaissance of the Twelfth Century*. 2nd. ed., New York, 1959.

Honig, E., *Dark Conceit, the Making of Allegory*. London, 1959.

Hopper, V. F., *Medieval Number Symbolism*. New York, 1969.

Jauss, H. R., "Entstehung und Strukturwandel der allegorischen Dichtung," *Grundriss der romanischen Literaturen des Mittelalters*, Vol. 6, Part I, pp. 146-244. Heidelberg, 1968.

Jeanroy, A., *La Poésie lyrique des troubadours*. 2 vols., Paris, 1934.

——, *Histoire sommaire de la poésie occitane*. Toulouse, 1945.

Jung, M.-R., *Études sur le poème allégorique en France au moyen âge*. Berne, 1971.

Lafont, R., and Anatole, C., *Nouvelle histoire de la littérature occitane*. Paris, 1970.

Langlois, E., *Origines et Sources de la Roman de la Rose*. Paris, 1890.

——, *Table des noms propres de toute nature compris dans les chansons de geste*. Paris, 1904.

Lazar, M., *Amour courtois et "fin'amors" dans la littérature du XIIᵉ siècle*. Paris, 1964.

Lewis, C. S., *The Allegory of Love*. Oxford, 1936.

Lot, F., "La Chanson de Landri," *Romania*, 32 (1903), pp. 1-17.

——, "Notes historiques sur Aie d'Avignon," *Romania*, 33 (1904), pp. 145-162.

Muscatine, Ch., "The Locus of Action in Medieval Narrative," *Romance Philology*, 17 (1963), pp. 115-122.

Neilson, W. A., *The Origins and Sources of the Court of Love*. Boston, 1899.

Nelli, R., *L'Erotique des troubadours*. Toulouse, 1963.
——, *Le Roman de Flamenca, un art d'aimer occitanien du XIIIe siècle*. Toulouse, 1966.
Parducci, A., "La 'lettera d'amore' nell'antico provenzale," *Studi Medievale,* n.s. 15 (1942), pp. 69-110.
Paris, G., "Les Cours d'amour au moyen âge," *Journal des Savants* (1888), pp. 664-675, 727-736.
Pépin, J., *Mythe et allégorie. Les origines grecques et les contestations judéo-chrétiennes*. Aubier, 1958.
Robertson, D. W., Jr., *A Preface to Chaucer. Studies in Medieval Perspectives*. Princeton, New Jersey, 1962.
Schwarze, C., "Pres, Amor, Gelosia," *Zeitschrift für romanische Philologie,* 83 (1967), pp. 280-305.
Thomas, A., *Francesco de Barberino et la littérature provençale au moyen âge*. Paris, 1883.
Tuve, R., *Allegorical Imagery. Some Medieval Books and their Posterity*. Princeton, New Jersey, 1966.
Wettstein, J., *"Mezura": l'idéal des troubadours, son essence et ses aspects*. Zurich, 1945.
Zumthor, P., *Langue et techniques poétiques à l'époque romane (XIe-XIIIe siècles)*. Paris, 1963.

VI. DICTIONARIES

Battisti, C., and Alessio, G., *Dizionario etimologico italiano*.
Levy, E., *Provenzalisches Supplement-Wörterbuch*. 8 vols., Leipzig, 1894-1924.
——, *Petit dictionnaire provençal-français*. 3rd. ed., Heidelberg, 1961.
Monaci, Ernesto, *Crestomazia italiana dei primi secoli con prospetto grammaticale e glossario*. 2nd. ed., Rome and Naples, 1955.
Raynouard, F.-J.-M., *Lexique roman ou dictionnaire de la langue des troubadours*. 6 vols., Paris, 1844.
Wartburg, W. von, *Französisches Etymologisches Wörterbuch; eine Darstellung des galloromanischen Sprachschatzes*. Bonn and Basel, 1928-.

VII. BIBLIOGRAPHIES

Brunel, C. F., *Bibliographie des manuscrits littéraires en ancien provençal*. Paris, 1935.
Jeanroy, A., *Bibliographie sommaire des chansonniers provençaux*. Paris, 1916.
Pillet, A., and Carstens, H., *Bibliographie der Troubadours*. Halle, 1933.

VIII. TEXTUAL STUDIES

Bühler, C. F., "The Phillipps Manuscript of Provençal Poetry," *Speculum,* 22 (1970), pp. 305-323.
Mussafia, A., *Beitrag zur der norditalienischen Mundarten im XV. Jahrhundert*. Reprint, Bologna, 1964.
Pfister, M., "Die Anfänge der altprovenzalischen Schriftsprache," *Zeitschrift für romanische Philologie,* 86 (1970), pp. 305-323.

Suchier, H., "Il Canzoniere Provenzale di Cheltenham," *Rivista di Filologia romanza,* 20 (1875), pp. 49-52, 144-172.
Voelker, P., "Die Bedeutungsentwicklung des Wortes *Roman,*" *Zeitschrift für romanische Philologie,* 10 (1886), pp. 485-525.

CONTENTS OF THE *CORT D'AMOR*

The text is incomplete at the end

EDITION AND TRANSLATION OF THE
CORT D'AMOR

[S]einor, vos que volez la flor
E la corteszia d'amor,
E non avez soing d'autr'aver,
Mas ab ioi voletz remaner, ★
5 Auzatz un romanz bon e bel,
Bastit de joi fin e novel, ★
E gardatz quant l'auresz auszit,
Non metatz los motz en oblit;
Que za negus hom no fara
10 So que.l romanz comandara,
No sia plenz de corteszia, ★
E que non guerrez Villania. ★
Que lo be que lo romanz di
Fasson las dompnas e.l drut fi,
15 E gardon se de la folia,
Que.l romanz deveda e castia;
Que vos sabetz qu'ab Desmeszura
Perd Amors a tors sa dreitura, ★
Que Malvestat e Putaria
20 No.l laisson tener dreita via. ★
Per so han fag novella amor
D'una domna de gran valor.
Viij. xx. que donas qe pulsellas,
Q'an trobat lurs raszons novellas
25 Coment Amors sia lials,
Fugon s'en las falsas e.ls fals,
Qa cant Amors parlament, ★
No.s taing haza galiament.
Ora zuzatz coment araszona ★
30 Sa gent, Amors la dousa e la bona.
Mas premieramens vos dirai

Seigneur, you who require the flower
And the courtesy of love,
And have no care for other goods,
But wish to remain with *joi*, ★
5 Listen to a good and beautiful romance, ★
Built of fine new *joi*,
And beware, when you have heard it,
That you do not forget the words;
Because never will any man do
10 What the romance commands,
If he is not filled with courtesy,
And if he does not fight Villany.
May the good of which the romance speaks
Make the ladies trust the lover, ★
15 And preserve themselves from folly,
Which the romance forbids and chastizes;
Because you know that with Excess
Love wrongly loses its direction,
For Wickedness and Prostitution
20 Do not permit one to stay on the straight path.
For this reason they have made a new love
For a lady of great merit. ★
Eight score ladies as well as maidens ★
Who have found their new arguments
25 How loyal Love can be,
Flee away from false men and women,
For when Love holds parliament, ★
It is not suitable that there be trickery.
Now hear how she spoke
30 To her people, Love the sweet and good. ★
But first of all I will tell you

Sos conpainons, ni hon estaz, ★
Ab cui faz acordament ★
D'amor lo lial zutgament.

35   [E]l temps qe.l roissignol faz nausa,
     Qe de nueit ni de zor no pausa ★
     Desots la fuella de cantar
     Pe.l bel temps que vei refrescar,
     Aven que Fin'Amors parlet ★
40   Ab sos barons en son rescet
     En som del puei de Parnasus. ★
     Zoi e Solasz foron laisus,
     E Ardimenz e Corteszia
     Qe de flors l'enzonchon la via.
45   Bon'Esperancha e Paors ★
     Li portent de denant las flors.
     D'autra part Larguesza e Domneis
     Lo meton en un leit d'orfreis. ★

fol. 31v   Celars e Dousa Conpania
50   Geton desus roesa floria. ★
     Lo cortes pueih, de l'autra part,
     De.l fuoch d'amor relusz ez art. ★
     D'aqui mou tota la ioza ★
     Qu'Amors per mez lo mond envoza.
55   E d'autra part son las floretas,
     La ruosas e las violetas,
     Qi trameton lor gran douszor
     Denant lo leit de Fin'Amor; ★
     E d'autra part ha cent pulsellas
60   Q'anc negus hom non vi plus bellas,
     E chascuna ha son amador,
     E son vestu d'una color;
     Baison ez braisson soven, ★
     E mantenon pretz e ioven.
65   Totz temps han aital desdug ★
     Ad aital gen vai be, so cug.
     E d'autra part hac un ombrage
     On hac maint auzel saulvatge ★
     Que cantent la nueit e lo zor

Her companions, and where she is,
With whom she is in agreement
In the loyal judgment of love.

35 In the time when the nightingale makes his noise,
Who pauses neither night nor day
From his singing among the leaves
In the lovely season that I see re-budding,
It happened that *Fin' Amor* spoke ★
40 With her barons in her refuge
On the summit of the mountain of Parnassus.
Joi and Solace were up there,
And Boldness and Courtesy
Who strewed the way with flowers.
45 Good Hopes and Fear
Brought them the flowers from below.
In another place, Largesse and *Domneis* ★
Place her in a bed of gold cloth. ★
Discretion and Sweet Company
50 Strew red flowers on the floor.
In another place, the courtly mountain ★
Shines and burns with the fire of love. ★
From here moves all the joy ★
That Love sends throughout the world.
55 And elsewhere are the little flowers,
The roses and the violets,
That send forth their great sweetness
Around the bed of *Fin' Amor*;
And in another place there are one hundred maidens
60 More beautiful than any man has ever seen,
And each one has her lover, ★
And they are dressed in one color;
They often kiss and embrace,
And they maintain merit and youth.
65 They continually have such pleasure
As suits such people, so I believe.
And in another place there is a shady wood
Where there are many wild birds
That sing night and day

70 Voltas e lais de gran dousor.
   Ze.l mei loc ac un castel ★
   Q'anc negus om non vi plus bel,
   Qe non ha una peira e.l mur
   Non luisza con d'aur o d'azur.
75 D'aqi guerezon Vilania.
   Las claus son Pretz e Drudaria, ★
   E.l gaita q'es e.l castel cria: ★
   "Esta lo drutz contra sa mia, ★
   E la mia contra son drut. ★
80 Era non sera ia sauput. ★
   Ar es lo luochs e la saiszos
   Qu'ieu haz endormitz los gilos." ★
   Davant la porta hac una font,
   E non a tan bella e.l mont,
85 Qi sortz en una conca d'aur.
   De tot lo mont val le tesaur. ★
   N'a om e.l mont, si n'a begut, ★
   Que cant qe es e cant fut, ★
   Non sapchza de be e d'onor,
90 Qe non oblit ira e dolor.
   Claus es de lauries e de pis, ★
   E de pomiers de paradis.
   De flors de lizs es coronada,
   Que nais menudet en la prada.
95 Aqi s'asis a parlament
   Amors, e parlet bellament
   Enaissi con deu far lo seingner
   Qe tot lo mont ha a destreigner. ★
   Esgardet vas terra un petit,
100 Con sabis om, e pueis ha dit:
    "Seinors, eu me lau be de vos,
    Mas vos sabetz qe totz om pros

fol. 32r   Deu gardar q'en sa senioria ★
              Fassa om sen e lais folia,
105 Qe vos sabetz q'ab obs d'amar
    No val re que vol folleiar, ★
    Que l'autrer nos dis Iohanitz ★
    Que leons aucis la formitz.

70 Songs and lays of great sweetness.
And in the middle of the place there is a castle ★
More beautiful than any man has ever seen, ★
Which has not one stone in the wall ★
Which does not shine like gold and azur.

75 From here Villany is waging war.
The keys are Merit and Intimacy, ★

Watchman: And the watchman who is in the castle cries:
"Here is the lover with his lady,
And the lady with her lover.

80 Now it will never be known.
Now is the place and the season
Because I have lulled the jealous ones to sleep."

Fountain: In front of the door there is a fountain,
And there is none other so beautiful in all the world,

85 Which spurts from a golden shell.
It is worth the treasure of all the world.
There is no man in the world, if he has drunk from it,
Whatever he is or whatever he was,
Who does not know good and honor,

90 And who does not forget anger and sorrow.
It is closed in by laurel trees and pines, ★
And by the apple trees of paradise.
It is crowned with fleurs de lis,
Which grow very tiny in the meadow.

Fin'Amor: 95 Here, seated in Parliament
Is Love, and she speaks beautifully
As must the seigneur ★
Who has the entire world to rule. ★
She looked toward earth for a moment,

100 Like a wise man, and then she said:

Fin'Amor's
first speech
to Joi: "My lords, I praise myself greatly because of you,
But you know that each man of merit
Must keep watch so that in his seigneury
Men behave seriously and leave folly,

105 Because you know that where love is concerned,
Nothing is of value that requires acting foolishly,
For recently Johanitz told us ★
That the lion kills the ant. ★

Don Iois, aisso dig contra vos, ★

110 Que vos faitz aitant fort ioios ★
Us vassal qe no er cellatz. ★
Si domna li fai sos agratz, ★
Si a el non s'ennanara, ★
E lo blasme li remanra,

115 Vec vos la fromitz e.l leon.
La domna es morta pe.l garchon.
Eu.s comanc: non fassatz mais re,
Mas donatz zoi lai on conve.
Als enfantz fatz con a d'enfans,

120 Als parladors donatz parlans,
E metetz en tot tal meszura
Q'eu no i perda ma dreitura,
Que pros om i a grand onor
Qan fai be l'afar son seinor."

125 [A]pres araiszonet Solaz.
Tota la cort estet en paz.
"Seinor, mout si deur'om sofrir, ★
Qe mout deu om son cors cobrir, ★
Qe non diga tot son coratge,

130 Ni non mostre grand alegratge,
Mas lai on es luechs e meszura,
Q'amors per be cellar meillura,
Qe l'auzel, cant el ve lo latz,
S'en fui d'aqi tost e viatz.

135 Tot altretal fai de manes,
Vilans qant vei ome cortes,
Que viu de ioi e de solatz ★
E porta trezador ni laz,
Quant el lo ve serra sa porta ★

140 E sa moiller es pesz qu'a morta. ★
Aisso dic per vos, don Solatz,
Qu'ez mos amig e mos privatz, ★
Ez affi vos la mia fe,
Qe tot lo mon non am tan re

145 Mas voill qe laissetz la gaiessa

Sir *Joi,* this I say to you,
110 That you in the same way make most joyous
A vassal who was not discreet.
If the lady gives him his pleasure,
If to him she does no dishonor,
And the blame remains with him,
115 Here you have the ant and the lion.
The lady died because of that miserable man.
I command this: do not do anything else,
But give *joi* there where it is fitting.
Toward infants, behave as with infants,
120 To those who talk, give speech,
And in everything observe such measure
That I do not lose my jurisdiction,
Because the worthy man has great honor in it
When he conducts the business of his lord well."

125 Then she addressed Solace.

Fin'Amor's
second speech
to Solace:
The entire court was silent.
"Seigneur, often one will have to suffer,
For often one must cover his heart,
So that he does not tell his feelings,
130 Nor does he show his great happiness,
Except there where there is occasion and measure,
Because love through being well hidden improves,
Like the bird, when it sees the trap,
Flies away from that place quickly and lively.
135 In quite the same way and immediately, behaves
The base man when he sees a courtly man,
Who lives with *joi* and solace
And carries a crossbow and trap,
When he sees him close his door,
140 And his wife is worse than dead.
This I say for you, Lord Solace,
Who are my friend and confidant,
And I confide my faith to you,
Than whom in all the world I love nothing better.
145 But I want you to leave the gaiety

Qan non es luechs qe, si be.us pesa, ★
Vos ensegnarai vostre pro
Qar eu n'ai fort bel gaszardo.
Qe vos faitz amors comenssar,
150 Vos faitz l'un a l'autre agradar.
Vos non voletz envei ni plors; ★
Viulas, dansas e tanbors ★
E Ioventz vos fan compania. ★
Seigna vos qi no sab la via ★
155 D'amor, qe vos lo metretz lai
On om non meissaona mas iai." ★

fol. 32v   [A]pres parlet ab Ardiment:
"De vos me lau eu ben e gent,
Que vos fatz toszeta ardida
160 Q'a paors neis d'aucel qant crida.
Pueis la fassaitz vos tan segura ★
Q'a son drut vaz de nueit oscura,
Qe non tem marit ni parent
Batre ni menassar sovent.
165 E faitz a paubre drut enqerre
Domna q'a gran fieu e gran terre. ★
Qe.l ditz: "Se no.m laissas estar, ★
Eu te farai ton envei far." ★
E cel que de re non s'esfreda,
170 Sitot, s'a petit de moneda,
S'adoba ades de ben servir.
Pueis la fatz tant enardir ★
Qu'ella oblida son lignatje,
Sa riqesa e son parate, ★
175 E torna tot son cor en lui,
E son bon amic ambedui. ★
E per vos vai a parlament
Drutz a si donz ardiment. ★
En amor, non val re paors;
180 Ardimentz es la claus d'amors."

[C]orteszia, de vos non sai
Dir lo bens qe de vos hai, ★

For this is not the place so that, even if that weigh upon
I will teach you your rôle   [you,
For I have in the affair a very pretty recompense.
In order to make love begin,
150 You make them please each other.
You do not want envy or tears;
Violas, dances and drums
And Youth keep you company.
Learn the name of him who does not know the way
155 Of Love, so that you shall put him there
Where no one any longer harvests."

Fin'Amor's
third speech
to Boldness:
Next she spoke to Boldness:
"For you I praise myself well and nobly,
Because you make the young girl bold,
160 She who has the same fears as a little bird when it cries.
Then you make her so secure
That she goes to her sweetheart in the dark night,
And she fears neither husband nor relative
Will beat or threaten [her] often.
165 And you make the poor lover seek
A lady who has great fiefs and great lands.
Let him say to her: 'If you do not let me remain,
I will certainly make you do what you desire.'
And he, who is not afraid of anything,
170 Soon, if he has a little money,
He then equips himself to serve well.
And then you make her so bold
That she forgets her lineage,
Her wealth and her rank,
175 And turns her entire heart toward him,
And they are both of them good lovers.
And through you the lover goes to converse
With his lady so boldly. *
In love, fear is worth nothing;
180 Boldness is the key to love."

Fin'Amor's
fourth speech
to Courtesy:
"Courtesy, as far as you are concerned I do not know
How to describe the good things that I have had from
                                                [you, *

Ni non sai grazir las onors
Q'ieu haj de vos, ni las lauszors,
185 Q'ab plana razon de sofrir,
Me fatz a totz mon abellir.
Ab lo sofrir avetz mesura
Per qe vostre bon pretz meillura.
Vos metetz mesura en parlar,
190 Envez no sabetz vos ia far, ★
Ni ia negus om non er pros ★
Si non ha compania ab vos,
Que aqel que i a conpania
Non fara orguoill ni follia."

195 "[B]on' Esperansa, grand aiuda
Me fatz, qar vostre cor no.s muda ★
Q'al premier que vol faire druda,
El ven a leis, si la saluda,
E pueis comensa la pregar ★
200 Per Deu q'elle lo deia amar. ★
Bon' Esperansa la lo guida,
E sitot noncha l'es gracida
Sa pregueira al comensar,
Ades lo faz ben esperar
205 Qe greu verreis novella amia
Q'a premier non se fassa enia. ★
'Domna, per q'es q'altr'amic hai?' ★
Qe.l dira: 'Ges no.us amarai,'
fol. 33r   O dira: 'Ges no.us amaria
210 Q'onor e marit en perdria,' ★
O dira qe: 'Plens es d'engan,
Vos amador, per qe.us soan,' ★
Bon' Esperansa, ditz c'aison ★
Non cal tot preiar un boton. ★
215 Qant el se desditz ne s'orguella,
Q'adoncs se descausa e despuella."

"[P]aors, vos siatz benedeita!
Per vos vai drutz la via dreita,
Qe, qant vai a si dons parlar,

Nor do I know how to thank you for the honors
That I have had from you, nor for the praises,
185 For with full reason to suffer,
You make me much embellished by everyone. *
With suffering you have moderation
Through which your good merit increases.
You place measure in speaking, *
190 Envy you do not know how to cause,
And never was any man ever worthy
If he did not keep company with you,
For he who has you as companion
Will not become proud or foolish."

Fin'Amor's
fifth speech to
Good Hope: 195 "Good Hope, great help
You give me, for your heart does not change
So that to the first whom he wishes to make his sweet-
The lover goes and greets her,   [heart,
And then he begins to beseech her
200 In the name of God that she deign to love him.
Good Hope guides him there,
And although his prayer is never granted
In the beginning,
You make him hope immediately
205 So that only with difficulty would he see a new lady,
Because he did not become angry with the first.
'Lady, why is it that you have another sweetheart?'
If she say to him: 'Certainly I will not love you,'
Or if she say: 'Certainly I would not love you
210 If I should lose honor and husband by it,'
Or if she say: 'You are full of deceit,
You lovers, so that I scorn you,'
Say, Good Hope, that that
Must not be considered worth a button.
215 When he contradicts himself and becomes proud,
Let him then take off his shoes and undress."

Fin'Amor's
sixth speech
to Fear: "Fear, may you be blessed!
Through you, the lover goes the right way,
Because, when he goes to his lady to talk,

220 Q'el li cuida desmostrar
E dire qe per s'amor mor,
E vos li donatz ins e.l cor
Si q'el non sab dire razo,
Ni sab detriar oc ni no.
225 qe qant ha trestot iorn parlat,
Non cuia aver dit mas foudat. ★
E qant l'a trames son message
Et el pensa en son corage:
'Las! aiso.l mandetz solamen! ★
230 Ben sabra q'eu hai pauch de sen. ★
Jamais non virara sol l'uel.
Aiso se tenra az orguel.
Catieu! qe faras si.t soana? ★
O si tos messages t'engana?
235 O qe faras si desir lonia? ★
O.l messages te dis mensonia? ★
Ben saz qe m'escanara, ★
E mon message me batra.
Non fara qe tan ez cortesa. ★
240 Ja non fara aital malesa.
Caitieu! mala la vi'enanch!
Sa plaia me tol tot lo sanch. ★
Be.m pesa qar lo i ai trames,
Que sos maritz es malares.
245 E Dieus! com aura vergoinat ★
Si mon message auci ni bat.'
Aici vos dic on nos estem:
'Re non ama om qe non tem.' "

"[L]argueza, vos voell castiar
250 E si.m fatz vos tot mon afar,
Qe greu pot haver gran pesa ★
Negus om si non ha larguesa,
Ni causa no pot om trobar
Qi tant vailla ad obs d'amar.
255 Mais no.u cell qe votre pesa ★
Metas en orba Cobetsa, ★
Ni.u cell qe dones largament ★

220 He believes he demonstrates to her,
And says that for her love he is dying,
And you inspire him deep in his heart
So that he does not know how to speak rationally,
Nor does he know how to distinguish between yes and
225 And when he has spoken for the entire day,   [no.
He does not believe that he has said so much folly.
And when he has sent his messenger to her,
And he thinks in his heart:
'Alas! I sent her only this!
230 Well she will know how little intelligence I have.
Never again will she turn even her glance toward me.
This will seem like pride.
Miserable me! What will you do if she refuses you?
Or suppose all the messengers deceive you?
235 Or what will you do if desire escapes?
Or the messengers tell you lies?
You know perfectly well that she will torment me,
And she will beat my messenger for me.
240 Never will she do such an evil thing.
She will not do it because she is so courteous.
Miserable me! A difficult road henceforth!
Her wound took all my blood from me.
It weighs upon me because I sent him there,
Because her husband is vile.
245 Oh God! How ashamed she will be
If he kills or beats my messenger.'
Then you say to him right here where we are:
'A man loves nothing who fears nothing.'

Fin'Amor's
seventh speech
to Largess: "Largess, I want to instruct you
250 And thus you do all my business for me,
For hardly can any man have great prowess
If he is not generous,
Nor can a man find anything
That is worth so much where love is concerned.
255 I do not conceal from you that your merit
Blinds Covetousness, *
Nor do I hide from you that you give largely

A neguna dompna qe.s vent,
Qe qant il vos atrai, ni.us tira,
260 Ni de.l cor de preon sospira. ★
Il non o fai mas feintament
Per so que.l dones de l'argent,
E.l iois qan cobeesa aiuda ★
Non es res mas amor venduda.

fol. 33v   265 Per q'ieu vos prec qe.l fals sospir
No.us puoscan l'aver escotir,
Mais qant veires domna de pretz,
Digas li vos eissa en privetz,
· Qe si.l donas, il vos dara,
270 E de confundre.us gardara,
E pueis dara vos largament
Joy e proesa e ardiment."

"[D]omneis, qui.us vol mal si 'aonitz. ★
Per vos vai paubres drut garnitz,
275 E vai en invern a la bisa ★
Qe non ha freig en sa camisa,
E conten se plus bellament
Qe tals qe ha trop mais d'argent.
E cel es richs, el fara cort, ★
280 E torneiament e beort,
E parla plus bellament ★
Ab lo paubre q'ab lo manent,
Per so qe chadaus om diga ★
Ben de lui a sa dousa amiga."

285 "[C]elamens, vos es la flors ★
Don nais e creis la ioy d'amors.
Vos non voles envei ni bruda, ★
Ni ia domna no er batuda ★
Per re qe vos digatz en fol.
290 Vos non li viratz sol lo col
Qant om o ve, ni fatz semblant
Qe de ren mens alatz calant. ★
E qant es la sasons ni.l locs,
Vos fatz pareiser vostre iocs.

To any lady that comes,
Because when she ressembles you, she draws it from you,
260 And she sighs from the bottom of her heart.
She does not do it except by pretense
So that you will give her money,
And the *joi*, when covetousness is added,
Becomes nothing more than purchased love.
265 Therefore I beg you that the false sighs
May not have hidden you from her,
But when you see a lady of value,
Tell her that she comes from you in secret,
That if you give to her, she will give to you,
270 And she will keep you from perishing,
And then she will give you widely
Joi and merit and boldness." ⋆

Fin'Amor's
eighth speech
to Domneis:

"*Domneis*, whoever wishes you evil dishonors himself.
Through you poor lovers are armed,
275 And they go about in winter in the wind ⋆
In only their shirts and they are not cold,
And they behave more brilliantly
Than those who have too much money.
And if he is rich, he will pay court,
280 And take part in tourney and joust,
And he will speak more politely
With the poor man than with the rich,
In such a way that every man speaks
Well of him to his sweet lady."

Fin'Amor's
ninth speech
to Discretion:

285 "Discretion, you are certainly the flower
From which is born and grows the *joi* of love.
You do not want envy or rumor,
Nor was any lady ever beaten
Through anything that you said foolishly.
290 You do not even turn your neck to her
When someone is looking, nor do you pretend
That for nothing less you go about content.
And when it is the time and the place, ⋆
You make your games appear.

295 Qan es partitz, cuza cascus
     Qe siatz monges ou resclus.
     Vos voletz vostre ioi en pasz; ★
     Vos mantenes ioi e solasz. ★
     Per cortesia e per onor
300 Vos doin la baneira d'Amor." ★

     "[D]olsa Compania, fina druda
     Es soven per vos ben venguda,
     E cela res qi plus li platz, ★
     Son bel amic entre sos bratz.
305 E.l baisza mil ves en la boca,
     Qe qant sos bel cors al sieu toca, ★
     Ella li ditz per plan solaz:
     'Amics, enveia vos mos braz?' ★
     El li respon: 'Domna, el non.
310 Tan qan vos mi faitz m'es tan bon.
     M'arma, mos cors, so m'es avis,
     Es e.l mei luec de paradis.'
     'Bels amics, coindes e ioios, ★
     S'ieu ren vaill, so es per vos,
315 Q'anch Galvains ni Soredamors, ★
     Ni anch Floris ni Blanchaflors,
     Ni l'amor Ysolt ni Tristan,
     Contra nos dos non valg un gan.'

fol. 34r   'Bella domna, tant qant vivrai ★
320 Sachas de fi vos servirai,
     Q'ieu non voell qe a mort ni a vida
     La nostra amors sia partida.'
     E volrion mais esser mort
     Q'entre lor agues un descort.

325 "[D]rudaria, vos es Dons Pres ★
     Qe del castel las claus tenes,
     Gardas qe s'aqest dez baron ★
     Vos aduiszon negun preszon, ★
     Qe lo metas en fuec d'amor,
330 Gardan la nueit e lo zor, ★
     E zamais non haion be ★

295 When it is gone, each one thinks
That you are a monk or a hermit.
You require your *joi* in peace;
You maintain *joi* and solace.
Through courtesy and honor
300 I give you the banner of Love."

Fin'Amor's
tenth speech
to Sweet
Company:

"Sweet Company, a fine mistress ★
Is often welcomed through you,
And that thing which pleases her most,
Her handsome lover in her arms.
305 And she kisses him a thousand times on the mouth,
And when her beautiful body touches his,
She tells him for pure solace;

The lady: 'Lover, do you dislike my arms?'

The lover: And he answers her: 'Lady, not at all.
310 All that you do for me is very good.
My soul, my body, so I think,
Is in the middle of paradise.'

The lady: 'Handsome friend, gracious and joyous,
If I am worth anything, it is so through you,
315 For never Gawain nor Soredamors, ★
Never Floire nor Blanchefleur, ★
Nor the love of Yseult and Tristan,
Compared to we two, were worth a glove.'

The lover: 'Beautiful Lady, as long as I shall live
320 You know that I will serve you purely,
For I do not wish that living or dead
Our love should be divided.'
And they preferred to be dead
Rather than have a disagreement between them.

Fin'Amor's
eleventh speech
to *Drudaria*
and Merit:

325 "*Drudaria*, you and Lord Merit
Who hold the keys to the castle,
Watch so that if these ten barons ★
Bring you any person,
You set him afire with love,
330 Watching night and day,
And may they never have any peace

Tro lor domnas n'aion merce. ★
Si prenon domnas dos tans plus fort ★
Las conduisetz trus q'a la mort
335 Tro qe'z mandon a lur amics ★
Qe non lor aion cor enics,
Qe fort fer deu om tormentar
Las domnas car se fan pregar.
E si chai venon amador,
340 Domnas ni drutz de gran valor,
E vos lo fatz fort bel ostal: ★
Asetzes los as deis rial
E colgas los lai dins la tor
En la mia cambra de flor."

345 [Q]ant Amors hacs a gran leszer ★
Comandat e dit son plaszer,
Las domnas l'an ben autreiat
Qe d'aco qe ha comandat
Li faran de tot son talan,
350 Qe ia mot non traspassaran. ★
Mais de leis volrion saber:
Qal amor deu hom mais tener,
E preigan lo com lor seignor
Q'el las engart de desonor,
355 Qe tant pros domnas com ellas son ★
Non haion blasme per lo mon, ★
Ni qe lor pretz ni lor valor
Non lur destrua Fals'Amor,
E qe lur diga soltiment ★
360 Per razon e per iugament, ★
So qe fai d'amor e gardar,
E aco q'hom en dei ostar.

[S]o dis Amors: "Bon conseil sai.
Na Corteszia, q'eu vez lai,
365 Voell q'en fassa aqest iutgament, ★
Qe sab per on monta e disent
Amors, e qar sab ben q'il es
Del mont la plus adreita res.

Until their ladies have mercy on them.
If they take ladies two times stronger,
You will lead them to their death
335 Until they assure their lovers
That they do not have hearts hostile to them,
For very cruelly must men torment
The ladies, for they require much persuading.
And if lovers come here,
340 Ladies and lovers of great value,
You must make a very good welcome for them.
Seat them at the royal dais
And give them beds there in the tower
In my chamber of flowers."

The ladies'
Request:
345 When Love had with great leisure
Commanded and spoken her pleasure,
The ladies assured her
That all that she had ordered
They will do according to her desire,
350 So that they would not pass over a word.
More from her they wanted to learn: *
Which love one must hold more dear,
And they begged her as their seigneur *
That she protect them from dishonor, *
355 So that such worthy ladies as they are
May have no blame in all the world,
And so that neither their merit nor their value
Be destroyed for them by False Love,
And that she tell them subtly
360 Through reason and judgment,
What to do in order to keep love,
And that which one must avoid.

Fin'Amor's
request of
Dame Courtesy:
Thus spoke Love: "I know good advice.
Lady Courtesy, whom I see there,
365 I require that she make this judgment,
Because she knows through what Love increases and
And because she knows well that it is   [decreases,
The most correct thing in the world.

Il lo fera be ses engan." *
370 Cortesia pleigua son gan
E doba se de iugar, *
Q'om cortes se fan pauch pregar *

fol. 34v

Qant vei q'es luecs es avinents. *
Molt es grantz e preon sos sens. *
375 Puis parlet com savis e pros, *
Gent fon auszida sa razos:

"[S]einors, per dreig e per usage
Deu Amors gardar son parage,
Qe paubresza ab gentilesa *
380 Val mais q'orgueill ab riqesa, *
Ni a sa cort non am res at *
Mais servir ab humilitat.
Eu vos o dirai breu e bon, *
E breuiar vos hai la raszon. *
385 Fin'Amors es de qatre res: *
La premiera es bona fes,
E la segona lialtatz, *
E sos afars sia cellatz.
E la terza es mesura *
390 De parlar per la gad tafura, *
E la qarta sapchas es sens
Ab q'Amors fai tots sos talens.
Aqesta devem mantener *
E gardar de nostre poder;
395 Mais la falsa via bastarsa
Qe sec la gent q'e.l fuec fos arsa,
Las trairitz e las venals,
Las canaritz e las comunals, *
Qe lor femm'es e lors amors, *
400 Es tot chaitiviers e dolors.
D'aqellas non devem parlar, *
Mas qant solament de blasmar.
Aqest iutgament, fait d'Amor, *
Dreitz es com no.l pot far meillor,
405 E qi desdire lo volia,
Ben sapchas q'eu lo il defendria,

She will do it well without deceit." *

370 Courtesy pledged her glove
And prepared to judge,
For the courteous man has himself beseeched but little
When he sees that the place is suitable.
She is very great and her intelligence is profound.

375 Then she spoke wisely and worthily,
Carefully were her reasons heard:

Lady Courtesy's
speech:

"Seigneurs, through right and custom
Must Love guard her peerage,
For poverty with gentleness

380 Is worth more than pride with wealth,
Nor at her court does she need anything
But service with humility.
I will tell it to you briefly and well,
And I am right to abbreviate for you.

385 Fin'Amor is made of four things:
The first is good faith,
And the second is loyalty,
That her affairs may be hidden.
And the third is moderation

390 In speaking before knavish joking,
And the fourth you know is intelligence,
With which Love accomplishes all her desires.
This we must maintain
And guard with all our strength;

395 But the false bastard way, *
That is followed by the people who were burned in the
The traitoresses and prostitutes,   [fire, *
The fickle and vulgar women,
Who are their women and their love,

400 Is quite miserable and sorrowful.
Of them we must not speak,
Except only to blame.
This judgment, made by Love, *
Is just, and no one can make a better one,

405 And he who wishes to contradict it,
You know very well that I would defend it against him,

E.n rendria mon cavalier,
Si.n trobava encontra guerier."

[L]as domnas han ben entendut,
410   E an en lor cor retengut
Lo zutgament, e mes en brieu
Per so qe l'oblide plus greu. ⋆
Amors lo lor ha saiellat ⋆
Ab son anel d'or niellat, ⋆
415   E segnet lo de sa man destre, ⋆
Met li n'en paradis terrestre. ⋆
La Cortesa d'Amor lo pren
En una caisa dousamen.
L'a mult bellament estuzat
420   E.l mei loec d'un samis pleiat, ⋆
E dis als barons en rient:
"Aves ausat lo zutgament ⋆
Qan adreitaments an jutgat, ⋆
Mas — qar sai qe m'en sabreitz grat — ⋆
425   Vos dirai d'amor de tal loc
Don maint plor tornaran en ioc, ⋆

fol. 35r

E maint ioc tornaran en plor,
Q'aital usatge han amador,
Qe gai son qant be lor estai,
430   E qant han tant ni qant d'esmai,
Li plaint e li plor e ill sospir
Lur aduiszon trues q'al morir. ⋆
Mas drutz q'amors vol conqistar
Deu de mantenent demonstrar
435   A si dons son cor ses taina. ⋆
Sera plus rica qe.l reina,
Q'una non trobares en mil
Qe no.us en tengua per gentil,
E q'e.l cor no.us en sapcha grat, ⋆
440   Si ben non fai semblant irat, ⋆
Q'il pensara: 'Ges non soi laida, ⋆
Pos aqest s'en vol metre en faida,
E molt faria qe felnesa
S'aqest gentils om de mi pensa, ⋆

And I would offer my champion,
If a knightly encounter take place."

Signing and
sealing of
Judgment:

The ladies have understood very well,
410 And in their hearts they retained
The judgment, and put it into a chart
So that they could forget it less easily.
Love has sealed it for them
With her ring of gold engraved with black enamel,
415 And she signed it with her right hand,
And placed it in the Earthly Paradise.
There Courtesy took it from Love ⋆
Gently in a casket.
She placed it very elegantly
420 In a place draped with samite,

Courtesy's
speech:

And smiling she said to the barons:
"You have heard the judgment
That they have judged correctly,
But — for I know that you will be grateful to me for it —
425 I will tell you of such a place for love
Where many tears will turn into games,
And many games will turn into tears, ⋆
For such is the custom lovers have,
That they are gay when things are good,
430 And when they have the least little bit of disquiet,
The laments and the tears and the sighs
Bring them nearly to death.
But the lover who wishes to conquer love
Must from now on demonstrate
435 His heart to his lady without complaint.
Thus she will be richer than the queen,
For you will not find one in a thousand
Who would not consider you as noble,
And who in her heart is not grateful to you,
440 So much so that she will not pretend to be angry with

The lady:

Because she will think: 'Certainly I am not ugly, [you,
Since this man is willing to begin a vain wait,
And I would behave like a criminal
Since this gentle man thinks of me,

445 S'ieu non pensava de lui.
     C'aisso non sap re, mas no.s duj, ★
     Q'el es coberts en son coratge,
     Q'anch no.m volg trametre messatge, ★
     Ants m'o dis tots sols de sa boca.
450 Ben conosch qe m'amors la toca.
     Ben ai pus dra cor d'un leon ★
     S'el m'ama ez eu non voell son pron,
     E molt fazia gran pecat ★
     S'el moria per ma beltat.
455 Q'el non sembla ges traidor,
     Qe qan mi demonstret l'amor, ★
     Mudet tres colors en una ora,
     Q'el devenc pus ners d'una mora; ★
     Aqi eus devenc pus vermels ★
460 Q'e.l mantz qan leva solels; ★
     Aq'eus devenc pus blancs ★
     Qe.l color li fugi e.l sancs.'
     Vec la vous entrada en consir,
     Adoncs s'adobe de servir
465 Lo drutz. E si plus non l'eschai,
     E.l li soplei ab cor verai,
     E digua q'il o puosca auszir,
     E fasa semblant de morir:
     'Domna, ben vous dei adorar
470 Per la gran beltat q'en vos par,
     E.l terra es santa, q'ieu o sai,
     Qar anc sostencs vostre cors gai.'
     E las lacremas iescan for,
     Per so q'el puesca emblar lo cor, ★
475 E giet s'als pes de genoilos,
     E digua: 'Dieus, reis glorios,
     Salv'a mi dons la gran pesa ★
     En la beltat q'en lei s'es mesa,
     E voillatz q'el haza merce
480 De.l caitiu qe vez denant se.

fol. 35v
     Dompna, Dieus e merces mi vailla! ★
     Gitas me d'aqesta batailla!
     Non vezes qe denant vos mor? ★

445 If I did not think of him.
But that I do not know since he does not reveal [it],
Because he is hidden in his feelings,
For never does he wish to send a messenger to me,
But on the contrary, he told it to me all alone with his
450 Well do I know that my love touches him. [own mouth.
Certainly I have a heart harder than a lion's *
If he loves me and I do not want his service,
And I would commit a great sin
If he should die for my beauty.

455 But he scarcely seems a traitor,
Because, when he was declaring his love to me,
He turned three colors in an hour, *
For he became blacker than a mulberry;
Then he became redder
460 Than the morning sunrise;
Then he became whiter
So that the color fled from him and the blood.'
There you are taken into her consideration.
Thereafter, the lover prepares to serve.

465 And if it no longer happens to him.
And he supplicates her with a true heart,
And says so that she can hear it,
And pretends to die:
The lover: 'Lady, certainly I must adore you
470 For the great beauty that appears in you,
And the earth is sanctified, I know,
Wherever it has held your gay person.'
And the tears pour forth, *
So that he can hide his heart,
475 And he throws himself to his knees at her feet,
And he says: 'God, glorious king,
Protect for my lady her great worth
And the beauty that was placed in her,
And permit her to have mercy
480 On the miserable man that she sees before her.
Lady, may God and mercy aid me!
Deliver me from this battle!
Do you not see that I am dying in front of you?

L'uels mi volon saillir del cor,
485 Tant vos haz cellada l'amor. *
Mais s'un pauch d'aqesta dolor
Sentis lo vostre cors cortes,
Ben sai qe mi valgra merces.
Las! qe hait dit? be fas a blasmar! *
490 Bella dompna, Dieus vos enguar *
Qe za, per mi, laisor color
Vezas en vostre mirador.
De me non podes haver tort,
Mais l'oill traidor qe m'an mort
495 Veiramen son ill traidor:
Mais aimon vos qe lor seinor, *
Mais ill se raszonon vas me
Q'enquera mi fares gran be,
Qe tan bel cors com m'han mostrat
500 No fo anch ses humelitat."
Dompna, aiso soj per l'asaiar. *
Ab un mot mi podez ric far;
Qe sol qe m'apelletz 'amic,'
Vas mi son paubre li plus ric.'

505 [L]a dompna responda causida:
'D'una re non soj ges marrida, *
Q'al mie semblan be fora mesa *
En voz, si.ll cor al re no pensa,
L'amors de meillor q'eu non soz. *
510 Mais si eu.s o dic, no voz enoj *
Ni me perpens qe vos diraj
Ab altra vez quan vos veraj, *
Qe vos, drutz, quan vos es jauszit, *
Metes las dompnas en ublit,
515 E tota dompna fora druda
Si non fos per aqella cuda.
A altra vez, nos veirem be. *
Ez e.l mez membre vos de me
Que.us faraj de vostre plazer
520 Que.m plaira, si.m venes vezer.'
Qe pro ha drutz ab domneiar *

The eyes are leaping from my body, *

485 So much have I hidden my love from you.
But if a little of this sorrow
Were felt by your courteous self,
I am convinced that it would earn me mercy.
Alas! What have I said? I am certainly to be blamed!

490 Beautiful Lady, may God protect you
From ever, through me, seeing
An uglier color in your mirror.
Toward me you can never be guilty,
But the treacherous eyes that have killed me, *

495 They are truly traitors.
They love you more than their seigneur.
But they argue with me
That you will do great good for me,
Because such a beautiful person as they have shown me

500 Was not ever without humility.
Lady, so am I for attempting it.
With a word you can make me rich;
If only you call me 'lover,'
Compared to me the richest are poor.'

The lady: 505 The lady answers carefully:
'Concerning one thing I am not at all distressed,
Because in my opinion it would be well placed
In you, if your heart thinks of nothing else,
The love of a better one than I am.

510 But if I tell you so, I do not annoy you,
Nor do I think that I will tell you
At another time when I see you,
Because you lovers, when you are happy,
You forget the ladies,

515 And every lady would be a sweetheart
If it were not for this belief.
At another time we shall certainly see.
Remember me within the month
So that I will do for you your pleasure,

520 Because it will please me, if you come to see me.'
For the lover has an advantage to court

De si dons et ab gen parlar,
E qant l'a un lonc temps servit,
E.l baisa, ben l'a enriquit; ★
525　Qe.l menre amors qe si dompna fassa ★
A son drut es qant vol qe jiassa. ★
Qe drutz de si dons arozinatz, ★
El deve vilas e malvatz, ★
E ublida se de donar,
530　De servir e d'armas portar. ★
E si lo vol tener vaillent,
Ab respeig lo fasa jausent,
E qant li dara son bel don,
Fassa o qe.l sapcha tan bon, ★

fol. 36r　535　Qe qant l'aura entre sos braz,
El non cug que.l sia vertatz.
Aiso queron li drutz leial;
Qui pus en demanda fai mal.

[A]pres aqist bon convinent, ★
540　Conve q'il tenga sor cor gent, ★
E qe se gart de fol parlar,
Q'hom non puesca en lui re blasmar.
E d'una causa sia tricx:
S'es paubre qe se fengua ricx,
545　Q'ab un petit de bel garnir
Pot hom sa paubreza cobrir;
E gard dommentre q'er iraz
Sa dompna no.l veia en la faz, ★
Q totz hom, men q'es ioios, ★
550　N'es trob plus belle sa faissons. ★
Als messages de sa maison
Serva e prometa e don,
E acuella plus bellament ★
Qe s'eron sei privat parent,
555　Per so qe sa dompna la bella
Auia de lui bona novella ★
E haia message cortes. ★
Mais gart qe hom non sia ges
Qe miels dis dompna son talent,

THE "CORT D'AMOR" 129

His lady well and with gentle speech,
And when he has served her for a long time,
And she kisses him, well does she enrich him by it;
525 For inferior love that the lady gives *
To her lover, is when he wishes to go to bed.
When the lover makes arrangements with his lady,
He becomes vile and miserable
And he forgets to give,
530 To serve and to bear arms,
And if she wishes to hold him as worthy,
With respect she may make him rejoice,
And when she gives him her beautiful gift, *
She may do what she knows so well,
535 So that when she has him in her arms,
He does not believe that it is true.
This is what loyal lovers claim;
He who asks for more does wrong.

After this good covenant,
540 It is fit that he keep his heart gentle,
And avoid speaking foolishly,
So that no one can blame him for anything.
And in one thing should he be a deceiver:
If he is poor, let him pretend to be rich,
545 For with a little beautiful embellishment
A man can cover his poverty;
And let him beware while he is angry
Lest his lady look him in his face,
Because every man, as soon as he is happy, *
550 Is much more gracious in his manners.
To the domestics of her house
He promises and he bestows and serves,
And he greets them more courteously
Then if they were his close relatives,
555 So that his beautiful lady
May hear good news of him
And have courteous messengers.
But he must beware that no man
Speak better to his lady of his desire,

560 A femina qe ad'autra gent.
     E fassa a ci dons cembel, ★
     Manias, e cordon et anel, ★
     Qe tuit sabem ad esient
     Q'amistat creis per l'ausiment.
565 E una causa non oblit:
     Ausen leis lause son marit
     E digua qe molt fora pros
     Si non fos un petit gilos,
     E s'ill s'en blasma, tant ni qant, ★
570 Cel li pot be dir aitant: ★
     'Dousa dompna, fei q'eu dei Deu,
     Vos lo conoissetz miels qe eu,
     Mais totz temps creirai q'el es pros
     Qar Dieus volc alte qu'es a voz.' ★
575 E anso ven lai on estai, ★
     E si per aventura eschai
     Qu'el al trob sola mantenent,
     La bais e l'embras sovent.
     E s'ill se suffre a forsar ★
580 Prenda son ioi ses demorar, ★
     Qe dompna vol per dreita escorsa ★
     Q'hom la fasa un petit de forsa,
     Q'ill no dira ia: "Faces m'o." ★
     Mais qui la forsa; sofre s'o. ★
585 Soven deu a si dons parlar,
     Si pot, o de loing esgardar,
     E mostre semblant cellador,
     Q'ill sapcha q'el viu de s'amor.

fol. 36v   Enaisi deu son ioi noirir ★
590 Drutz qe d'amor se vol iausir.

     [La] dompna qe vol esser druda ★
     Deu enansi esser tenguda
     Con gentils om se dompna soin ★
     Del sparvier qant l'a en son poin ★
595 Qe garda qe la plus ma non fraina. ★
     Deu ill gardar qe non remaina
     En sa cara q'il desconveigna,

560 Or to womenfolk as well as to other people.
And he should give his lady gifts, *
Sleeves, necklaces and rings,
Because everyone knows from experience
That friendship grows from praises. *

565 And do not forget one thing:
Hear her praise her husband,
And say that he would be very worthy
If he were not a little jealous man,
And if she blames herself, however little,

The lover:

570 The lover can tell her as well:
'Sweet Lady, by the faith I owe God,
You know him better than I do,
But I still believe that he has merit
Because God requires otherwise in what belongs to you.'

575 And with that, he arrives there where she is,
And if by chance it happens
That he finds her alone now,
He kisses and embraces her often.
And if she suffers herself to be forced *

580 He takes his *joi* without waiting,
For the lady requires for her correct exterior
That the man use a bit of force with her,
That she not even say: 'Do it to me.'
But that he force her and she permit it.

585 Often he must talk to his lady,
If he can, or gaze at her from afar,
And show himself discreet,
Because she knows that he lives by her love.
Thus must the lover nourish his *joi,*

590 He who wishes to enjoy love.

Courtesy's
advice to the
lady:

The lady who wishes to be a sweetheart
Must be held henceforth *
In the same way that a noble man is careful
Of the sparrow hawk when he carries it on his fist,

595 And watches that the plumage not be harmed.
She must watch that there not remain
In her face that which is not suitable,

Mas tota causa q'ez aveigna,
No ie meta causa qe i nosa, *
600 Mais be pot gitar aigua rosa
Qe qui la baiza per gran dousor, *
Cug q'haia.l cors plen de flor. *
De si meteissa sia gilosa,
Tant vol esser coinda e ginnosa, *
605 Qe tota dompna es bella e cara
Qe se ten cointamen et esgara. *
E es de tot en tot perduda
Si car e gent non es tenguda,
E l'oills sapchon retener grat *
610 D'aco q'il aura esgardat.
Ab vertat e ses tricaria
Demostro bella compainia, *
E ill paresca sots la gimpla
Gaire e cortetsa e simpla; *
615 E qui ven a leis corteiar *
Sapcha gen respondr'e parlar,
E gart per plana gentilesa
Qe non diga mot de malesa,
Ni de folia ni d'orguell.
620 Qui gent parla semena e cuell
Q'el semena ensenhaiment
E cuell laus e prez de la gent.
E gars q.il mot sian causit, *
Per so qe meills sion graszit,
625 Ab vertat e ses tricaria. *
Si cors consen e coindia, *
Qe gen parlars creis son seinors, *
Si com rasa creis e la flors, *
Per qe dompna gen enparlada
630 Sera totz temps pros e onrada. *
E sapcha tan gen acuillir
Qe, qant venra al departir,
Qar sol auran ab leis parlat,
Cuidon li fol esser senat,
635 E.l savi digan: 'Dousa res,
Mult es vostre cors de ioi ples. *

But everything that is attractive,
And that she not put anything on it that harms it,
600 But well may she sprinkle it with rose water
Because he who kisses her, overcome by great sweetness,
Believes she has a body full of flowers.
Of herself she should be jealous,
She wants so much to be clever and ingenious,
605 Because every lady is pretty and dear
Who behaves carefully and attentively.
And she is entirely lost
If she is not treated well and nobly,
And her eyes should know how to please
610 What she will have seen.
With virtue and without trickery
She should demonstrate good company,
And below her wimple she appears
Merry, courteous and modest;
615 And he who comes to court her
Ought to speak and respond gently,
And must avoid through pure gentleness
Speaking a single word of impoliteness,
Of folly or of pride.
620 He who speaks gently both sows and reaps
Because he sows good instruction
And reaps praise and merit from people.
And he must watch that the words be chosen,
So that they will be better received,
625 With virtue and without trickery. *
And she consents and is polite
Because her noble speech increases the number of her
Just as the rose grows and the flower,   [suitors,
Because a well-spoken lady
630 Will always be valued and honored.
And she must know how to welcome so gently
That, when the time for departure arrives,
Because they will have spoken with her, *
The fools believe they are wise,

The wise: 635 And the wise may say: 'Sweet thing,
Your person is very full of *joi*.

Molt sabes mesclat cointamen ★
Corteszia, foudat ab sen,
Ez urguell ab humilitat.
640 Ancheis hauri'hom fait privat ★
Un roissinol, com vos auies, ★
Far ni dir qe.us desconvenies. ★

fol. 37r

Vostre dit han aitan d'onor:
L'un son bon e l'autre meillor.'
645 Son amic non tricha ges, ★
Ni.l digua mais so qe vers es,
Que dompna e polpra e samit
Trobares alques d'un aqit, ★
Qe la porpra, pois es solada,
650 Non pot esser iamais gensada, ★
On plus la non lai sezes. ★
E dompna puis engans i es
Ni pot esser d'engan represa, ★
Jamais non pot esser cortesa,
655 Ni pus, com pot estain durar, ★
Non pot iamais son prez cobrar." ★
"E ill cabeill ssion coindament
Estretz ab fil d'aur on d'argent.
Una sotilleta garlanda
660 Gart qu'uns pel front no s'en espenda, ★
E sion per plana gardat,
Enolt de polpra o de cendat, ★
Mais un sol petit c'om en veia ★
Qe.l mons digua de fina enveia:
665 'Ben han l'onor e la proesa
Dompna, del mon qi vos adesa.'
E anon dreit e per un fil
E coindament sion sotil
Li sobrecil sotz lo bel front.
670 Lo mentonet bel e rodont,
Las dents paucas e menudetas. ★
Bel nas e bocas vermelletas
Ben faitas ad obs de baisar
Cui Deus volria tan onrar.
675 Blanc col e porte sas bellas mans ★

Very well do you know how to gracefully mix ★
Courtesy and folly with intelligence,
And pride with humility.

640 Never would any man have tamed ★
A nightingale, such as you hear,
In order to do or say anything that is not suitable to
Your words have so much honor,   [you.
Some are good, the others are better.'

645 She never deceives her lover at all,
And never may she speak anything but the truth,
Because a lady and purple cloth and samite
You find [have] something of the same nature,
Because the purple, once it is sewn

650 Can never again be cleaned,
And no longer do you sit there upon it.
And a lady, once there is deception
Can not be taken again by deception;
Never again can she be courteous,

655 Nor, in the same way that one can gild tin,

Another's
advice to
the lady on
grooming:

Can she ever recover her merit."
"And her locks are very prettily
Bound with a golden filet or one of silver.
A fine garland

660 Should prevent one curl from spreading over her fore-
And they should be held together by a comb   [head,
And laced with purple or silk,
Except for a single curl, that one can see
So that everyone says with pure envy:

665 'Certainly they have honor and prowess,
Lady, those people whom you sustain.'
And very straight and like a thread
And prettily subtle are
The eyebrows on her pretty forehead.

670 Her little chin is pretty and round,
Her teeth are hidden and small.
She has a pretty nose and red lips
Well made for kissing
Those whom God wishes to so honor.

675 She has a white neck and wears on her pretty hands

En gans qe no.ls veza vilans. ★
Bella borsa, bella centura
Com s'era tot fait en peintura
E paresca bella e dolguda ★
680 Sotz la bella boca daurada. ★
D'una re se deu donar cura,
Com l'estei be sa vestidura,
Gent vistent e gent afublans,
Amorosa e totz sos semblas.
685 Bel sion li vestit defors:
La camisa qe toca.l cors
Sia bella, sotils se blanca, ★
Co.l neus en uvern sor la branca. ★
Gent se cals e gent port sos pes.
690 E an ab dompnas de gran pres, ★
Am gentils omes qi q'en gronda.
Parle gent et digua e responda.
La gimpla non sia ges mesa
E.l cap a gisa de pagesa,
695 An sia coindamen pausada ★
Sobre las bellas crins planada,
fol. 37v   E si deu anar en coasa,
D'un cordonet daurat la fasa,
Que l'aur, pel e li boton ★
700 Rescemblon tuit d'una faison.
Gent si tengua, sovent se bain,
E ab nedesa so compain. ★
Ves tot lo mont cuberta e cellada, ★
Mais son amic sia aizinada
705 Quant sera luecs ni d'avinent.
Eu haz ben dig al parlament
So qe li bon drut tenran car,
E fara.l gilos enrabchar."

[C]ortesia ditz: "Dompn pros, ★
710 D'aiso m'acort eu ben ab vos,
Qe molt es gilos en gran pena
Qe, s'el bat sa moiller, forsena.
Adoncs pens'ella: 'Ar amarai

Gloves so that the villain may not see them.
She wears a pretty purse and belt *
As if she was made in a painting,
And she appears pretty and slender
680 Below the pretty golden buckle. *
Concerning one thing she must take care,
That she be well dressed,
Nobly appearing and nobly cloaked,
Attractive by all appearances.
685 Her outer clothes should be beautiful:
The chemise that touches her body
Must be beautiful, fine and white,
Like the snow in winter on the branches.
Nobly she must be shod, and gently place her feet,
690 And she should go with ladies of great merit,
And with gentlemen who chide her.
She must speak sweetly and talk and respond.
The wimple should not be placed on her head
In imitation of a rich peasant woman,
695 But rather it should be prettily fixed
Over the beautiful combed hair,
And if she must go about with her hair in a braid,
She ties it with a red gold cord, *
Because gold, her hair and the spring buds
700 All resemble each other in the same way.
She should keep herself sweet and bathe often,
And she must be accompanied by cleanliness.
Toward everyone she ought to be restrained and dis-
But her friend may be welcomed   [crete,
705 Where there is occasion and it is suitable.
I have clearly told the convocation
What the good lover will hold dear,
And what will make the jealous man become enraged."

Courtesy:

Courtesy said: "Worthy Lady.
710 I am quite in agreement with you about this,
For certainly the jealous man is in great torment
Because, if he beats his wife, he is out of his senses.
Then she thinks: 'Now I will love

Pois atrestant de blasme n'hai.' ⋆

715 E puis c'ave tot en trait ⋆
Qe dis: 'Mals es ma parte fait,' ⋆
E el la baisa e la percola; ⋆
Adons la destrui e l'afola
Q'ella pensa: 'Molt m'aima fort.

720 Ben sufriria dreig e tort.'
Per nient serion gellos; ⋆
Batre ni blandir non ges bos, ⋆
Mais lais lor on anar los pe, ⋆
E venia lui bona merce." ⋆

725 Amors, aiso qe.ls ven a grat, ⋆
E ha devant se esgardat,
E vi Merce venir corrent
Qe volg esser el parlament.
E quan l'an vista li baron

730 No i a cel non sapcha bon. ⋆
Mont polsa son caval lo flancs; ⋆
Per un pauc qe non es stancs. ⋆
Aqest trameto.l amador ⋆
Per faire clam a Fin'Amor

735 De las dompnas des cominals.
Molt cuitas c'a tost le vasals. ⋆
A tant es a cort desendutz.
Tuit diçon: "Ben siaz vengutz."
E el respon: "E deu sal vos,

740 Amors, e tots vostre baros,
E confonda aquiels qes eu vei, ⋆
La Cobezesa ez Orguei, ⋆
Q'entro c'aici m'an encausat.
A qant loncs temps m'an trabaillat!

745 Amors, tot lo mont han delit;
Dompnas vos an mes en oblit.
Qe c'era fils d'emperador, ⋆
S'es paupre, gens non a d'amor, ⋆
Mais aqell es onratz ses failla

750 Qe promet los diniers e.l bailla. ⋆

fol. 38r

E qant ha lors diniers pagat,
E.l fausa los ha escuchat,

Since I already have as much blame for it.'
715 And then it happens suddenly
That he says: 'Badly is my part played.'
He kisses her and embraces her;
He then disturbs her and drives her mad
So that she thinks: 'He loves me a very great deal.
720 He would suffer both right and wrong willingly.'
For nothing should one be jealous;
Beating and courting are scarcely good,
But let them go wherever their feet take them,
And may good grace come to him."
725 Love, whom this pleased,
Has looked around her,

Arrival of
Mercy:

And she saw Mercy enter at a gallop
For she wished to be at the convocation. *
And when the barons saw her
730 There was not one whom she did not know well.
Often she spurred the flanks of her horse;
Hardly could she stop.
She was sent by the lovers
To make a claim of *Fin'Amor*
735 Against the ladies of the communities.
All the vassals had many thoughts.
Then she dismounted to the court.
They all say: "You are most welcome."

Mercy:

And she responds: "And God save you,
740 Love, and all your barons,
And confound those that I see,
Covetousness and Pride,
Who up to this place have pursued me.
Ah, what a long time they have tormented me!
745 Love, they have damaged everybody;
Ladies have forgotten you.
Even if he were the son of an emperor,
If he is poor, he has no love at all,
But that one is honored without fault
750 Who promises money and gives it.
And when he has paid them their money,
And the false woman has put it away,

Il dis: 'Enqer non es sasons
Autra ves trametrem per vos.' *
755   E.l ten l'e aquella balansa, *
E confont la bona esperansa,
E qant non ha plus qe donar, *
Il lo gaba e laissa.l estar,
L'orgoilosza, cui Deus abata!
760   Qant vei lo mantel d'escarlata,
E lo var e lo cenbelin,
La pols qe mena lo train....
La filla d'un villan caitiu
Vos fara de mil drutz esqiu.
765   E amors deu esse umils *
On plus es rica e plus gentils.
E s'er filla d'un cavaler
E negus autra om l'enqer,
Ela dira: 'Ges no.m eschai
770   Ne ia vilan non amarai.'
E fai pecat s'enaisi i clama, *
Qe totz om val lo rei qe ama. *
Aici.m trameton l'amador *
Qe vos regardetz lur dolor:
775   Per vos son mort et enganatz.
De lor avetz torts e pecatz,
E fares mal vostra fasenda
Si de vos non han bella esmenda.
E c'om digua q'a bon signor
780   Han servit, membre.us de lor."

[S]o dis Amors: "Las dompnas son
Tota.ls plus dousa res de.l mon.
Eu soi lor et ellas son mias,
E be conois qe lur follias
785   Lor tolon garen de lur pron *
Qe quant om dis: 'A vos me don,
Bella dousa res, ses engan.
A Dieu et ab vos mi coman,
Dompna. Vezas ma bona fe.
790   Si no.m retenes, morai me.

She says: 'Now is not the season,
Another time we will send for you.'

755 And she holds him in that balance,
And confounds his good hopes,
And when he no longer has anything left to give,
She mocks him and lets him so remain,
The proud one, may God strike her!

760 When I see the mantle of scarlet,
And the vair and the silk,
The dust that rises from her train...
The daughter of a miserable villain
Will make you lose a thousand lovers.

765 And Love must be humble
Where she is richer and more gentle.
And there was the daughter of a knight
And no other man sought her love,
She will say: 'Certainly it does not happen to me,

770 Nor will I ever love a villain.'
And he who so claims commits a sin,
Because each man is worth the king when he loves.
The lovers send me here to you
So that you may see their sorrow:

775 Through you they are dead and deceived.
Concerning them you are wrong and sinful,
And you perform your duty badly
If they do not have good reparation from you.
So that one may say that they have served

780 A good seigneur, remember them."

Fin'Amor's response:

Thus spoke Love: "Ladies are
All the sweetest thing in the world.
I am theirs and they are mine,
And I know well that their follies

785 Remove protection from their affairs,

The lover:

Because when a man says: 'I give myself to you,
Beautiful sweet thing, without deceit.
I recommend myself to God and to you,
Lady. See my good faith.

790 If you do not accept me, I will die.

Caitiu, q'hai dit? Dompna no.us pes
Qe.l grans deszirers qe.m ten pres ★
Me fai lo maltrait descobrir.
E si vos mi fazes morir
795 Mi plaz, mas no i haures honor
S'auciez vostre servidor,
Q'eu sai be qe per vos servir
Nasqiei. E qant li dous sospir
Me coiron tan qe per vos plor, ★
800 Beu las lagremas de dousor,
E dic: "Oillz, bona feses anc nat ★
Qar haves per mi donz plorat
Q'en val mens." ' S'ella.l respont gent, ★
E ce merceira coindament, ★

fol. 38v 805 E dis: 'Amicx, eu vos fai grat ★
De co qe m'avetz presentat. ★
Eu voell qe per me siaz pros,
E vos tenrai gai e ioios.' ★
Ez haurai son pres retengut,
810 E l'autra aura fait coinde drut,
E pueis s'il en conois s'onor,
Pot en faire son amador.
Merces, aitant farai per vos,
Qe dopnas metran orguel jos, ★
815 Mais amara.l plus orguilosa
Son drut que cel cui esposa, ★
E li drut seran lur senior.
E portas lur aqesta flor,
Per entresenia q'ieu lur man
820 Q'ill auran tot so q'ill voran.
Las cobezesas, don vos clamaz,
Jamais non vos entremetaz.
Cortezia las atzinadas. ★
Aquellas qi qeron soldadas ★
825 Er getat de ma companna. ★
Non voell c'om lur son en la via,
Qe dompna qe diniers demanda
Es traitris e mercaanda,
E non sau bon tant de raubar

Miserable me, what have I said? Lady, may it not weigh
That the great desire that holds me captive [upon you *
Makes me discover suffering.
And if you make me die,
795 It pleases me, but you will have no honor from it
If you kill your servant,
Because I know well that in order to serve you
I was born. And when the sweet sighs
Torment me so much that I weep for you,
800 I drink the tears of sweetness
And I say: "Eyes, it is good that you were never born,
For you have wept for my lady
So that she is worth less for it.' Thus she answers
And thus prettily she grants him mercy,   [gently,

The lady: 805 And says: 'Friend, I am grateful to you
For what you have presented to me.
And I wish that through me you may be of merit,
And I will keep you gay and joyful.'
And I will have retained his merit,
810 And the other will have made a gracious suitor,
And then if she knows wherein lies her honor,
She can make him her lover.
I will do as much through you, Mercy,
So that ladies put down pride,
815 But the proudest lady will love
Her lover rather than him whom she married,
And the lovers will be their seigneurs.
And bring them this flower,
As a sign that I send them
820 That they will soon have what they wish.
The Covetous of whom you complain,
Concern yourself no longer with them.
Courtesy has judged them.
Those who seek wages
825 I have rejected from my company.
I do not wish that anyone be in their path,
For the lady who asks for money
Is a traitoress and a merchant,
And the pirates from overseas

830 Li galiot de sobre mar.
E s'ela me faz mon plazer
Als diners en dei grat saber.
A leis non dei portar onor
Segond lo jutguament d'Amor."

835 [A]mors levet del parlament
E tuit li baron eissament.
La Cortesa d'Amor lo sona:
"Seiner, qar non portes corona ★
Qe reis es de trastota gent
840 Apres Christus l'omnipotent?"
La corona l'han aportat,
Jois l'a mantenent coronat.
La fontaina pres a bruir, ★
E la conca a retenir, ★
845 C'om no sat negus estrument
E.l mo qa s'acordes tan gent. ★
L'arbre l'encoron a sopleiar
Qe l'avia vist coronar. ★
Del prat li sailon per lo vis,
850 Violetas et flor de lis,
E en tot lo mon non a flor
No.l fasa tant qant pod d'onor.
Qant venc al intrar del castel,
Comenson a cantar li aucel,
855 El foc d'amor ad abrasar,
E las donzellas a dansar,
E l'amador canton dous lais.
Tan rica cort no er iamais. ★

fol. 39r   Pe.ls deis si asezon matenent. ★
860 Las flors e.ls ausels mesclament.
E.l mon no es volta ni lais
L'ausel non canto en palais.
Del maniar ia no er parlat, ★
C'om no sap poison ni dintat
865 Qe a cors d'ome fasa ben
No i aia tan quan i coven. ★
Qant son asis, la guaita cria:

830 Do not know as much about robbery as she.
And if she gives me my pleasure
I must thank her in money.
I must not bring her honor
According to the judgment of Love." *

The Coronation
of *Fin'Amor*:

835 Love stood up in the council
And all the barons did the same.
There Courtesy speaks of Love thus: *

Courtesy:

"Seigneur, why do you not wear a crown
Since you are king of all people
840 After Christ omnipotent?"
They brought a crown to her,
Now *Joi* has crowned her.
The fountain began to flow,
And the shell to catch water,
845 So that no one knows anything
In the world that reconciled so many people.
The trees went to meet her in order to bow
Because they had seen her crowned.
From the meadow, violets and fleur de lis
850 Jumped toward her face,
And in all the world there was not a flower
That did not do what it could to honor her.
When she came to the entrance of the castle,
The birds began to sing,
855 And the fire of love to burst into flames,
And the maidens to dance,
And the lovers sing sweet lays.
Never was there such a powerful court.
They are seated at the dais now,
860 The flowers and the birds mix together.
In all the world there is neither song nor lay
That the birds do not sing in the palace.
Eating was not yet mentioned,
For no one knows potions or delicate foods
865 That are good for the bodies of men
That were not there in fit quantities.
When they are seated the watchman cries:

"Cobezesa es morta e aunida,
E havem Orguel abatut. ★
870 Ara si guardon li cornut,
Qe mon senior porta corona. ★
Alquel han ioi cui el en dona, ★
E totz om es malauros
Que non s'acompania ab vos.
875 Nos havem fag lo iugament ★
D'Amor: fols es qui non l'aprent."
Amors comencet a seinnar,
E anceis que volges maniar ★
El dis: "Senior Deu glorios,
880 Tot aquest ioi teng eu de vos. ★
Seiner, la vostra gran merces
De l'onor qu'ieu hai e de.l bes."

[Q]ant han le premier mes aiutz ★
Ris e Deport i es vengutz.
885 Joglar foron a Fin'Amor,
Ab Na Coindia sa seror,
Qui vai per sol molt coindament,
Dansan ab un cimblos d'argent.
Tan gai son qe lor cor lur vola:
890 L'us ag arpa, l'autre viola.
Per las taulas viras los drutz, ★
De la gran dousor esperdutz.
Las donzellas cuion sautar ★
Fors de las taulas per dansar,
895 Mais Amors o ha conogut
Qe ha por rire son cap mogut.
Pel seneschal lur a mandat:
"Qe.l ioglar sion escoutat ★
Q'el vol, pueis a tot lur plaszer
900 Se deporton a lur voler,
E fe qu'il devon non lur pes ★
Q'am.l coffrir vez om li cortes. ★

[L]i ioglar se proschon del rei ★
... ...

The Watchman:
"Covetousness is dead and dishonored,
And we have defeated Pride.

870 And now the cuckolds are careful,
Because my seigneur wears the crown.
Those have *joi* to whom she gives it, ⋆
And every man is unhappy
Who is not accompanied by you.

875 We have made the judgment
Of Love: a fool is he who does not learn it."
Love began to make the sign of the cross,
And before she started to eat

Fin'Amor's prayer:
She said: "Glorious Lord God, ⋆

880 All of this *joi* I hold from you.
Lord, I thank your very great mercy
For the honor and the goods that I have."

Arrival of the jongleurs:
When they have heard the first message
Laughter and Amusement came there.

885 They were jongleurs to *Fin'Amor*,
With Dame Grace their sister,
Who moves so gracefully,
Dancing with cymbals of silver.
They are so merry that their hearts fly from them:

890 The one had a harp, the other a viola.
Among the tables the lovers turn,
Bewildered by the great sweetness.
The maidens want to jump
From behind the tables in order to dance,

895 But Love has realized
That from laughter she has moved her head.
Through the seneschal she ordered them:

Seneschal:
"Let the jongleurs be heard,
For she wishes it, then at their entire pleasure ⋆

900 They may amuse themselves at their will.
And may the faith that they owe not weigh upon them
For in suffering one sees the courtly man!" ⋆

The jongleurs approached the king, ⋆
… … … … … … … … … … … …

Rire parlet enantz Deport:
905 "Amors, molt vos fan estrain tort
Li lausengiers de lin iutas, ★
Qui mal fuecs las lenguas abras,
Qe li phylosof e.l doctor
Jutguon lausengiers per traidor;
910 Sia breus sa raszon ou longa
Lo tot o.l plus sera mensonga.
Ai Dieus! con lait han desconfit!

fol. 39v   Com han dompnas e drutz partit!
Qe.l drutz dis: 'Dousa res causida,
915 Mout vos avia ben servida.
Totz mos avers e mos tesors
Era lo vostre gentil cors.
Er non seretz iamai laidida ★
E doncs, dompna, qe.m val ma vida?
920 Ben m'er dura res ez amarai
Se lla vostra convinens cara, ★
Qe fai tot lo mon resplandir,
Se laissa qe vas me no.s vir.
Faita an li lauzeiador ★
925 Com aqel qe danmia la flor ★
Del vergiez qe vol sordeiar, ★
Qe non puesca pois frug far.
Zois era floritz antre nos,
Mais lausengiers l'en han secos
930 Qe no i han laissat flor ni foilla,
Per qe l'aigua del cor mi moilla
Mos oills. Mas cant a trop tengut
Lais temps, e qe za feit plogut, ★
Plaz mais lo soleals, el bels iorns ★
935 Ez es a tota gens sozorns.
Atressi creis e dobla zais
Apres lo maltraig, e val mais.
Per q'eu, dompna, no.m desesper,
Ni la Dieus no m'en don lezer ★
940 Qe de vos sparton mei deszir, ★
Nes lo zorn qe volrai morir,
Qe qan per aventura ven

Laughter:

Laughter spoke before Amusement:

905 "Love, much cruel wrong is done you *
By the malicious gossips of the line of Judas. *
May an evil flame burn their tongues, *
For the philosophers and the doctors *
Judge gossips as traitors;

910 Whether their arguments are brief or long,
The whole or more will be lies.
Ah, God! How wrongly they have undone!
How many ladies and lovers have they parted!

The lover:

Let the lover say: 'Sweet chosen thing,

915 Much have I served you well.
All my goods and treasures
Will be your gentle self.
Now you will never be insulted
And so, Lady, what is my life worth to me?

920 Certainly it will be a hard thing for me and I will love
[Even] if your lovely face,
That makes the entire world resplendent,
Allows itself not to turn toward me.
But the gossips have done

925 Like the one who ruins the flowers
In the orchard which he wants to sell,
So that they cannot bear fruit.
Joi was in bloom between us,
But the gossips have shaken it

930 So that they have left there neither flower nor leaf,
And so that the water that comes from the heart
My eyes. But when the bad weather   [dampens *
Has lasted too long, and when it has rained very hard,
The sun and the pleasant days are more pleasing,

935 And for everyone it is a respite.
Similarly *joi* grows and doubles
After suffering, and it is worth more.
Therefore I, Lady, do not despair,
Nor does God ever give me leave *

940 That my desires may separate from you,
Even on the day that I will be ready to die,
Because when by chance it happens *

Q'eu dorm ez estau tan ben,
Dompna, q'adonc soz eu ab vos, ⋆
945   E remir las vostras faisos,
E cug ades ab vos parlar
Privadamens, si com soil far,
E cug q'ades siatz enblada
De la cambra en qe es gardada.
950   Lo grans zoi me fai ricedar, ⋆
E quant eu non vos puosc trobar
Tan granda dolor emdeven ⋆
Q'ieu me mervell qar non forsen.
E Dieus! Qe me pod conortar?
955   Qan mi soven de l'embrasar
E del dous baiszar e del rire,
Amiga, ben deuria ausire, ⋆
Qe vos estaz ma dousa amiga,
Aisi com la raza ab ortiga, ⋆
960   Qe vos es dousa e plazens
Ez es pauzada entr'avols gens.'
Enaisi plaing lo drutz e.l druda
Es mil aitans morta e venduda ⋆
Q'el non ausa ab omen parlar, ⋆
965   Ni gen vestir ni gen causar,
Ni s'ausa deportar ni rire,

fol. 40r

Qe non haia paor d'aucire. ⋆
Ez esta en gran penssamen,
E ditz en son cor mout soven:
970   'Bels amics, haurai iamai aisze
Qe vos percolle ni vos baisze?
Eu non. Faillit, son mez deport. ⋆
Me e vos han lauzengiers mort.'
Amors, penren en ia veniansa, ⋆
975   Ni.n portarem escut ni lansa ⋆
Sobre.ls lausengiers traidors
Qe tolon las dousas amors."
Plasers lo senescals d'Amor,
Parlet en luoc de son seinor.
980   Molt fo pros e cortes e viastes
E savis hom e bon legistes.

That I sleep and I feel so good,
Lady, then I am with you,
945 And I contemplate your forms,
And I believe immediately that I speak with you
Privately, thus as I used to do,
And I believe that already you are taken
From the chamber in which you are secluded.
950 The great *joi* makes richness for me,
And when I cannot find you
Such a great sadness comes upon me
That I marvel that I am not out of my senses.
Ah, God! What can comfort me?
955 When I remember the embrace
And the sweet kiss and the laugh,
My Beloved, well I ought to faint,
Because you are my sweet friend,
Like the rose with its thorns, *
960 Because you are sweet and pleasant,
And you are calm among vile men.'
Thus sighs the lover, and the beloved
Is so much dead and cheapened
That she does not dare to speak with anyone, *
965 Nor gently dress nor gently speak,
Nor does she dare amuse herself or laugh,
Fearing that she murders him.
And she is in deep thought,
And in her heart she very often says:
The lady: 970 'Handsome Lover, will I ever be at ease
Unless I kiss or embrace you?
Not I. My amusements are failures.
The gossips have killed you and me.'
Love, we will certainly take vengeance on them,
975 And carry shield and lance
Against the treacherous gossips,
Who take away the sweet loves."
Pleasure, the seneschal of Love,
Spoke in place of his seigneur.
980 He was very gallant, courtly and prompt,
And a wise man and a good lawyer. *

[E] ha li dit: "Bels amics bos, ★
Gent aves dig vostras razos,
Mais tot quant aves devizat,
985 Ha hoi Cortezia iugat, ★
Q'ill ditz q'ab sen et ab mesura
Pot hom aver amor segura,
E si lausengier son Marcos
Hom lur deu esser Salamos.
990 Ja no er qe gilos non sia,
Mais ieu dic qe re non enbria
Qe mos seihner es poderos
Qe ia luszengiers ni gelos
No ceran dan a drut cortes. ★
995 Ans lur pro mas be lur pes ★
Qar en luoc fan tan gran paor,
Q'el non parlara auien lor, ★
E si con l'aurs e.l fluec s'escura, ★
Aqesita paor los meillura
1000 Q'el si gara de fol parlar,
E fai ab sen tot son afar.
E s'il van si don espian,
Ill faz vezer lur bel semblan. ★
Ab tal don gaere no li cal
1005 A qe cobre son ioi coral."

[A]pres ditz Deportz: "Gran faillida
Fai aqel qe si donz oblida,
Qan de son gent cors onrat, ★
El non la trait ni galiat, ★
1010 Antz l'a tengut gai e iausen. ★
Fait tan enveios prezen ★
Coves de son bell acuillir,
E l'a volgut tan enreqir
Qe si ag maltrait de s'amor.
1015 Ar lo j ha tornat en dousor, ★
E donat de sas bellas res,
Mangas, cordos et orfres,
E si.l mostra puei cor truan, ★
No se pot desfendre d'engan. ★

Pleasure, the
seneschal:

And he said to him: "Handsome good friend,
Gently have you spoken your discourse,
But all that you have recounted,
985 Courtesy has already judged today,
For she said that with intelligence and moderation
A man can have secure love,
And if the gossips are Marcos, *
One must play the part of Salamos.
990 Nor will it ever be that the jealous man does not exist,
But I say that nothing matters
Because my seigneur is powerful,
So that never will either gossips or the jealous man
Pose any danger to the courtly lover.
995 On the contrary, their affairs weigh better upon them
For sometimes they cause such great fear,
That he will not speak where they can hear,
And just as gold is purified in the fire, *
So this fear improves him
1000 So that he will avoid speaking foolishly,
And with sense he will conduct all his affairs,
And if he comes looking for his lady,
She shall assume a welcoming expression.
To such a lady, it is scarcely a matter of concern
1005 With what he covers his heartfelt *joi*."

Amusement:

Then spoke Amusement: "Great fault
Is committed by him who forgets his lady.
When he is honored with her gentle self,
He neither betrays nor deceives her,
1010 But, on the contrary, he has kept her gay and joyful.
He makes very enviable gifts
According to her sweet welcome,
And he wanted to enrich her so much
That he has suffered from his love.
1015 Now she has turned it into sweetness for him,
And she has given of her beautiful possessions, *
Sleeves, necklaces and embroidered bands,
And if then he shows a truant heart,
He cannot defend himself against deception.

1020 Antz contrafai lo traidor
Qu'es rics de l'aver son seinhor,
E pueis met contra luei l'aver,
Es pena de lui decacer.
Ges non deu haver cor colatge.
1025 Antz deu tener ferm coratge, ★
Qe bona dompna non peiiura.
Antz enancha ades e meillura, ★
Q'eu prez mais la valor e.l sen ★
De dompna non faz lo ioven,
1030 E si com frugs val mais qe flor, ★
Val mais qe beltat la valor, ★
Mais cant es bona la canchos,
La laissa.l ioglar enoios, ★
Aital sai qe tota sazon ★
1035 Non fai si donz qe.l sapcha bon, ★
E si fai apres autra mia, ★
Ni autra, qi cosapchatz, si fia. ★
Ell'apella son amador ★
... ...
Qe totz temps es de ioi deiuna ★
1040 La boca q'ez enqier mas una."
"[S]i m'aiut Dieus," so dis Coindia, ★
"Ben fai mal qe si donz oblia,
E mal fai dompna qe delonza ★
Son amic, pois per lui es conia, ★
1045 Qe ia non sera tan zinnosa, ★
Daus pueis qe si fai vergoinosa,
D'aqel qe volria aver pres.
Non faza lo vilan cortes
E percaz son ben e s'onor ★
1050 Q'enantz qe li lauzeniador ★
O haion saubut ni sentit, ★
Deurian haver son ioi complit.
Qar tost passon li mercadier
Lo pas on tornan li stradier, ★
1055 E qan ill son en via segura,
Ill van bellamen l'anblaura.
Atressi dompna non deu alen ★

1020 On the contrary, he imitates the traitor
Who is rich with the goods of his seigneur,
And who then uses his wealth against him,
And tries to destroy him.
Certainly he must not have a fickle heart.
1025 On the contrary, he must keep his heart firm,
So that a good lady does not worsen.
On the contrary, she advances and improves steadily,
For I prize more the value and intelligence
Of the lady, than I do youth,
1030 And just as fruit is worth more than the flower,
Value is worth more than beauty,
But when the song is good,
The bored jongleur leaves it.
Such a one I know who each season
1035 Does not do for his lady what he knows is pleasing,
And he takes for himself later another girl friend,
And the other, who knows this, trusts him.
She calls him her lover,
... ...
For it is continually starving for *joi*.
1040 The mouth that always demands more."

Dame Grace: "If God help me," said Dame Grace,
"Very badly behaves he who forgets his lady,
And badly behaves the lady who turns away
Her lover, then is left by him,
1045 For never will she be so clever,
Once she becomes dishonored
By the one whom she would like to have taken.
She does not make the villain courtly
And seek his goods and his honor,
1050 So that before the gossips
Have known or sensed it,
They would have his *joi* accomplished.
As the merchants pass by quickly
On the path where the narrow streets turn,
1055 And when they are on a secure road,
They go gaily walking on it.
In the same way, the lady must not slowly

Penre son ioi, mas torne son gen, ★
E deu gardar qe Fin'Amors gaia, ★
1060 Per lonc enplaidar non dechaia, ★
E no.s deporton nos oimais. ★
E.ll auzell movan tut lur lais,
E veian si s'acordon gen, ★
L'auzell e nostri estrumen.
1065 Qi apres aisso au las voz ★
E.l ioi qe menon entre.ls totz, ★
Ben ha pus dur lo cor d'oziman," ★
… … … … … … … … … …

[H]onors e Valors e.l baillessa ★
D'Amor, qe re mas ioi non pessa, ★
1070 Son vengudas ad auzir los chan.
E son vestudas d'un semblan,
D'un blanc samit ab floretas
D'aur; capelz han de violetas.

fol. 41r   Qant ellas entron e.l palais
1075 Sapchatz qe.l cortz en val mais.
La baillessa d'Amor a presa
Honor; deiost'Amor l'a mesa. ★
El ac gran ioi qan l'ag veszuda. ★
Vas si la streing, baisar la cuda,
1080 Mais sas gen lo feiron suffrir
Per paor q'en fezes murir,
De plan'enveia, dos o tres, ★
Qe la dompna es tan bella res,
E ditz: "Dompna, ben foz onrada ★
1085 Ma bocca, si.us hages baisada,
… … … … … … … … … …
Q'ieu non soi dignes, dous'amiga
Qe tanha d'onor vostra boca ★
Qe tot es sans qant a leis toca.
Vos mi tenes en tal liam,
1090 Con pus m'aucises, no m'en clam.
Per q'auciretz vos, Dompna bella,
Celui qi vas vos no.s revella?
Vostra dousa amors m'esperona.

Take her *joi,* but should shape her ruses,
And she must watch that *Fin'Amor* be kept gay,
1060 And that *Fin'Amor* not suffer by long pleadings,
And they do not amuse us henceforth,
And the birds are sending forth all their lays,
And they see if they gently blend,
The birds and our instruments.
1065 He who after that hears the voices
And the *joi* that they produce among themselves,
Certainly he has a heart harder than a diamond," ★

... ...

Arrival of
Honor, Valor
and the
Bailiff of
Love: Honor and Valor and the Bailiff
Of Love, she who discerns nothing but *joi,*
1070 Came to hear the song.
And they are dressed in one fashion,
In a white samite with little flowers
Of gold; they have crowns of violets.
When they enter the palace
1075 You know that the court increases in value.
The Bailiff of Love has taken
Honor; up to Love she has led her.
She had great *joi* when she saw her. ★
She clasped her to her bosom, intending to kiss her,
1080 But her people make her suffer
For fear that she cause death among them,
Two or three, from pure envy,
Because the lady is such a beautiful thing.
Fin'Amor's
speech to
Honor: And she said: "Lady, well would
1085 My mouth be honored, if it had kissed you,

... ...

But I am not worthy, sweet friend,
That your mouth touch me honorably,
For everything that touches it is pure.
You hold me in such a bond,
1090 That the more you kill me, I do not complain of it.
Why, beautiful lady, would you kill
The one who does not revolt against you?
Your sweet love spurs me.

Pos bella es, siatz me bona,
1095 E non fassatz l'auszellador
Q'apella e trai ab dousor
L'auszel tro qe l'a en sa tela,
Pueis l'auci e.l destrui e.l pela.
Dompna, l'uell pus luszent qe stela,
1100 Regardon, pus son cor no.us cela,
Le vostre sers qe tant vos ama. *
Per Dieu e per vos se reclama.
Per mil vez siatz ben venguda
Gran joia m'es al cor creguda,
1105 Qar es tant fina e tant liaus.
Ja mos cors non haura repaus
Tro qe.m digas coment sera
Si'll vostre bel cors m'amera,
Q'ieu soi vostre hom en tota guisza,
1110 Qe Fin'Amor e.l cor m'astiza *
Un fuec don m'es suaus la flama,
Qe de.l vostre bel cors m'aflama.
E regardatz lo vostr'honor,
Qe diguen li fin amador,
1115 Q'en vos non sap om blasmar re,
Qe bella es e de gran merce. *
De paor no.us aus dire pus,
Mais vostr'amor ni don Christus,
Aissi con ieu, per bona fe,
1120 L'aus qer, mi don, e.l de vos be, *
Q'ieu no.m puesc ges de vos defendre.
Enguazar mi podes o vendre.
Faitz en faire cartas e brieus.
Mos cors prenc de vos e mos fieus, *
1125 E qar eu soi sener d'amor,
Hai causit lo pus ric seinhor."

[A]jlors respon ela: "Soi ben vostra, *
fol. 41v   Q'ieu non soi ges aqil qe mostra *
Orguell mentre q'es iovecenlla *
1130 Qi a la color fresca e novella,
E qant aqil colors li fail,

Since you are beautiful, be good to me,
1095 And do not be the bird hunter
Who calls and deceives the bird with sweetness,
Until he has it in his net,
Then he kills it and destroys it and plucks it.
Lady, with your eyes brighter than a star,
1100 Look, since she does not hide her heart from you,
At your servant who loves you so much.
She recommends herself to God and to you.
You are welcome a thousand time.
Great joy has grown in my heart,
1105 For you are so fine and loyal.
Never will my heart find repose
Until you tell me how it will be
If your beautiful self will love me,
For I am your man in all ways, *
1110 Because *Fin'Amor* stirs up in my heart *
A fire whose flame is sweet to me,
And which your beautiful self inflames.
And consider your honor,
What true lovers say,
1115 For in you no one can blame anything,
Because you are beautiful and very merciful.
For fear I do not dare tell you more,
But may Christ give me your love,
As I, in good faith,
1120 Dare seek it, my lady, and the good from you,
So that I cannot struggle against you.
You can pledge me or sell me.
Have charts and letters made of it.
I took my body from you and my fiefs,
1125 And because I am the Seigneur of Love,
I have chosen the most powerful seigneur."

Lady Honor: Honor then answered: "I am certainly yours,
Because I am not at all one of those who shows *
Pride while she is a young lady
1130 With fresh new color,
And when these colors fail her,

Ez el se vei en son mirail,
E conois qe trop s'es tarzada,
Ill qier so don era pregada
1135 E ditz: 'Ben hai mon tenps perdut.
Ja mais non poirai haver drut.'
Adoncs oing sa cara e la freta,
E cuida se faire toseta,
E on pus se gensa e.l peizura. ★
1140 Qe.l beutat non ven per natura,
Qe domnas i ha d'autre fuel, ★
Qe paron laide ande non vuel, ★
Qe negus gentils hom si fi
En dompna qe laidura di.
1145 Ants se devont d'aitant veniar, ★
Qe francs hom non la deu baiszar.
Dompna non deu parlar mas gent
E suau e causidament,
E deu tant sos mots assire
1150 Qe totz hom son solaz desire,
Qe las pauraulas qe son fors
Demostran los talens del cors,
Per qe non deu dire folor,
Dompna qe s'enten en valor."

1155 [L]a baillessa d'Amor s'assis
Davant las pulsellas e dis:
"Sabetz qe deu faire doncella
Qant sos bos amicx es ab ella,
E Fin'Amors l'a tant onrada
1160 Q'ab son bon amic l'a colgada?
Lor coven q'al comensamen
Li fassa d'un baisar presen,
E pueis ab rire ez ab solaz
Qe.l faissa coisin de son braz,
1165 Ez ab l'autre ves si l'estrenia, ★
E digas: 'Grans onors vos venia, ★
Amors, e gran bonaventura!
Fols es qe de vos se rancura,
Qe s'anc me venc maltrac de vos,

And she sees herself in her mirror, *
And she knows that she has waited too long,
She looks for that for which she had been sought,
1135 And says: 'I have certainly wasted my time.
Never will I be able to have a lover.'
Then she anoints her face and rubs it,
And believes she makes herself young,
And she decorates herself more and besmears it,
1140 Since the beauty does not come naturally.
Since these ladies have other follies,
And since they look ugly and repugnant,
May no gentleman trust
A lady who speaks outrageous words.
1145 On the contrary, they must avenge themselves all the
Because an honest man must not embrace her.   [more,
A lady must not speak in any way but gently
And sweetly and thoughtfully,
And she must compose her phrases so gently
1150 That every man desires her company,
Because the words that are strong
Reveal the desires of the body.
For that reason she must not speak foolishly,
The lady who strives for value."

Advice of the
Bailiff of
Love to the
maidens:
1155 The Bailiff of Love sat down
Before the maidens and said:
"You know what a young lady must do
When her good friend is with her,
And Fin'Amor has so honored her
1160 That she has been in bed with her sweetheart? *
It is suitable for them that at the beginning
She give him the gift of a kiss,
And then with laughter and solace
That she make a cushion of her arm,
1165 And with the other she embrace him closely,
The lady:
Then she says: 'May great honor come to you,
Love, and great good fortune!
A fool is he who complains of you, *
Because if ever suffering comes to me through you,

1170 Bon m'en es rendutz gazardos.
Bels amics, vos podez veder
Q'ieu soi tota al vostre plazer,
Qe vesetz q'eu no.m gard de vos,
E vos es tan bels e tan bos,

1175 Qe gardaretz de vilania
Vostre bel cors e vostra amia.
Endreit vos non desir lo rei.
Al vostre causiment m'autrei,
E vos sabetz qe de toseta,

1180 No i ha onor cel qe l'abeta.
Gran maltrait hai per vos haiut; *

fol. 42r   Soven n'hai lo maniar perdut, *
E quant eu cuiava dormir, *
M'esvellavon li dous sospir,

1185 Qe pensava, bels amicx dous
… … … … … … … … … …
E qant eu era desidada,
Disia: "Mala fui anc nada,
Seinher Dieus, qar non dura totz temps,
Q'adoncs sivals estiam emsens,

1190 Eu e mos amicx per cui plor.
Non puesc pus soffretar l'ardor
Q'Amors m'auci de fina enveia." *
Mais ia non er qe Dieus non veia, *
Amis, se vos m'aves traida.

1195 Q'ie.us hai de mon poder servida,
Non faissaz lo lairon, qe di
Qant s'encontra ab lo pellegri:
"De sains tenez, bels amics, *
Sains es vostre dreit camis." *

1200 E quant l'a mes el bois preont,
Li tol son aver e.l confont.
Amics, non si'eu confonduda
Atressi, qar vos hai seguda.
Davant m'estava ben e gent,

1205 Mais era perd lo cor e.l sen.
Non puesc pus la dolor suffrir
Qi.m fai la color laideszir.

1170 Good from it is given to me as recompense.
Dear Friend, you can see
That I am completely at your pleasure,
For you see that I do not keep myself from you,
And you are so handsome and so good,
1175 That you will keep from villany
Both your handsome self and your beloved.
In comparison to you, I do not want the king.
To your discretion I give myself,
And you know that where a young girl is concerned,
1180 The man who abuses her has no honor.
Great suffering I have had because of you;
Often have I lost my appetite because of it, ★
And when I thought I was asleep,
Sweet sighs awakened me,
1185 Because I was thinking, dear sweet friend, ★
... ...
And when I was awakened,
I said: "Unhappy that I was ever born,
Lord God, because it does not last all the time,
For then, at least, we were together,
1190 I and my friend for whom I weep.
I can no longer bear the ardor
For Love kills me with perfect lust."
But it never happens that God does not see,
Friend, if you have betrayed me.
1195 Since I have served you with all my power,
Do not act the thief who says, ★
When he encounters the pilgrim:
"You resemble a saint, good friend,
Your straight path is safe."
1200 And when he has led him into the deep woods,
He takes his goods from him and kills him.
Friend, may I not be killed
In the same way, for I have obeyed you.
Before I felt good and gentle,
1205 But now I lose my heart and mind.
I can no longer suffer the sadness
Which makes my complexion turn ugly.

Aqest mal hai haiut per vos, ★
Amics, e Dieus q'es francs e bos,
1210 E pius e plens de corteszia,
Sab q'eu.s hai amat ses bauzia, ★
E vuella q'entre mi e vos,
Vivam lonc tenps ez amen nos. ★
Tenes lo man q'eu vos o iur, ★
1215 Ez enasi vos asegur, ★
Qe za totz los iorns de ma vida ★
No.us farai de m'amor genchida, ★
E vos iuras m'o atressi, ★
Qe non fassas lo bel mati,
1220 Qe tramet el miez luec del iorn ★
La plueia e.l vent e.l tenps morn.' ★
Ez el responda qe cortes : ★
'Dompna, ben conosch qe dretz es, ★
E dic vos per los sans qe son,
1225 Qe tant qant vivrai en est mon, ★
Non amarai autre mas vos,
Ni a present ni a rescos.
Amors e Ious si iugirent ★
Mi e vos d'aqest convinent.
1230 Aissi con son bon e privat,
Vuellon qe tengam lialtat, ★
E q'entre nos non haia engan. ★
A Dieu et a vos mi coman,
E baisem nous en, qar cove, ★
1235 E nom de tota bona fe.' ★
fol. 42v   Enaissi deu esser segura
Dompna de drut s'i met sa cura. ★
E quant verra al departir, ★
Sitot lor es mal a sufrir,
1240 Cant ab hora s'adobes li ★
E parta de lui tant mati,
Qe za non sapcha mals ni bos,
Mais com assi anc re non fous. ★
E sapchia mesatge causir
1245 Qe lapsapchia tan gen cubrir ★
Qe pauraula sia cellada, ★

This evil I have had through you,
Friend, and God, who is honest and good,
1210 And merciful and full of courtesy,
Must know that I have loved without falseness,
And he will require that, between me and you,
We live a long time and love each other.
Take my hand that I may swear it to you,
1215 And thus I assure you,
That for all the days of my life
I will not refuse you my love,
And you will swear to me the same,
That you do not sleep until late in the morning,
1220 For it brings in the middle of the day
The rain and the wind and the gloomy weather.'
And he answers like a courtly man:

The lover:
'Lady, I know well that it is right,
And I tell you, by the saints that be,
1225 That as long as I shall live in this world,
I will love none other than you,
Neither publicly nor in private. *
Love and *Joi* judged
Me and you by this covenant.
1230 Just as they are good and discreet,
They require that we keep loyalty,
And that between us there be no deceit.
To God and to you I commend myself,
And let us embrace, for it is fit,
1235 In the name of all good faith.'
Thus the lady must be sure
Of the lover if she places her care in his hands.
And when it comes to departure,
Immediately there is pain for them to suffer,
1240 When sometimes he dresses
And departs from her so early in the morning,
So that one knows neither evil or good,
But [it is] as if nothing ever was.
And she knows how to choose a messenger
1245 Who knows how to protect her so gently
That the word may be secret,

Q'hom non sapcha qant n'er tornada.
El matin si vei en la plasa
Son amic, ia semblan non fasa *
1250 Qe anc enqera no.l veges, *
Ni qe sapcha de lui qi es,
Qe.l ious d'amor, fruita e floris, *
Qi ab sen lo garda e.l nouris." *

[L]a cortesa vallen Valors
1255 Enseina e ditz als amadors:
"Mult deu esser vallens e pros
Totz hom pois se feing amoros,
Desqe pois ha vist los bels mans *
De si dons per qi pn'es villans *
1260 Qe prous dompna ab fresca color
Es ruesa del vergiers d'Amor
E deu prenre de chausiment
Tant de leis e d'enseinhament,
C'om digua: 'Ben tenc per onrada
1265 La dompna don aqist s'agrada,
E cill qe l'ama a ben causit, *
Pro drut e vallent e ardit
E homen q'ades se mellura; *
En bon lou ha tornat sa cura.' *
1270 Apress fasa tant de proessa
Qe sa dompna franca e cortesza
Parle privadamens ab lui,
Qe qant ill seran ambedui
Emsens, mout dousamen li diga: *
1275 'Dieus vos sal, bella dousa amiga,
Cona la pus ben ensenhada
E la genszer q'anc fos amada *
E pos Dieus ha en vos tramessa
Honor e beutat e franquessa,
1280 Merces non sia ia ostada. *
Amors, enpert tanta velada, *
E per tant angoissus martire
M'es enmenda q'ella mi vuella rire, *
O qe la dousa man del gan

[And] that one not know when he had returned.
And in the morning, if she sees in the square
Her lover, she should give no sign
1250 That she has ever seen him before,
Nor that she knows who he is,
Because of the *joi* of love, the fruit and flower,
That with intelligence protects him and nourishes him."

There courteous noble Valor
1255 Teaches and says to the lovers:

Lady Valor: "Each man must certainly be noble and valiant
Once he takes pains to be a lover,
When once he has seen the beautiful hands
Of his lady through whom he is not villainous,
1260 Because the excellent lady with fresh color
Is a rose from the orchard of Love,
And she must make a choice
Of so many laws and so much teaching,
That they say: 'Certainly the lady is considered
1265 Honorable, whom these men please,
And he whom she loves she has chosen carefully,
An excellent lover, noble and bold,
And a man in whom there is always improvement;
She devoted her care in a good place.'
1270 After being chosen, he shall display so much prowess
That his frank and courteous lady
May speak privately with him,
So that when they are both
Together, very sweetly he may say to her:
1275 The Lover 'God save you beautiful sweet friend,
As the best instructed
And the sweetest that ever was loved.
And since God has transmitted to you
Honor and beauty and honesty,
1280 Grace will never be taken from you.
Love, I lose so many evenings,
And for so much martyred agony
I am compensated that she may want to smile at me,
Or the sweet hand from the glove

1285 Me lais baiszar en sospiran.
Bella dompna, vostra faissos
Me fai ardit e paoros.
Non soi ben arditz q'en tal loc
Ausei qerre solas ni ioc. *

fol. 43r 1290 Mei uell non s'auszon enardir
D'esgardar tro qe.m sen murir,
Adoncs vos esgar de paor,
Com lo sors son irat seinhor *
Qe non l'ausza merce clamar

1295 Mais plora e pensa: "S'ieu l'esgar,
Ades l'en venra pietatz
Qant veira lo gran dol q'eu fatz."
Ja non aurai ioi ni salut *
Tro qe vostre bel cors m'aiut, *

1300 Qe, per ma fe, trop m'es pus bon *
Qe.m permetaz q'altra mi don.
Bella dousa res, cui reblan, *
Totz tenps vos semblarai l'enfan
Qe plora per la bella re

1305 Totas las oras q'il la ve *
Entro qe l'ha. Aital farai, *
E si no.us puesc haver, morrai.
E diran totz qant m'aures mort:
"Sa dompna l'aucis a grant tort,

1310 Mais sals er al dia del iuzizi, *
Qe mort es per son bel servizi." *
Grans merces vos clama vostre sers *
Qe per vos lo ten en gras fers, *
Don zamais non sera fors *

1315 Tro qe l'engent vostre bels cors. *
Ses engan e ses cor volatge, *
M'autrei e.l vostre seinhoratje;
Las mans iointas, a genolos, *
A Deu me coman e a vos,

1320 Qe anc pos vos me donestes jorn, *
Non estet mos cors en soiorn. *
Antz se Dieus de vos m'aconsel,
Hai pregat la luna e.l solel,

1285 She lets me kiss with a sigh.
Beautiful lady, your manners
Make me bold and fearful.
I am not so bold that in such a place
I dared seek company and games.
1290 My eyes do not dare be so bold
As to look until I feel myself die.
Therefore I contemplate you with fear, ★
Like the serf [looks at] his angry seigneur,
Because he dares not ask for mercy.
1295 But he weeps and thinks: "If I look at him,
Then pity will come from him
When he sees the great sorrow that I suffer."
Never will I have *joi* or happiness
Until your beautiful self aids me,
1300 Because, by my faith, it is much too good for me
What you permit me than what another [woman] gives
Beautiful sweet thing, whom I serve, 　　　　　　[me.
I will always seem to you an infant
Who cries for the beautiful thing
1305 All the while that he can see it
Until he has it. So will I do,
And if I cannot have you, I will die. ★
And everyone will say when you have me dead:
"His lady was very wrong to kill him,
1310 But he will be saved at the Judgment Day,
Because he died for his good service."
Your servant claims your great mercy
Because you keep him in great irons,
From which he will never be freed
1315 Until you deliver him with your beautiful self.
Without deceit and without fickle heart,
I give myself to your seigneury.
With hands joined, upon my knees
I commend myself to God and you,
1320 For never since you have given me an interview,
Has my body been in repose.
Rather, if God gives me counsel concerning you,
I have asked the moon and the sun,

E drieg coma bons mos seinors, ★
1325 Per Dieu que.m breu gesson lo iors, ★
Q'ieu vos volia vezer tan
Q'us pauchs jorns me scemblan a un an. ★
Ja per mal qe.m fassas suffrir,
No.m laissarai de vos servir. ★
1330 A la gran valor et al sen
Ez al bel cors de vos mi ren.' "

[E]nasi ha parlat Valors.
Auien totz, l'en merceia Amors. ★
Apres lui comencet Proessa,
1335 E dis: "Eu no.m soj entremessa ★
Ad aquesta cortz de parlar,
Ez hai auzit a totz comtar,
Per Crist, bonas raszos e bellas,
Mais eu vos comtarai novellas
1340 Qe no.s taignon ges entre vos,
Qe fan li fol drut nuallos;
Q'ara venra per aventura
Un drutz enqer bonaventura, ★
fol. 43v   E.l ious de Fin'Amor entratz, ★
1345 Ez ira qerre son solatz
A dompna qe.z er coinda e joiousa, ★
E trobara la angoisosa,
E comensera a rogir.
... ...
Et il fara o de talant,
1350 E ben leu respondra.l aitant:
'Amicx vos non sabetz ab cuj ★
Parlatz; q'anc vos ni autruj ★
Non amei, ni non sai qes es. ★
Mais s'ieu m'en entremeses ★
1355 Vos es ben tan bels e tan pros
Q'ieu fera mon amic de vos.
E si voletz haver mon grat,
Ins aisi on es comensat, ★
Si lasat q'eu vos vencus, ★
1360 Qe per lo mens ni per lo pus, ★

With justice, as my good seigneurs,

1325 In the name of God, to shorten the length of my days,
For I want to see you so badly
That a few days seem to me to be a year.
Even in spite of the evil that you make me suffer,
I will not stop serving you.

1330 To your great value and to your intelligence
And to your beautiful self, I give myself.'

Thus spoke Valor.
Within the hearing of all, Love thanked her.
After her began Prowess,

Prowess: 1335 And she said: "I did not enter
This court to speak,
And I have heard everyone present,
In the name of Christ, good and beautiful arguments,
But I will tell you new ones

1340 That are not at all suitable among you,
About what the foolish indolent lovers do;
For now there will come perhaps
A lover seeking good adventure,
Entered into the *joi* of *Fin'Amor*,

1345 And he will go to seek his solace
Of a lady who is pretty and joyful,
And he will find her full of agony,
And he will begin to blush,
... ...
And he will do it with skill,

1350 And very gently she will answer thus:
The lady: 'Friend, you do not know with whom
You speak; for never you nor any other
Have I loved, nor do I know what it is.
But if I undertake it,

1355 You are certainly so handsome and so valiant
That I will make of you my sweetheart.
And if you wish to have my gratitude
In it, right here where it is begun,
So bound as I conquered you,

1360 [Behave] so that in the least things and in the greatest,

Non er fachs e dic vilania,
Qar eu non es devenc vostra amia.'
Ez el parra s'en vergoinos. ★
E.l dompna q'es valents e pros
1365 Tenra lo per avilanit,
E dira: 'Ben valra petit
Aqela qe vos amara.
Mais valriatz ad ermita,
Vos es be d'aqel lignatje
1370 Don son li fol drut salvatje.'
E vechs la bon'amor perduda ★
Qar non es qi l'aia seguda, ★
Qe drutz j ha qe per folor ★
Demandon o qeran amor: ★
1375 'Qe ben sapchatz q'eu amaria ★
Volenters si trobes amia.'
Venga sai cel qe vol amar,
Q'ieu sai q'el en porra trobar,
Qe s'el j vol metre s'ententa, ★
1380 S'el ne vol una, en haura trenta.
De drut conven q'al comensar ★
En prec tan o fassa pregar
Tro qe s'avenga e s'eschaja ★
En pro dompna valent e gaia.
1385 E si non la pot tan tost trobar, ★
Ges per so no.s deu esfredar,
Qe cel qe cercha l'aur tant lava ★
Lo lot e trastorna la grava
Tro qe truoba lo luzant aur ★
1390 Don es rics e don fai tesaur.
Per qe non deu haver nuala
Qe precs e servir e trabala.
S'era del mon la pus estraigna
Si li.n fara dousa compaigna. ★
1395 Ez apres q'aiha tal messatje ★
Qe.l diga e.l man son coratje
A cellas q'han d'amor talan,
fol. 44r   Mas bellamen e ses malan
E trobera aitant d'aqelas ★

Villany will not be done or spoken,
For I have not [yet] become your beloved.'
And he will look ashamed because of it.
The lady who is worthy and excellent
1365 Will consider him as abased,

The lady:

And she will say: 'Certainly of little worth
Is she who will love you.
You would be worth more to a hermit.
You certainly belong to that lineage
1370 To which the foolish and wild lovers belong.'
And so was good love lost
For there is no one who has pursued it,
Because there are lovers who from folly
Demand or seek love:

The lover:

1375 'Because you know very well that I would love
Willingly, if I found a sweetheart.'
He who wants to love may come here,
Because I know that he will be able to find one,
For if he wants to place in it his aspirations,
1380 If he wants one, he will have thirty.
It is fit for the lover that in the beginning
He ask much or send his prayers
Until it happens that he merits
A worthy lady, excellent and joyful.
1385 If he cannot find her so soon,
He must not in the least lose courage for that,
For he who looks for gold washes
The mud so much and turns over the gravel
Until he finds the shining gold
1390 With which he is rich and with which he makes his
Therefore he must not be indolent,   [treasure.
Where prayers and service and tribulation are concerned.
She will be the strangest in the world
If she will not give him her sweet company.
1395 And after he has such a message
Let him speak and send his feelings
To those women who have desire for love,
But prettily and without evil intent,
And he will find as many of these

1400   Com le cels pod haver estelas,
       Q'una non trobares a dire
       Qi no am lo solaz e.l rire
       D'amor, si noncha vol lo pus
       E diga: 'Ja no.m sal Christus,
1405   S'ieu non sai, bella dompna e bona, *
       Qi porta de ioi la corona *
       Sobre lous amadors.'
       'E vos bauszares m'en lo fron *
       Senpres qant eu lo vos dirai
1410   Qe lo joventz q'en vos estaz *
       E.l vergoigna qi ren non tria
       Vos en fara faire folia
       Q'el n'es be de xx parts semos,
       Mais eu lo lauzava a vos,
1415   E dic vos qe sots lo solel
       Non haura bazaler parel.
       Ben seriatz de ioi la soma. *
       De dous arbre chiaj dousa poma, *
       Qe ambedui es molt avinent.
1420   A com sa conten ricament!
       Qe sel vol haver bon solatz, *
       Ja hom non sera enoiatz, *
       E quant es ab sabia gen, *
       Los aprodera totz de sen. *
1425   Anc els mieus zorns non fo tan bos,
       Ni tan bels, tan pauc orguolos.
       Eu saz q'ins el cor vos sab bon *
       So q'eu dic, e si dizes non,
       Eu sai qe vos non dizes ver.
1430   E.uz metrai aisz e lezer,
       E progaraj tan lo sejnor *
       Si Dieus plaz, vos darai s'amor *
       E si tant fatz qe.l bel e.l bon,
       Vos am, e lo mieus gazardon *
1435   Non sia ges mes en oblit,
       Q'ie.us darai gran re per petit.
       Q'ieu lo mogui l'altre de loin, *
       Per saber si n'hauria soin.

1400 As the sky can have stars,
For you will not find one to speak of
Who does not love the solace and the laughter
Of love, if ever she does not want it more,

The lover:
And he may say: 'Certainly Christ will not save me,
1405 If I do not know, good and beautiful lady,
Who wears the crown of *joi*
Over all the lovers of the world.'

Messenger:
'And you will kiss my forehead
Quickly when I tell you,
1410 For the youth that is in you
And the modesty that cannot distinguish anything
Will cause you to commit folly
Until it is thoroughly blamed twenty times,
But I praised him to you,
1415 And I tell you that under the sun
There will not be a similar bachelor.
You could well be the summit of *joi*.
From sweet tree falls sweet apple
Which is quite welcome to both.
1420 Ah, how richly they behave!
So that if he wants to have good society,
Nobody will ever be bored,
And when he is with wise men,
He will benefit them all by reason.
1425 Never in the best days was one so good,
Nor so handsome with the least bit of pride.
I know that in your heart you know well
What I am telling you, and if you say no,
I know that you are not telling the truth,
1430 And I will put you at ease and leisure,
And I will beseech the seigneur so much
If it please God, that I will give you his love,
And if you do much that is beautiful and good,
I love you, and may my recompense
1435 Never be forgotten,
For I will give you great things for small.
I moved him the other day from afar,
In order to know if he would care for it.

E j dis, ses vostre saubut, ★
1440 Qe vos li mandavatz salut,
E qant el s'auzi saludar
De part vos, non poc mais sonar ★
D'una pessa, pueis respondet:
"C. milia merces li ret.
1445 Con desson sers endompneiatz, ★
Ab son rire.m teing per pagatz. ★
Anc mais no.m entremis d'amor
C'aqesta.m fai gran paor,
Qe m'ausi ab un dous esgart
1450 Qe dompnas han en l'uel dart
Ab qe naffron tan dousament

fol. 44v

Qe mentre q'hom mor, non o sent,
Qe.l gaz cors ausi drut cortes
Com lo rossinol qant es pres
1455 Qe non pot esser ab sa par.
Per qe vaj a mi dons pregar ★
Si com ell'es francha e cortesza,
Non per me mais per gentilesza, ★
M'acuella, qe sos ser se mor,
1460 Si no me girofla.l cor
Ab un baiszar, sa dousa alena,
Q'enaissi.m pot gitar de pena." ★
Lo zou de vos mi faj plorar ★
Quant eu lo vi color mudar,
1465 Qar conogui a son soenblan
Qe.us amaria ses engan.
Aitant n'hai comensat ses vos.
Amatz lo qe bels es bos,
E no.l fassatz la vilania
1470 Qe fan las dompnas per folia ★
Qi.s fan pregar un an o dos,
Q'ez aqell pregar enojos,
Qe cuzon qe lur onor sia,
Lur tol lor pretz e.l desenbria.'

1475 [L]a dompna dira: 'No.us mais pes. ★
Sembla qe.l faz vos trameses, ★

And I said to him, without your knowledge,
1440 That you sent him greetings,
And when he heard himself greeted
On your part, he could not speak
For some time, then he answered:

The lover: "A hundred thousand thanks I give her on my part.
1445 As must the faithful servants,
With her laughter I consider myself paid.
Never more will I undertake love
For that causes me great fear, ⋆
That she might kill me with a sweet look
1450 For ladies have a dart in their eyes
With which they sweetly wound
So that although a man dies, he may not feel it,
For the merry person kills the courteous lover
Like the nightingale when it is caught
1455 And cannot be with its partner.
Why do I go to beseech my lady
If, since she is honest and courteous,
Not for my sake but for the sake of gentility, ⋆
She greets me while her servant is dying?
1460 If she does not perfume my heart
With a kiss, her sweet breath,
So that thus she can deliver me from pain?"
The *joi* because of you, made me weep
When I saw him change color,
1465 For I knew by his pallor
That he would love you without deceit.
So I have begun without you.
Love him because he is handsome and good,
And do not do that villany to him ⋆
1470 That women do through folly
Who have themselves petitioned for a year or two,
Because it is this wearisome beseeching,
Which they believe does them honor,
That takes their merit from them and diminishes it.'

The lady: 1475 The lady will say: 'Do not let it weigh upon you.
It seems that fate sends you back,

E per mesatje logaditz *
Fan mantas dompnas fols arditz.
En son repszas e traidas. *
1480 Ben hai vostras raszos auzidas,
E quant eu lo porai vezer,
Eu sabrai si vos dizes ver,
Qe s'ieu parle veszent la gent,
Ab lui, fols es que m'en repren.'

1485 '[D]ompna, ben sai qe pels truans
Qe fan las falas e.ls engans, *
Son li bon homen mescreszut;
Mais dompna, si Dieus ja m'azut,
Sitot me soj de paubra gent. *
1490 Lial homen son miei parent, *
Ez eu soj de lur parenta, *
Q'ieu vos dic, bella dompna e genta,
Qe si vos en fizavaz en me,
Eu vos irai per bona fe *
1495 Q'el vos amara e vos lui,
Q'ieu vez que morez ambedui
D'amor. Orus vos non sintez re *
Mai si vos vos veizatz be *
A la color qu'havetz perduda,
1500 Vos diriatz: "Por Deu, m'ajuda *
Q'el m'am." Non digas oc ni no,
Q'ieu parlaraj oimais d'aiso, *
E farai vos la pus onrada
Dompna de tot'esta contrada.'

1505 [L]a dopna dira: 'Tot veiraj *
A qual part vostre cor metrai,
E engan ou en liautat. *
Si.m enganatz, fares pecat.'

'[D]ompna, ans percas lo vostre be.
1510 No.m en crezes? Vec vos ma fe,
Q'ieu j regarde vostre onor. *
Maldit sion li traidor,

fol. 45r

And through mercenary messengers
Many ladies commit bold follies.
They are blamed for them and betrayed.
1480 Well have I listened to your arguments,
And when I am able to see him,
I will know if you speak the truth,
Because if I speak within sight of people,
With him, It is foolish because they will blame me.'

The Messenger: 1485 'Lady, well I know that it is through the truands
That fables and deceits are made,
And good men are discredited;
But Lady, if God help me,
I too am of poor origin.
1490 Loyal men are my relatives,
And I am of their lineage,
For I tell you, beautiful and gentle lady,
That if you trusted in me,
I would tell you in good faith
1495 That he will love you and you, him,
For I see that you will both die
Of love. Now you do not feel anything of it
But if you saw yourself clearly
By the color that you have lost
1500 You would say often: "For God's sake help me
That he may love me." Do not say yes or no,
For I will speak further of this,
And I will make you the most honored
Lady of all this country.'

The lady: 1505 The lady will say: 'Soon I will see
In what part I will place your heart,
In deceit or in loyalty.
If you deceive me, you commit a sin.'

The Messenger: 'Lady, on the contrary, I seek your good.
1510 Do you not believe me? Here is my faith,
For I see in it your honor.
Cursed be the traitors,

Qe par lur soi mescrezuda. ★
Anseis fos ma lenga perduda,
1515 Q'ie.us hages dit mas so qe.us taing.
Si tant fatz q'ieu vos acompaing
Ab lui, una causa vos dic:
Amatz lo mais c'Aia Landric, ★
E qe val qant viu ses amor? ★
1520 Dompna q'es de vostra valor?
Tot'es vostra color mudada. ★
Eu cug qe vos es soclamada, ★
Q'el frons vos no.s gieta calor. ★
Non es; anz es lo mal d'amor,
1525 Qe.us ha tenguda longament. ★
Mota es qi consol no j prent. ★
Ja vostra mort non soffriraz; ★
A Dieu vos coman. Vau men lai
Pregar lo franc e.l amoros,
1530 E si tant faz q'el parl'a vos,
Non li siatz ges presenteira,
Mais vergoinosa e pauc parleira;
Con pus seres enveiosa ★
De lui, feines vergoinosa,
1535 Mais no.l laises ges famar ★
A re qe.l sapchia demandar,
Q'adorar deu hom e grazir
Dompna qan sab gen acuelir.
S'ieu podia aiso acabar
1540 Mais cuiaria conquistar ★
Qe s'era oultra mar romeva.
Ja negus om no.m en don trieva.
Qi volra vostra amor blasmar
Mais vengan a mi parlar. ★
1545 Q'ambedui es molt avinent,
Bel et enfant e covinent,
E tota gens la lausaria,
La vostra amor, si la sabia.
Per estiers non er za saubut,
1550 Ni ja.l veszin non faran brut,
Ni non sabra hom vostr'afaire ★

Because through their efforts, I am discredited.
Thus was my discourse lost,
1515 Because I have told you often that which is suitable for
If you command that I accompany you   [you.
With him, I tell you one thing:
Love him more than Aia [loved] Landric, *
And what is a lady worth when she lives without love?
1520 A lady of your merit?
Your color has changed entirely. *
I believe that you are suffering from a fever,
But your forehead does not give off heat.
You are not; on the contrary, it is the sickness of love,
1525 Which has held you for a long time.
Dead is he who does not take advice.
Assuredly you will not suffer your death;
I commend you to God. It is of less value there
To beseech the honest and the amorous,
1530 And if you behave so that he speaks to you,
Be not at all of easy access to him,
But modest and of few words;
And the more desirous you will be
Of him, feign modesty,
1535 But do not let him die of hunger
For anything that he knows how to request,
Because a man must adore and give thanks
To the lady when she knows how to receive gently.
If I could obtain this
1540 I would believe I had conquered more
Than if I had made a pilgrimage overseas.
Never does anyone give me truce.
He who would want to blame your love,
May rather come to speak to me.
1545 Because you both are very comely,
Handsome and young and well formed,
Everyone would praise it,
Your love, if they knew about it.
Furthermore, it will never be known,
1550 Nor will the neighbors ever gossip about it,
Nor will anyone ever know of your affair *

Mais nos tres q'em coma fraire,
Ez Amors qi fara lo qart *
Qi nos gitara de regart.'
1555 E qant venra a l'avesprar,
Veigna tot son senor comdar *
Qant haura lo zorns espleitat.
Ja anseis non sia laisat *
Tro qe s'eschiaza a Fin'Amor *
fol. 45v 1560 Puis am ses cor galiador."

[Q]ant Proessa hag dit son agrat,
L'amador son en pes levat,
E fetz caschus a si dons un gin.
Adoncs foròn uberts escrin,
1565 E joas donadas e preszas. *
Qi non son ges en perdos meszas *
Qe hom non sap lo prez adismar. *
Cor e Deszir e Dous Esgar, *
E Plaszer, tug cil q'ho demanda, *
1570 E Baiszar ab q'Amors abranda *
Lo coratje dels fis amans
E lur fai faire sos comans,
Ad Amor han dig en rient:
"Nos volem nostre convinent,
1575 Seiner, e per onor de vos
Dansar veian vostres baros." *
Amors lur o ha autrezatz,
E apres lur ha comandatz:
"Anatz suau e bellament
1580 E cantatz clar et aut e gent."
Trenta cofres totz ples de flors
Lor fetz per sol gitar Amors
Qe fez traire de son tesaur,
Q'el no j ten argent ni aur, *
1585 Ni non toca aur ni argent,
Si non sei joias q'hom no vent *
Qe non son ges per aur gardadas.
Ans son per Fin'Amor baiszadas
Et envoutas de drap de seda.

Beyond we three who are like brothers,
And Love who will be the fourth,
Who will give us a glance?'
1555 And when it comes to evening time,
Her seigneur shall come soon to chat
As soon as he will have spent the day.
Before [this] he will not be tranquil,
Not until he belongs to *Fin'Amor*
1560 Since he loves without a deceiving heart."

The lovers' ritual:

When Prowess had spoken her mind,
The lovers rose to their feet,
And each one bowed to his lady.
Then the caskets were opened,
1565 And jewels were given as gifts and admired.
Those who were not considered pardoned,
Let no man know how to esteem them.
Heart and Desire and Sweet Regard
And Pleasure, all those that asked it,
1570 And Kissing with which Love brands
The heart of the true lovers
And causes them to obey her commandments,
To Love they said with laughter:
"We want our agreement,
1575 Seigneur, and in your honor
To dance within the view of your barons."
Love granted it to them,
And then commanded them:
"Go sweetly and prettily
1580 And sing clearly, loudly and gracefully."
Thirty coffers all full of flowers
Were ordered thrown on the floor by Love
Who had them drawn from her treasury,
For it held neither silver nor gold, ★
1585 And she does not touch either gold or silver,
But only those jewels that one does not sell,
That are not kept for gold.
On the contrary they are kissed by *Fin'Amor*
And wrapped in silk cloth.

1590 Plaçer faire sensa moneda, *
Ses tot aver, fai sa fazenda
Q'el ha tot qant se vol de renda
Qe tot qant tenon l'amirant *
Ni.l rej, tot es a sson comant, *
1595 Ni negun de mer non adesa *
Qar dompnas en fan cobeesa.
Cascus drutz si dons la flor lansa.
Dopneis se vai penre en la dansa
Q'es adretz et ag cor isnel,
1600 E porta cascus un capel
De ruesza pueis dis en rizent:
"Amors, fols es qi se deffent *
E qui totz los jonrs de sa via *
Non es en vostra seinhoria.
1605 Qi, apres aiso, au los sons
E.ls novels motz de las chansons,
E regarda la gran coindia
Qe cascus drutz fai ab sa mia, *
E los dous rires e.ls solatz,
1610 E.ls gins e los baiszars enblatz,
E las frescas colors q'el hant,
E la beutat q'en lor resplant,
E las bellas crins entreszadas, *
... ...

fol. 46r   Ben es sers e plens de felonia, *
1615 Qi ves Amors non s'umilia."

[L]j baron han Amor pregat *
Per Dieu qe.l bal sion laisat
Qe non podon lo zou soffrir
Qar ab pauc non volon morir.
1620 Qant lur soven de las onradas
... ...
Qe non auszon far bel semblant
A lur drutz com aqestas fant.

[A]mors comandet a Plaszer
Qe las fassa tornar sezer, *

1590 Giving pleasure without money,
Without possessing anything, she conducts her business
Because she has all that is required in revenue,
For all that the emir owns
And the king, all is at her command,
1595 Nor does she take from anyone pure,
For ladies make of them great covetousness.
Each lover tossed a flower to his lady.
Domneis went to take part in the dance
For he is skillful and has a lively heart,
1600 And he brings each one a chaplet
Of roses, then he said with laughter:

Sir *Domneis*: "Love, a fool is he who forbids himself
And who every day of his life
Is not within your seigneury.
1605 Whoever, after that, hears the melodies
And the new words of the songs,
And sees the great gentleness
That each lover observes with his lady,
And the sweet laughter and the society,
1610 And the reverences and the hidden kisses,
The fresh complexions that they have,
And the beauty that shines in them,
And the pretty plaited coffers,
... ...
Certainly he is a villain and full of felony,
1615 He who does not become humble before Love."

The barons had beseeched Love
In the name of God, that the dances be ended
Because they could not suffer the *joi*
For they will nearly die
1620 When they remember the honored ladies
... ...
So that they do not dare give good greeting
To their lovers as these do.

Love commanded Pleasure
That he have them return to be seated,

1625 E qe lur fassa bellament ★
Ab drap de seda moure vent,
O de l'aigua rosa gitar
En lur caras per reffrescar
Q'en la dansa han ajut calor. ★
1630 Molt se dompna gran soing de lor. ★
E pueis ha dig: "Za Dieus non veia, ★
Cortesa gens, qi vos gerreia! ★
Qe re non de hom tant onrar ★
Com bona dompna a fin amar,
1635 Mais per aqest mieu blonde cap,
Be.m peszara s'Orguels non sap,
E.l garsona la q'el mante ★
Lo poder qe ha contra me, ★
Qe za non er longa sazons
1640 Qe l'en veran mil gonfanons ★
Qe volrian en un gran soil
De clamar eser ab un oil. ★
Q'ieu non voell soffrir la clamor
Qe fan dompnas e amador.
1645 E si vos, seinhor, m'o laissatz
Non lor er pus suffert en patz."

[S]ens estet en un farestol
E plaz li molt qar Amors vol
Gerreiar per tenir dreitura. ★
1650 El pensa qe sos fieus pejura ★
E al dig: "Anseis qe movatz, ★
Ad aqest besoing me sonatz,
E castias una folor
Qe fan li fol drut feinedor,
... ...
1655 Qe qant ill ha si donz conqes, ★
El se feing tan fort e s'aplaigna
Q'el non cuida ges q'hom remaigna
En la vila qant el s'en eis,
E passa soen davan leis,
1660 Entro qe la gens en fai brada ★
E q'hom dis: 'Aquella es sa druda,'

1625   And that he have them prettily
Fanned with silken cloth,
Or splash rose water
On their faces to refresh them
For in the dance they have been warm.

1630   He takes great pains for them,

Sir Pleasure:

And then he said: "Certainly God has not seen,
Courtly people, who wages war against you!
For there is nothing that a man must honor as much
As a good lady to love truly,

1635   But by this my blonde head,
It will weigh heavily upon me, if Pride does not know
And the maid whom he maintains,
The strength that he has against me,
Because it will not be long

1640   Before they will see a thousand banners
[As many] as they could wish on a large field,
To claim to see with a clear eye.
Therefore I do not want to suffer the tumult
That ladies and lovers make,

1645   And if, Seigneur, you leave it to me,
It will no longer be permitted them in peace."

Sense was seated on a throne
And it pleases him much that Love wants
To wage war to maintain justice.

1650   He thinks that he endangers his fiefs

Sir Sense:

And he said: "Before you move,
You call me to this need,
And you punish a folly
Committed by the foolish presumptuous lovers,
... ...

1655   Who when he has conquered his lady, *
Pretends to be so strong and boasts
So that one does not believe a man remains
In the city when he departs,
And he often passes before her,

1660   Until the people gossip about him *
And they say: 'She is his mistress,'

E el ten la bruit ad onor,
E fan lo cer qe.l casador ★
E.l lebrier veinon ateignen,
1665 Ez el vaz s'en seguramen
E pot se denants tot garir,
E platz li tant qant l'au glatir

fol. 46v   Los cans qe torna e non sap mot, ★
Tro q'es mort e retegutz de tot.
1670 Aital faz cel qe com zauzis ★
Fol brut, si e si donz trais, ★
Q'ans dieu esser d'aital escuoil
Qe s'amor soisep tant son oil,
E.l fassa si dons esgardar.
1675 Tost en deu la cara virar,
E Folz Semblantz torna e nient ★
Amors, e blasme de la gent,
E ben sapchiatz qe Malparler
Estai enaissi con l'archier
1680 Qe trai e naffra ab son qairel
Dementre qe canta l'aucel. ★
Atressi naffron l'enozos
Malparler los amans zoios ★
Ab lor lengas, cui Dieus azir;
1685 E los fan en viven murir.
Per qe.lz ne castias, bel Seinher? ★
Qe laisson e.l fol brut e.l feiner? ★
Qe.l mon non es tan folla res
Com feing drutz peintenat plaides
1690 E la dompna q'en lui se fia
Sera grieu q'al derer s'en ria.
Eu vos en hai dig mon vejaire, ★
E vos fai oimais vostre afaire
E qant comandares: "Montatz!"
1695 Eu serai dels premiers armatz.
Totz francz hom veia la vejansa ★
E perda Dieu qe no los lansa ★
En foc, envolz, sebelis unis, ★
Los traitors lausengiers caitis, ★

And he considers the gossip honor,
And he behaves like the stag that the hunter *
And the greyhound have just reached,
1665 And it moves away confidently,
And it can escape from in front of everyone,
And it pleases it so much when it hears the baying
Of the dogs that turn and know nothing,
Until it is dead and restricted by all.
1670 So in the same way he behaves when he rejoices at
Foolish rumor; he betrays himself and his lady,
For indeed he ought to be of such conduct
That should his love draw his eye so much,
And make him look at his lady,
1675 He must quickly turn his face,
And False Appearance turns Love into nothing,
And into blame by the people.
And you know well enough that Slander
Is just like the archer
1680 Who draws and wounds with his arrow
While the bird is singing.
In the same way the wearisome Slanderers
Wound the joyous lovers
With their tongues, may God hate them!
1685 And they make them die while they are living.
Why do you not punish them, good Seigneur?
Why do you permit both the foolish brute and the
[pretender?
For in the world there is not such a foolish thing
As the lover who feigns querulous penance [penitent de-
1690 And the lady who trusts him, [fense?]
Will be displeased that people laugh at her behind her
I have told you my view, [back.
And henceforth you conduct your affairs.
And when you give the command: "Mount!"
1695 I will be among the first ones armed.
May every honest man see the vengeance
And lose God if he does not throw them
Into the fire, enveloped, buried together,
The traitorous cowardly slanderers,

1700   E las trairitz desonradas
       Don li drut han avolz seudadas ★
       Qer cujon trobar bona fe ★
       E.l falsa lengua ditz lor be.
       E van simplas com una monza ★
1705   E.l fals cor es plens de mensonza.
       Oi! bona gens, fins amador,
       Tug es mort qi non vos secor!
       E vos es plenz de gentilesa,
       E trobas engan et amalesa!
1710   E qi pot soffrir la dolor
       Qe l'uel de bella dompna plor ★
       Per manasas e per malditz?
       E deves l'autra part l'amictz, ★
       Qar sap q'hom la destreing per lui
1715   Totz los deportz q'el ha s'en fui. ★
       Amors si aiso non venjatz,
       Totz es vostre prez abaissatz."

       [A]pres Sens, ha parlat Zovens. ★
       Molt fon adretz, francs e valens.
1720   Gent li destreis sor sas blozas cris ★
       La garlanda de flor de lis
       ... ...

1700 And the dishonored traitoresses
Whose lovers have avowed them sold
Because they believed they found good faith there
And the false tongue spoke to them of good,
And they go about simply, like nuns,
1705 And the false heart is full of lies.
Oh! Good people, true lovers,
All are dead who do not help you!
And you are full of gentleness,
And you find deceit and villany!
1710 And who can suffer the sadness
When the eyes of a beautiful lady weep
From threats and slander?
And on the other hand, the friend should [suffer]
For he knows that they torment her because of him,
1715 All the amusement that he has disappears.
Love, if you do not avenge all this,
Entirely is your merit abased."

Sir Youth:

After Sense spoke Youth.
He was very clever, honest and valiant.
1720 Gently pressed on his blonde hair,
The garland of fleur de lis
... ...

NOTES TO THE EDITION

4 *ioi*: Constans *joi*.

6 *joi*: Mahn *ioi*.

11 *plenz*: Mahn *plens*.

12 *guerrez*: Constans *queira*.

18 *a tors*: Constans *a cors*, Chabaneau *a tort*.

20 *no.l laisson*: Constans *nollaisson*.

27 *Qa*: Mahn *Qa tant*, Constans *Q[e] a tant Amors parlament*. Read *Qar cant Amors ten parlament*.

29 *Ora zuzatz*: Mahn *Or azuzatz*, Chabaneau *Or auzatz*.

32 *estaz*: read *estai*.

33 *faz acordament*: Constans *faz[ia]*, Chabaneau *acordadament*.

36 *nueit*: Mahn *nuetit*.

39 *parlet*: Mahn *parler*.

41 *som*: Mahn and Constans *son*.

45 *Bon'Esperancha e Paors*: Mahn *bon'esper ancha e paors*, Bartsch *Bos Espers, Ancha e Paors*.

48 *meton*: Mahn *meton*, Constans *meron*. Although both forms are attested in Old Occitan, Chabaneau preferred *meton*. The manuscript is not clear, and the copyist writes *r* and *t* similarly.

50 *roesa*: Mahn and Constans *idesa floria*. *Roesa* for *rosa* is regular in Upper Italy, east of Milan, cf. A. Mussafia, *Beitrag zur der norditalienischen Mundarten im XV. Jahrhundert* (reprint, Bologna: Arnaldo Forni, 1964), p. 13. Cf. also l. 56 *ruosas*, l. 628 *rasa*, l. 959 *raza*, l. 1261 *ruesa*, l. 1601 *ruesza*, l. 1627 *rosa*.

53 *mou*: Mahn *mou*, Constans *mon [ta]*?

54 *per mez*: Mahn *permez*, Constans *mei*.

58 *denant*: Mahn *deuant*. *lo leit*: Constans *l'oleil*.

63 *braisson*: read *abraisson*.

65 *Totz temps*: read *E totz temps* since the line is short one syllable.

68 *maint auzel*: Constans *maint [bel] auzel*.

71 *Z.el mei loc*: read *Ez e.l mei loc*.

76 *Las claus son*: Constans *Las clauson*.

77 *cria*: Mahn *tria*.

78 *Esta*: Mahn *esca*. *sa mia*: Constans *s'amia*.

79 *la mia*: Constans *l'amia*.

80 *ia*: Constans *ja*.

83 *la porta*: Constans *la porte*.

86 *le*: Constans *lo*.

87 *om e.l*: Chabaneau *om'el*.

88 *Que cant qe es e cant fut*: read *Que cant qe es e cant que fut*.
91 *lauries*: read *lauriers*.
98 *Qe tot lo mont ha a destreigner*: Constans *Q'a tot lo mont a des-treigner*, Mahn *ad estreigner*.
103 *senioria*: Mahn *semoria*, Constans *seinoria*.
106 *que vol folleiar*: Constans *que vol follejar*, Chabaneau *qui*.
107 *Iohanitz*: Constans *Johanitz*.
109 *Don Iois*: Constans *Don ieu*. For *Iois* read *Jois* (vocative).
110 *ioios*: Mahn *joios*.
111 *Us*: Levy *un. cellatz*: Mahn *tellatz*.
112 *Si*: read *Sa*.
113 *Si a el non s'ennanara*: Mahn *s'en vanara*, Chabaneau *Sia el jou* (= *joi?*).
127 *deur'om*: Constans *deura*.
128 *cors*: Chabaneau *cor*.
137 *ioi*: Constans *joi*.
139 *serra*: Constans *serra[r]*.
140 *es pesz*: Mahn *espesz*.
142 *Qu'ez mos amig e mos privatz*: Constans *Qu'ez mos amig[s] e mos prevatz*.
146 Manuscript *Qā*.
151 *envei*: Constans *enuei*.
152 *Viulas, dansas*: Constans *Viulas e dansas*.
153 *Ioventz*: Constans *Joventz*.
154 *Seigna vos*: Chabaneau *Segua vos*.
156 *Meissaona* is an irregular form of *meisonar*. The dipthonguization has not been explained so far. Italianism?
161 *la fassaitz*: Constans *laffasseitz*.
166 *gran terre*: read *gran terra*, although this destroys the rhyme and meter.
167 *no.m*: Constans *non*.
168 *Eu te farai ton envei far*: Chabaneau *Eu be farai con eu vei* and *ton enuei*.
172 *Pueis la fatz tant enardir*: Constans *Pueis [el] la fatz tant enardir*, Chabaneau *[E] pueis* and *Pueis [vos]*.
174 *riqesa*: Constans *riquesa. parate*: Mahn *paraie*; read *paratje*.
176 *ambedui*: Mahn *ambeduz*.
178 *a si donz ardiment*: Constans *ab ardiment*.
182 *Dir los bens qe de vos hai*: Constans *Dir[e] lo[s] bens qe de vos hai*.
190 *ia*: Constans *ja*.
191 *ia*: Constans *ja*.
196 Chabaneau felt that at least two verses had been omitted here. His commentary is confusing since his correction deals with the two lines immediately following l. 206. I do not think that two lines could be missing after l. 196 or l. 206.
199 *comensa*: Constans *comens'a*.
200 *deia*: Constans *deja*.
206 *Q'a*: Constans *Qa[l]. enia*: read *enica*.
207 *Domna, per q'es q'altr'amic hai?*: Chabaneau "—*Donna, per qu'es? —Q'altr'amic hai.*"
210 *en perdria*: Constans *eu perdria*.
212 *Vos*: Constans *Vas*.

213 *Bon'Esperansa*: Constans *Bonesperansa*.

214 *preiar*: read *prejar*, or *pregar*.

226 *cuia*: Constans *cuja*.

229 *mandetz*: Constans *mandes*.

230 *eu*: Constans *ieu*.

233 *si.t soana*: Constans *sit forana*.

235 *desir lonia*: Constans *de tis lonja*.

236 *mensonia*: Constans *mensonja*.

237 *qe m'escanara*: Constans *q'e [la] m'escanara*.

239 *ez*: Constans *es*.

242 *plaia*: Constans *plaja*.

245 *com aura*: Chabaneau *co m'aura*.

251 *pesa*: read *proesa*. The scribe often abbreviated *pro* as $\bar{p}$, and *in* this case he forgot the notation. Cf. l. 255 and l. 477.

255 *no.u cell*: Chabaneau *non cal*. *pesa*: read *proesa*.

256 *orba*: Constans *orda*.

257 *Ni.u cell*: Chabaneau *Ni (or Nius) cal*.

260 *de preon sospira*: Constans *re prec on sospira*.

263 *iois*: Constans *jois*.

273 *si'aonitz*: Constans *sia onitz*.

275 *invern*: Constans *ivern*.

279 *cel*: read *s'el*.

281 *parla*: Constans *parlara*.

283 Chabaneau pointed out that *chadaus* has three syllables. That pronunciation produces a nine syllable line.

285 *vos es la flors*: Constans *vos es ben la flors*.

286 *ioy*: Constans *joy*.

287 *envei*: Chabaneau *enuei*.

288 *ia*: Constans *ja*.

292 Constans read *alatz calant*, but Chabaneau corrected it to *aiatz talant*. The manuscript clearly bears the first reading.

297 *ioi*: Constans *joi*.

298 *vos mantenes ioi*: Constans *vos mantenez joi*.

300 *doin*: read *don*.

303 Levy: *E ce (= se) la ren qi plus li platz, / Son bel amic a entrels bratz . . .?*

306 *Qe qant*: Levy *E qant*.

308 *enveia*: Chabaneau *enueja*.

313 *ioios*: Constans *joios*.

315 *Soredamors*: Constans *no saup re d'amors*.

319 *vivrai*: Constans *viurai*.

325 *vos es*: read *vos e*.

327 *Gardas qe s'aqest dez baron*: Constans *Car das qes aquest dui baron*.

328 *aduiszon*: Constans *adviszon*.

330 *Gardan la nueit*: Constans *Gardan lo la nueit*.

331 *haion be*: Constans *hazon [nul] be*.

332 *aion*: Chabaneau *ajon*.

333 *Si prenon*: Chabaneau *si son donnas*.

335 and 336 *amics* and *enics*: Levy *amic* and *enic*.

341 *lo*: read *lor*.

345 *Qant*: the initial was left blank for the illustrator. Mahn restituted *Cant*. *hacs*: Constans *hac*.

350   *ia*: Constans *ja.*
355   *com ellas son*: Constans *coma son.*
356   *haion*: Constans *hajon.*
359   *soltiment*: read *sotilment.*
360   *iugament*: Constans *jugament.*
365   *aqest iutgament*: Mahn *aquest*, Constans *jutgament.*
369   *Il lo*: Mahn *ille.*
371   *E doba se de iugar*: Constans *E a doba se de jugar*, Mahn *jutgar.*
372   *se fan*: Chabaneau *se fai.*
373   *q'es luecs es*: Constans *q'ez*, Mahn *q'ez*, Chabaneau *luecs es* and *quez* (for *quei*) *es luecs.*
374   *sos*: Constans *son.*
375   *savis e pros*: Chabaneau *savi'e pros.*
379   *paubresza*: Constans *paubrezta*, Mahn *paubrezta.*
380   *ab riqesa*: Mahn, Constans *ab riquesa.*
381   *res at*: Mahn *recat.*
383   *breu e bon*: Mahn *ben e bon.*
384   *breuiar*: Constans *breujar.*
385   *Fin'Amors es de qatre res*: Constans *Fin'Amors dis de qatre res.*
387   *la segona lialtatz*: Constans *la segonda li altatz.*
389   Constans *E la terza si es mesura*. The manuscript does not show *si.*
390   *gad*: read *gap* (joke, raillery), Mahn *gnt*, Constans *grant*, Chabaneau *gent.*
393   *Aqesta*: Mahn *aquesta.*
398   *canariz*: read *camjairitz* (a fickle or changeable woman), Mahn *camzairitz*, Constans *cantaritz.*
399   *Qe lor femm'es e lors amors*: Constans *Que lor femmes e lor amors*, Mahn *femes.*
401   *devem*: Constans *deven. aqellas*: Levy *aquella.*
403   Chabaneau believed that *Cortesia* had stopped speaking and that the following lines including l. 408, were spoken by *Amor*, and consequently he corrected l. 403 to read *Aquest jutgament, — fai s'Amor. iutgament*: Constans *jutgament.*
412   *oblide*: Constans *obliden.*
413   *saiellat*: Constans *sajellat.*
414   *niellat*: Mahn *mellat.*
415   *sa man*: Chabaneau *son man*, the noun being masculine in this case.
416   *Met li n'en*: Mahn, Constans *Met li non.*
420   *pleiat*: Constans *plejat.*
422   *Aves ausat lo zutgament*: Constans *Aves auszit lo jutgament*, Mahn *ausit.*
423   *Qan*: Constans *Qe*, Mahn *Qan. jutgat*: Mahn *zutgat.*
424   *sai*: Mahn, Constans, *saz.*
426 and l. 427 *ioc*: Constans *joc.*
432   *aduiszon*: Constans *advison.*
435   *dons*: Mahn *donz. ses taina*: Constans *s'esta[e]via.*
439   *E q'e.l cor no.us en sapcha grat*: Mahn *e qel non sis en sapcha grat.*
440   *non*: Chabaneau *von.*
441   *soi*: Mahn *soz*, Constans *soy.*
444   *pensa*: Levy *pesa.*
446   *no.s duj*: Constans *nos dui*, Mahn *nous dui.*
448   *no.m*: Mahn, Constans, *non.*

451 *dra*: Constans *dur*, Mahn *dru.*

453 *fazia*: Chabaneau *faria.*

456 *l'amor*: Chabaneau *s'amor.*

458 *ners*: Mahn *ners*, Constans *vers.*

459 *eus*: in Upper Italy, especially in the Venetian dialects, *ipse* serves also as third person personal pronoun, cf. *FEW*, IV, 810a. Or from French (*els*)?

460 *mantz*, masculine, singular of *man* (morning): Constans *maty.*

461 *Aq'eus devenc pus blancs*: Chabaneau *Et aqui eus devenc [tan] blancs.*

474 *emblar lo cor*: Constans *emba[r]locor.*

477 *pesa*: Constans *proesa.* Cf. l. 251 and l. 255.

481 *dompna*: Constans *dompne.*

483 *vos*: Constans *vous.*

485 *haz*: Constans *hay(z).*

489 *qe hai*: Constans *qu'hai.*

490 *vos*: Constans *vous.*

496 *aimon vos*: French form, read *amon*, Constans *aimon nous.*

501 *aiso soj per l'asaiar*: Constans *aisi soi per l'asajar.*

506 *soj*: Constans *soi.*

507 *mie*: read *mieu.*

509 *soz*: Mahn *soj*, Constans *soi.*

510 *enoj*: Constans *enoi.*

512 *Ab altra vez*: Constans *Ab altra voz.* Cf. l. 517.

513 *Qe vos, drutz, quan vos es jauszit*: Constans *Qe vous*, Mahn *Qe vous, drutz, quan vous esjausçit.*

517 *veirem*: Constans *veiren.*

521 *domneiar*: Constans *donnejar.*

524 *E.l baisa, ben l'a enriquit*: Constans *El baisa ben la en riquit.*

525 This line contains too many syllables. Constans read *Qel menre amors que si dons fassa*, and Chabaneau corrected it to *Qel menre amors que domna fassa*, both of which are still two syllables too long.

526 *qe jiassa*: Chabaneau *quei* (= *que i* = *que li*) *jassa.*

527 This line is certainly corrupt as it appears here and in the manuscript with nine syllables. *Malvatz*, l. 528, is correct but *arozinatz* is second person plural, present tense, even though a third person singular is required with *drutz* as subject. *Arozina* would destroy the rhyme. Constans read *aidzinatz.*

530 *d'armas*: Constans *dar mas.*

534 *Fassa o qe.l sapcha tan bon*: Constans *Fassa aquel [li] sapcha bon.*

539 *aqist bon*: Constans *aqist hom*, Chabaneau *aquest bon.*

540 *q'il tenga sor cor gent*: Constans *q'il tenga sor cor gent*, Chabaneau *qu'el.* For *sor* read *son.*

548 *la faz*: Constans *l'afaz.*

549 *men*: read *mentre* with Constans.

550 *belle*: Constans *bella.*

553 *E acuella*: Constans *Qels acuella*, Chabaneau *E acuella*, Levy *E[l]s.*

556 *Auia*: Constans *Aja*, Chabaneau *Auja.*

557 *haia*: Constans *haja.*

561 *ci*: read *si.*

562 *manias*: Constans *manjas.*

569 *s'en blasma*: Chabaneau *l'en blasma.*

570   *aitant*: Constans *al*[*tre*]*tant*.

574   *Qar Dieus volc alte q'es a vos*: Constans *Qar Dieus volc alt en qu'es a voz*, Chabaneau *attengues a vos*.

575   *E anso*: Chabaneau *E am so*.

579   *E s'ill*: Constans *sill*.

580   *ioi*: Constans *joi*.

581   *Qe dompna*: Constans *Or dompna*, Chabaneau *Qar dompna*.

583   *ia*: Constans *ja*.

584   *forsa; sofre s'o*: Constans *força, sofris o*.

589   *ioi*: Constans *joi*.

591   *iausir*: Constans *jausir*.

593   *dompna*: read *dona* with Constans.

594   *Del sparvier*: Chabaneau *D'esparvier*.

595   *plus ma*: read *pluma*.

599   Chabaneau (p. 93) remarked that *no ie* is an "exemple remarquable de la forme *ie*, si fréquente aujourd'hui dans les dialectes méridionaux." Constans read *noi*.

601   *Qe qui la baiza per gran dousor*: Constans *Qe quil baisza per gran dousor*, Chabaneau *Qe qui la baisza per dousor*.

602   *Cug q'haia.l cors plen de flor*: Constans *Cug q'haja l*[*o*] *cors plen de flor*, Chabaneau *Cuge qu'ajal cors*.

604   *Tant*: Chabaneau *Cant*.

606   *Que se*: Constans *Ques. cointamen*: read *coindament*? (Cf. 1. 626, *coindia*, but l. 637 *cointamen*). *t* for *d* is found also in Italian manuscripts, cf. E. Monaci, *Crestomazia Italiana dei primi secoli con prospetto grammaticale e glossario*, nuova editione riveduta e aumentata per cura di Felice Arese (Rome and Naples: Società Editrice Dante Alighieri, 1955), p. 625a.

609   *E l'oills*: Constans *E loing*.

612   *demostro*: Chabaneau *demostre*.

614   *gaire*: Constans *g*[*au*]*dire*.

615   *corteiar*: Constans *cortejar*.

623   *gars*: read *gart* with Constans.

625   This verse is a repetition of l. 611.

626   *e*: Constans *el*, Levy *et*.

627   *son*: read *sos*.

628   *rasa*: read *rosa*, cf. 1. 50. Chabaneau *Si com lo ros acreis la flor*.

630   *pros*: Constans *prous*.

636   *ioi*: Constans *joi*.

637   *cointamen*: read *coindamen*? Cf. l. 606.

640   *hauri'hom*: Constans *haurihon*.

641   *auies*: Constans *aujes*.

642   *desconvenies*: Constans *desconvenjes*.

645   *tricha*: Chabaneau *triche*. Constans inserted an initial *E*.

648   *alques*: Constans *al ques*.

650   *iamais*: Constans *jamais*.

651   *On plus la non lai sezes*: Chabaneau *On plus lav*[*ar*] *om lai* (= *la i*) *fezes*.

653   *Ni*: Constans *N'i*.

655   *com pot estain durar*: Chabaneau *c'om pot estain daurar*. The manuscript clearly bears the former although the latter is the preferable reading.

656   *iamais*: Constans *jamais*.

660   *s'en espenda*: Levy *s'en espanda*.

662   *enolt* (from *enoldar* 'to enlace'): Constans *ab vel,* Chabaneau *e volt* and *evolt de (involuti).*

663   *veia:* Constans *veja.* l. 664 *enveia:* Constans *enveja.*

671 and l. 672 Italianisms, *menudetas* and *vermelletas:* read *menudedas* and *vermelledas?*

675   *sas bellas mans:* Chabaneau *sos bels mans.* Cf. l. 415.

676   *no.ls:* Constans *nos.*

679   *dolguda:* Constans *delgada.* Read *dolgada.*

680   *boca:* Constans *boc[l]a,* Chabaneau *bloca.*

687   *se:* read *e* (*s* due to the laison with *sotils*).

688   *uvern:* Constans *ivern.*

690   *E an ab dompnas:* Constans *Can[t] [es] ab dompnas.*

695   *An:* Constans *Am[s],* Chabaneau *Ans.*

699   *l'aur, pel e li boton:* Constans *l'aur[i]pel e li boton.*

702   *so compain:* Constans *s'acompain.*

703-705   Chabaneau believed there was a lacuna before these lines. It is possible that these verses are corrupted.

709   *dompn:* read *dompna.*

714   *n'hai:* Constans *i hai.*

715   *en trait:* Constans *entre[es]ait.*

716   *Mals es ma parte fait:* Constans *Mals esma, part e fait.*

717   *E el:* Constans *Cel.*

721   *serion:* Chabaneau *seri'om.*

722   *non ges bos:* Constans *n'es ges bos.*

723   *los:* Constans *lor.*

724   *venia:* Constans *venja.*

725   *a grat:* Constans *agrat.*

730   *No i:* Chabaneau *Nol.*

731   *polsa:* Chabaneau *pols'a.*

732   *non es stancs:* Constans *non es [s]stancs.*

733   *trameto:* Constans *tramonto.*

736   *Molt cuitas c'a tost le vasals:* Chabaneau *Molt cuitas* (= *cuitatz*) *tost lo vassals.* Read *Molt cuitas an tot los vassals.*

741   *Aquiels qes eu vei:* Chabaneau *aquels ques eu vueil.*

742   *Orguei:* Chabaneau *Orgueil.*

747   *c'era:* read *s'era* with Constans.

748   *S'es paupre, gens non a d'amor:* Constans *Ses paupre gens non a d'amor.*

750   *e.l:* Constans *el[s].*

754   *trametrem:* Constans *trametren.*

755   *l'e:* read *l'en.*

757   *qe:* Constans *que.*

765   *esse:* read *esser.*

771   *e'enaisi i clama:* Chabaneau *s'enaisil.*

772   *qe:* Constans *qez.* The scribe wrote *q₃.*

773   *aici.m trameton:* Constans *aici intremeton.*

785   *garen:* Constans *ganre.*

792   *ten pres:* Constans *tenpes.*

799   *qe:* Constans *que.*

801   *bona feses:* Constans *bon(a) fosses.*

803   The manuscript, which bears a considerable variety of punctuation, clearly shows a period within the line after the word *mens,* which is the way

Constans also read the line. Chabaneau corrected it to *q'en val mens s'ellal respont gent?* and remarked that *Amors* has begun speaking again at this point.

804 *ce*: read *se*.

805 *fai*: Constans *sai*.

806 *co*: Constans *ço*.

808 *ioios*: Constans *joios*.

814 *dopnas*: Constans *dompnas*.

816 *cui esposa*: Constans *cui [es] esposa*.

823 *Corteszia, las atzinadas*: Chabaneau *Corteszia las a zujadas*.

824 *qeron*: Constans *queron*.

825 *Er getat de ma companna*: Constans *Ez getat de ma compania*, Chabaneau *Ei getat (habeo)*.

838 *Seiner*: Constans *Senier*. Chabaneau corrected *portes* to *portas* and translated *qar* as 'pourquoi.'

843 *fontaina*: Constans *fontania*.

844 *retenir*: Constans *reten[t]ir*.

846 *mo*: read *mon*. *qa*: read *que*.

848 *avia*: read *avian* with Constans.

858 *iamais*: Constans *jamais*.

859 *si asezon*: Constans *s'asezon*.

863 *maniar ia*: Constans *manjar ja*.

866 *aia*: Constans *aja*.

869 *havem*: Constans *haven*.

871 *mon senior*: Constans *mossenior*.

872 *ioi*: Constans *joi*.

875 *havem*: Constans *haven*.

878 *maniar*: Constans *manjar*.

880 *ioi*: Constans *joi*.

883 *aiutz*: Constans *a[u]jutz*, Chabaneau *ajutz*.

891 *viras*: read *viran*.

893 *cuion*: Constans *cujon*.

898 *ioglar*: Constans *joglar*.

901 *E fe qu'il devon*: Constans *E[l] fe[s] qu'il devon*.

902 *Q'am.l*: Chabaneau *Qu'al*.

903 *ioglar se proschon del rei*: Constans *joglar s'aprochon del rei*.

906 *Li lausengiers de lin iutas*: Constans *Li lausengier(s) de l'invitas?*, Chabaneau *del lin Judas*.

918 *iamai laidida*: Chabaneau *jamai l'ardida*.

921 *Se lla*: Constans *Sella*, Chabaneau *Se la*. *convinens*: Constans *convinent*.

924 *Faita an li lauzeiador*: Constans *Fait o an li lauze[n]jador*.

925 Possible metathesis: for *danmia* read *damnia*.

926 *sordeiar*: Constans *soldejar*.

933 *qe za feit*: Chabaneau *quez a fort*.

934 *iorns*: Constans *jorns*.

939 *ia*: Constans *ja*.

940 *Qe de vos sparton mei deszir*: Chabaneau *Qe de vos parton* and *De vos separton*.

944 *soz*: Constans *soi*.

950 *ricedar*: Chabaneau *ric e clar?* and *riche bar?* Ricedar is a scribal error *ricedat*.

952   *emdeven*: Constans *men deven*, Chabaneau *m'endeven*. Cf. Monaci, *op. cit.*, no. 24, l. 176: *m* for *n* is attested in the early thirteenth century in Italian manuscripts. Cf. also l. 1274.

957   *deuria*: Constans *devria*.

959   *raza*: Chabaneau *roza*. Cf. l. 50.

963   *venduda*: Chabaneau *vencuda*.

964   *omen*: Constans *ome*.

967   *haia*: Constans *haja*.

972   Constans read this verse as one sentence: *Eu non* (?) *faillit son mei deport.*

974   *penren en ia*: read *penrem en ja.*

975   *portarem*: Constans *portaren.*

982   *ha li dit*: Constans *li ha dit.*

985   *iugat*: Constans *jugat.*

994   *ceran*: Constans *feran*; read *seran.*

995   *Ans lur pro*: Constans *Ans [tol] lur pro.*

997   *auien*: Constans *aujen.*

998   *fluec* apparently represents a contamination of the word *fuec* with the word *flama.*

1003-1005   *Ill faz vezer lur bel semblan. / Ab tal don gaere no li cal / A qe cobre son ioi coral*: Chabaneau *El fai, vezen lur, bel semblan / A tal don gaire no li cal, / Ab que cobre son joi coral.*

1008   *de son gent cors onrat*: Constans *de son gen cors on[o]rat*, Chabaneau *et onrat.*

1009   Chabaneau wrongly remarked (p. 95) that "*El* est pour *il (elle).*"

1010   *iausen*: Constans *jauzen.*

1011-1012   *Fait tan enveios prezen, / Coves de son bell acuillir*: Constans *Fai de tan envejos presen, / Coves de son bell acuillir*, Chabaneau *E fait tan envejos presen / Con es de son bell acuillir.*

1015   *lo j*: Constans *loi.*

1018   *si.l*: Constans *s'il.*

1019   *desfendre*: Chabaneau *deffendre.*

1025   *Antz deu tener*: Constans *Antz deu [el] tener*, Chabaneau *Antz li deu tener.*

1027   *peiiura*: Constans *peijura.*

1028   *mais*: Constans *mai.*

1030   *qe*: Constans *que.*

1031   *qe*: Constans *que.*

1033   *ioglar*: Constans *joglar.*

1034   *Aital sai*: Constans *Aital fai.*

1035   *qe.l*: Constans *quel.*

1036   *autra mia*: Constans *autr'amia.*

1037-1038   *Ni autra, qi cosapchatz, si fia. / Ell'apella son amador*: Constans *Ni autra cosa cui si fia. / Ell'apella son amador*, Chabaneau *Ni autra, qi co sapcha, s'i fia / E l'apella son amador.*

1039   *de ioi deiuna*: Constans *de joi de l'una*, Chabaneau *de joi dejuna.*

1041   *m'aiut*: Constans *m'ajut.*

1043   *delonza*: Constans *de lonja.*

1044   *es conia*: Constans *esconja.*

1045   *ia*: Constans *ja.*

1049   *percaz*: Constans *perja(z)*, Chabaneau *perjaz*, "qui est *pour perchaz* (fr. *pourchasse*)."

1050   *li lauzeniador*: Constans *li lauzenjador.*

1051   *haion*: Constans *hajon.*

1054   *tornan*: Constans *torna[n]*, Chabaneau *torno.*

1057   *Atressi dompna non deu alen*: Constans *Atressi dompnan deu, alen,* Chabaneau (p. 95) "rétablir *non*, dont la suppression fait un contre-sens, et corriger *len.*"

1058   *ioi*: Constans *joi.*

1059   *E deu gardar qe Fin'Amors gaia*: Constans *(E) deu gardar que Fin'Amors gaia.* Chabaneau remarked "supprimer plutôt *que* ou *fin* que *E*," but the line remains too long in either case.

1060   *enplaidar*: Constans *en plaidar.*

1061   *E no.s deporton nos oimais*: Constans *E nos deport on [de] nos (oi)mais*, Chabaneau *deportem nos oimais.*

1063   *E veian*: Constans *En vejan*, Chabaneau *E vejam.*

1065   *au las voz*: Constans *aulaz vos.*

1066   *ioi*: Constans *joi.*

1067   Chabaneau remarked (p. 95) that "la lacune ne doit pas être très considérable. Peut-être ne manque-t-il qu'un vers, dont le sens doit être *s'il ne se laisse émouvoir ou si'il ne devient amoureux.*"

1068   *e.l*: Constans *e.*

1069   *ioi*: Constans *joi.*

1077   *deiost'Amor*: Constans *de jost Amor.*

1078   *ioi*: Constans *joi.*

1082   *enveia*: Constans *enveja.*

1084   *foz*: Constans *fos.*

1087   *Qe tanha d'onor*: Constans *Qe tanha d'Onor*, Chabaneau *Quem tanha donar.*

1101   *Le*: Constans *lo. qe*: Constans *que.*

1110   Levy (p. 239) preferred that *Fin'Amor* be written here in lower case.

1116   *Qe bella es*: Constans *Que bell'es.*

1120   *L'aus qer, mi don, e.l de vos be*: Constans *Laus qu'er mi don el de vos be*, Levy *L'aus querrem don el de vos be.*

1124   *Mos cors*: Chabaneau *Mon cors.*

1127   *[A] jlors respon ela: "Soi ben vostra"*: Constans *Amors respon: "Eu soi ben vostra,"* Chabaneau *Honors respon: "Ja soi ben vostra."*

1128   *aqil*: Constans *aquel.*

1129   *iovecenlla*: read *iovencella.*

1139   *peizura*: a combination of *pejurar* (< *pejor*) 'to worsen' and *peitz* (< *pix*, Old French *peiz*) 'pitch'? Or simply *z* for *j* /= dz/? This combination is not attested elsewhere.

1141   *Qe domnas i ha*: Constans *Que donnas i ha*, Chabaneau *E donnas i ha.*

1142   *Qe paron laide ande non vuel*: Constans *Que paron laiden de novel*, Chabaneau *Que parlon laid, e ja* (ou *laidang'e*) *non vuel. ande*: (*apud ab de*), cf. *FEW*, XXIV, 2, 63a. *nonvuel*: 'repugnance,' cf. *FEW*, XIV, 217a where Old French *desvueil* 'repugnance' is attested in the fourteenth century.

1145   *veniar*: Constans *venjar.*

1165   *estrenia*: Constans *estrenja.*

1166   *venia*: Constans *venja.*

1181   *Gran*: Constans *Grant. haiut*: Constans *hajut.*

1182   *maniar*: Constans *manjar.*

1183 *cuiava*: Constans *cujava*. l. 1185 *Qe*: Constans *Que*.

1192 *enveia*: Constans *enveja*.

1193 *Mais ia non er qe Dieus non veia*: Constans *Mais ja non er que Dieus non veja*.

1198 *De sains*: Constans *De segur*.

1199 *Sains*: Chabaneau *Desains*.

1208 *haiut*: Constans *hajut*.

1211 *Sab q'eu.s*: Constans *Sab qu'eus*, Chabaneau *queus*.

1213 *tenps*: Constans *temps*.

1214 *lo man*: Constans *la man*. *iur*: Constans *jur*.

1215 *enasi*: Constans *enaisi*.

1216 *Qe za*: Chabaneau *Quez a*.

1217 *no.us ... genchida*: Constans *vous*, Levy *jauzida*.

1218 *iuras*: Constans *juras*.

1220 *iorn*: Constans *jorn*.

1221 *plueia*: Constans *plueja*. *tenps*: Constans *temps*.

1222 *qe*: Constans *que*.

1223 *qe*: Constans *que*.

1225 *Qe tant qant vivrai*: Constans *Que tant qant viurai*.

1228 *Ious si iugirent*: Constans *Jous si jugirent*, Chabaneau *sion* (or *siam*) *guirent*.

1231 *qe*: Constans *que*.

1232 *haia*: Constans *haja*.

1234 *E baisem nous en, qar cove*: Constans *E baisem nous, enqar cove*.

1235 *E nom*: read *El nom*.

1237 *s'i*: Chabaneau *si i*.

1238 *verra*: read *venra*.

1240 *Cant ab hora s'adobes li*: Constans *Cant ab hora s'adob a li*, Chabaneau *Tant ab horas adobe ssi*.

1243 *com assi*: Constans *comassi*.

1245 *lapsapchia*: read *la sapchia*. The *p* inserted between these two words is inexplicable. Cf. l. 1259.

1246 *Qe*: Constans *Que*.

1249 *ia*: Constans *ja*.

1250 *Qe anc enqera no.l veges*: Constans *Que anc enquera nol veges*.

1252 *ious*: Constans *jous*.

1253 *nouris*: Chabaneau *nonris* (?).

1258 *los bels mans*: Constans *las bels mans*.

1259 *pn'es*: read *n'es* with Constans. The manuscript bears an illegible mark above the *n* and Professor André de Mandach, Habstetten (Berne, Switzerland), has conjectured that this represents an *o* which the scribe attempted to insert later, above the line, in order to suggest *noes* as one foot. Dr. de Mandach has suggested that the *p* at the beginning of the word is perhaps a scribal error, cf. l. 1245. Constans believed that there was a lacuna of two lines after this verse.

1266 *E cill qe l'ama*: Constans *E cill qu'el ama*.

1268 *E homen*: Constans *E hom en*.

1269 *lou*: Constans *loc*.

1274 Cf. l. 952; *m* for *n*.

1277 *E la genszer q'anc fos amada*: Constans *E la genszer, qant fos amada*.

1280 Chabaneau remarked (p. 96) that *non* = *no en*. *ia*: Constans *ja*.

1281   *Amors, enpert*: Constans *Amors en pert*, Chabaneau *Amors empert*.

1283   *M'es enmenda q'ella mi vuella rire*: Constans *Me sembla qu'el(la)*
mi vuella rire, Chabaneau *M'esmenda qu'elam vueilla rire*.

1289   *ioc*: Constans *joc*. Chabaneau suggested a question mark after *joc*.

1293   *sors*: read *sers* with Constans; cf. l. 1431 *progarai* for *pregarai*,
l. 1500 *por* for *per*. *e* for *o* is attested in Upper Italian texts, cf. Monaci,
op. cit., paragraph 102.

1298   *ioi*: Constans *joi*.

1299   *Tro qe*: Constans *Tro que*. *m'aiut*: Constans *m'ajut*.

1300   *Qe*: Constans *que*.

1302   *tenps*: Constans *temps*.

1305   *q'il*: Constans *q'el*.

1306   *qe*: Constans *que*.

1310   *iuzizi*: Constans *juzizi*.

1311   *Qe*: Constans *Que*.

1312   *Grans merces vos*: Constans *Gran merceus*.

1313   *Qe per vos lo ten en gras fers*: Constans *Que (per) vos lo ten[ez]*
en gra[n]s fers.

1314   *non sera fors*: Contans *non sera el fors*.

1315   *engent*: not attested elsewhere.

1316   *volatge*: Constans *volatje*.

1318   *iointas*: Constans *jointas*.

1320   *Qe anc pos vos me donestes jorn*: Constans *Q'anc, pos non me*
donesses (?) *jorn*, Chabaneau *pos von* (= *vos en*, or simply *vos*) *me dones*
(= *donetz*) *ces* (= *cest*) *jorn*, "c'est à dire, 'depuis que vous m'avez donné
un rendez-vous.' *Donar cest jorn* ou *aquest jorn* était une formule *juridique*
signifiant 'assigner un jour'."

1321   *soiorn*: Constans *sojorn*.

1324   *coma*: Constans *com a*. Levy remarked (p. 239) that *coma* was
preferable "puisqu'il y a au vers 1328 [Constans' numbering — here l. 1323]
la luna el soleill." The scribe may have inverted *bons* and *mos*. A more
normal word order would be *coma mos bons seinors*.

1325   *breu gesson*: read *breugesson*, imperfect subjunctive of *breujar*, 'to
abridge.' *lo iors*: Constans *lo cors*.

1327   *sçemblan a*: Constans *sçemblava*.

1329   *laissarai*: Constans *la(i)ssarai*.

1333   *Auien*: Constans *Aujen*. *merceia*: Constans *merceja*.

1335   *soj*: Constans *soi*.

1343   *Un drutz enqer*: Constans *Un[s] drutz, en q'er*.

1344   *ious*: Constans *jous*.

1346   *qe.z er*: Constans *q'er*.

1351   *cuj*: Constans *cui*.

1352   *autruj*: Constans *autrui*.

1353   *qes es*: Constans *ques es*.

1354   *s'ieu*: Constans *se ieu*.

1358   *Ins aisi on*: Chabaneau *Enaisi on*.

1359   *Si lasat q'eu vos vencus*: Constans *Si lasat z qu'eu vos u encus* (?),
"*U* prononcez *ou* = *hoc* latin," Chabaneau *Si fasatz qu'eu nos* (= *no vos*)
o encus.

1360   *Qe*: Constans *Que*.

1363   *parra*: Constans *pa[r]tra*.

1371   *E vechs*: Constans *E[c] vech(s)*, Chabaneau *E vech*, "ou mieux, *E veus*."

1372   *aia*: Constans *aja*.

1373   *j ha qe*: Constans *i ha que*.

1374   *qeran*: Constans *queran*.

1375   *Qe*: Constans *Que*. *q'eu*: Constans *q'ieu*.

1379   *j vol*: Constans *i vol*.

1381   *De drut conven q'al comensar*: Constans *De drut conven. Q'al comensar*.

1383   *Tro qe s'avenga e s'eschaja*: Constans *Tro ques avenga es eschaia*.

1385   *E si non la port tan tost trobar*: Constans *E si no. pot tan tost trobar*, Chabaneau "rétablir *non la* et supprimer *E* ou *tan*."

1387   *Qe*: Constans *Que*.

1389   *truoba*: Constans *trueba. luzant*: Chabaneau *luzent*.

1394   *Si li.n*: Constans *Si lui*.

1395   *Q'aiha*: Constans *q'ajha*.

1399   *d'aqelas*: Constans *d'aquelas*.

1405   Constans omitted the comma after *sai*.

1406   *ioi*: Constans *joi*.

1408   *bauszares*: Constans *baiszares*.

1410   *estaz*: Constans *estai(z)*.

1417   *ioi*: Constans *joi*.

1418   *chiaj*: Constans *chiai*. Constans felt that there was a lacuna after this line, of perhaps two verses.

1421   *sel*: Constans *s'el*.

1422   *Ja hom*: Constans *Jamais. enoiatz*: Constans *enojatz*.

1423   *E quant es ab sabia gen*: Constans *E quant el es ab sabja gen*.

1424   *aprodera*: Chabaneau *apodera*.

1427   *saz*: Constans *sai*.

1431   *progarai*: read *pregarai*, cf. l. 1293. *sejnor*: Constans *seinor*.

1432   *vos darai*: Constans *non dara i*, Chabaneau *von dara*, "à la rigueur, *darai* pourrait rester."

1434   *Vos am, e lo mieus*: Constans *Vos am e[n] lo mieus*.

1437   *l'altre*: read *l'altre[r]* with Constans.

1439   *E j dis*: Constans *E i dis*, Chabaneau *E li dis*.

1442   *mais*: Constans *mot*.

1445   *desson*: imperfect subjunctive for *deguesson. endompneiatz*: Constans *encompnejatz*.

1456   *Per qe vaj*: Constans *Per que vai*.

1458   Constans omitted this line.

1462   *Q'enaissi.m*: Constans *Qu'enaissim*.

1463   *faj*: Constans *fai*, Levy *fei*. Levy remarked (p. 239) that "M. Chabaneau a émis la conjecture que le discours de l'amant finit au vers 1469 [1463 in this text] avant lequel il y aurait une courte lacune, qu'il faudrait alors y transporter les points et les guillemets du vers 1468 [1462] et corriger *Clar conogui* au vers 1471 [1465]. M. Constans s'est ranger à cette opinion, et dans le tirage à part de son travail, il imprime comme suit:

Qu'enaissim pot gitar de pena

... ...

Lo zou[s] de vos mi fai plorar

et, au vers 1471 [1465], *Clar conogui*. ... Je crois que M. Chabaneau s'est trompé et que M. Constans a eu tort de changer la ponctuation. Le discours de l'amant finit au vers 1468 [1462]: 'Car ainsi elle pourrait me délivrer de peine.' La messagère, car c'est elle qui parle à la dame (cf. vers 1401, 1410), [1395, 1414 in this text], après avoir rapporté les propos de l'amant, continue: "La joie, à cause de vous, me fit pleurer quand je vis qu'il changea de couleur, car je reconnus à sa mine qu'il vous aimerait sans tromperie.'" In a note on the same page Chabaneau wrote: "M. Levy a raison. C'est le *fai* (indicatif présent) du vers 1469 [1463] rapproché de *vi* (parfait) du vers suivant, qui avait causé mon erreur. Grâce à la correction de notre ingénieux collaborateur, tout devient clair dans ce passage, et il n'y a plus de doute que la première leçon de M. Constans, sauf pour ce *fai*, était la bonne."

1470   *Qe*: Constans *Que*.

1475   *No.us mais pes*: Chabaneau *Mais nous pes* (or *mais pourvu que?*). "C'est une formule polie. Peut-être n'y a-t-il rien à changer, le sens au fond restant le même."

1476   *Sembla qe.l faz vos trameses*: Constans *Sembla quel sal vos trameses*, Chabaneau *qu'el sai*.

1477   *mesatje logaditz*: Constans *mesatje[s] logaditz*.

1479   *repszas*: read *represzas*.

1486   *falas*: Chabaneau *faulas*.

1489   *Sitot me soj*: Constans *Sitot me sai*, Chabaneau *Sitot me soi*. Old Occitan *sitot* 'also, too' is not attested elsewhere, but rather the synonymous *et tot*, cf. *FEW*, XIII, 2, 125.

1490   *Lial*: Constans *Li al*.

1491   *soj*: Constans *soi*.

1494   *irai*: read *dirai*.

1497   *D'amor. Orus vos non sintez re*: Constans *D'Amor. Or vos non sintez re*, Chabaneau *D'Amor, on* (ou mieux *e*) *vos non* (= *no en*). *Orus* is an inexplicable form; perhaps for *Ores?*

1498   *vos vos veizatz*: Constans *vos (nos) veiziatz*.

1500   *Por*: read *per*, cf. l. 1293. Chabaneau *Vos diriatz pro: Dieus m'ajuda...* The manuscript clearly bears a period after *diriatz*.

1502   *parlaraj*: Constans *parlarai*.

1505   *[L]a dopna dira: "Tot veiraj*: Constans *L[a] do[m]pna dira: "To[s]t veirai*.

1507   *En engan ou en liautat*: Constans *E[n] vengan [sa] on en liautat*, Chabaneau *En engan on en*.

1511   *j*: Constans *i*.

1513   *Qe*: Constans *Que*.

1518   *Amatz lo mais c'Aia Landric*: Constans *Amatz lo mais c'aja band ric*, Levy *Amatz la*.

1519   *E qe*: Constans *E que*.

1521   *Tot'es*: Constans *Tot es*.

1522   *qe*: Constans *que*. *soclamada*: Constans remarked (p. 271, n. 1) that this word is possibly derived from *subclamata* in the neuter sense of 'qui se plaint,' and seems to signify in this case 'qui a le délire de la fièvre.' Italianism, cf. Old Italian *socchiamare*, 'chiamare sotto voce,' 'to moan' (14th century, C. Battisti, G. Alessio, *Dizionario etimologico italiano*, V. 3522b).

1523   *vos no.s*: Constans *no vos*.

1525   *tenguda*: Constans *cenguda*.

1526   *Mota*: 'goat without horns'? Cf. *FEW*, VI, 3, 297b; hence, 'hornless,' or perhaps 'stupid'? Constans assumed that the scribe had omitted a letter and restituted *morta*. This is perhaps a preferable reading since the subject of the next verse is death.

1527   *soffriraz*: Constans *soffrirai*.

1533-1534   *Con pus seres enveiosa / De lui, feines vergoinosa*: Constans *Con pus d'el serez envejosa, / De lui serez mens vergoinosa*, Chabaneau *E on pus serez envejosa / De lui, feines vos vergoinosa*.

1535   *Mais no.l laises ges famar*: Constans *Mais no.l laises ges s'a [fa]mar*, Chabaneau *faniar, fadiar*? "*s'a [fa]mar* paraît inadmissable."

1540   *cuiaria*: Constans *cujaria*.

1544   *Mais vengan*: Constans *[Ja] mais vengan*, Chabaneau *Mais non venga*?

1551   *Ni non*: Constans *Si non*.

1553   *qi*: Constans *qui*.

1556   *comdar*: Constans *condar*.

1558   *Ja anseis*: Constans *Ja enseis*.

1559   *qe s'eschiaza*: Constans *ques eschiaza*.

1565   *joas*: Constans *joias*.

1566   *Qi*: Constans *Qui*.

1567   *prez*: Constans *pres*.

1568-1570   Constans printed the names of these personifications in lower case.

1569   *E Plaszer: tug cil q'ho demanda*: Constans *E Plaszer, cug, cil q'ho demanda*, Chabaneau *tug cil q'hom*.

1570   *q'Amors*: Constans *qu'Amors*.

1576   *veian*: Constans *vejan*, Chabaneau *vejen* or *vezen*.

1584   *j*: Constans *i*.

1586   *Si non sei joias*: Constans *Si non sol joias*, Chabaneau *Si non so joias*.

1590   *Plaçers faire sensa moneda*: Constans *Plaçers fai re sensa moneda* (?), Chabaneau *Plaçers faire son sa moneda* (?). "Le pluralité du verbe s'expliquerait par l'idée de pluralité contenue dans le sujet." Levy *Plaçers faire sensa moneda, / Ses tot aver fai sa fazenda* 'de faire des plaisirs sans monnoie [sic], sans avoir, cela fait son affaire'" (p 239).

1593   *Qe*: Constans *Que*.

1594   *rej*: Constans *rei*.

1595   *de mer*: Constans *d'amor*.

1602   *qi*: Constans *qui*.

1603   *jonrs*: read *jorns* with Constans.

1608   *sa mia*: Levy *s'amia*.

1613   Chabaneau remarked (p. 98) that "il ne paraît pas manquer ici plus d'un vers."

1614   *Ben es sers e plens de felonia*: Chabaneau *Ben es fers*.

1616   *[L]j*: Constans *[L]i*.

1624   *Qe*: Constans *Que*.

1625   *E qe*: Constans *E que*.

1629   *ajut*: Constans *azut*.

1630   *dompna*: read *dona* with Constans.

1631   *veia*: Constans *veja*.

1632   *qi*: Constans *que*, Chabaneau *qui. guerreia*: Constans *guerreja*.

1633   *re non de hom*: read *re non de[u] hom* with Constans.

1637   *E.l garsona la qu'el mante*: Constans *E[l]i garson als quals mante*, Chabaneau *El garsonala quel mante*.

1638   *ha*: Chabaneau *hai*.

1640   *Qe l'en*: Constans *Q'el en*.

1642   *eser*: read *veser*.

1649   *Gerreiar*: Constans *Gerrejar*.

1650   *pejura*: Constans *pezura*.

1651   *E al dig*: Constans *E el dig*, Chabaneau *E al dig* (= 'Et lui a dit').

1655   *Qe*: Constans *Que*. *conqes*: Constans *conques*.

1660   *Entro qe*: Constans *Entro que*. *brada*: read *bruda*.

1663   *E fan lo cer qe.l casador*: Constans *E fai lo cer, quel casador*.

1668   *qe*: Constans *que*.

1670   *com zauzis*: Constans *com auzis*, Chabaneau *com zauzis*, "c'est-à-dire *jauzis*."

1671   *si es si donz*: Constans *si es si dons*, Chabaneau "Faut-il entendre *si eis* ou *si e si dons?*" The latter is preferrable, the *s* of *es* being one of liaison.

1676   *E Folz Semblantz*: Chabaneau *Fals Semblantz torna a nient?* "Peut-être aussi *Que* pour *E?*"

1681   *qe*: Constans *que*.

1683   *zoios*: Constans *joios*.

1686   *bel Seinher*: Constans *(bel) seinher*, Chabaneau "rétablir la leçon du ms. *seiner* et *feiner* ont l'accent sur la première syllable."

1687   *Qe laisson e.l fol*: Constans *Que laissol fol*.

1692   *vejaire*: Constans *vezaire*.

1696   *veia*: Constans *veja*, Chabaneau *n'aja*.

1697   *E perda Dieu qe*: Constans *E prega Dieu que*, Chabaneau *E perda Dieu qui*.

1698   *En foc, envolz, sebelis unis*: Constans *En foc, (en)volz, sebelis, unis*, Chabaneau *En foc envolz, sebelis vius*.

1699   *caitis*: Chabaneau *caitius*.

1701   *seudadas*: Constans *soudadas*.

1702   *Qer*: Chabaneau *Qei* (= *que i*).

1704   *monza*: Constans *monja*.

1711   *Qe*: Constans *Que*.

1713   *amictz*: Chabaneau *amics* ou *amicx*. "Il y a d'autres exemples de *-icx* rimant avec *-itz*."

1715   *los deportz*: Chabaneau *lo deportz*.

1718   *Zovens*: Constans *Jovens*.

1720   *destreis*: Constans *destrein*.

NOTES TO THE TRANSLATION

4 *Joi* is untranslatable since there is no exact one-word English equivalent. In his *Joy d'Amor des Troubadours, jeu et joie de'amour* (Montpellier: Causse et Castelnau, 1965), Chapter VII, "Origine et définition du joy d'amor," p. 133, Ch. Camproux defines *joi* as "avant tout une activité, une force de vie, qui se manifeste par un exercice, un jeu, au sens profond du mot, un jeu, un exercice qui requièrent *Cor e cors e saber e sen / e fors e poder* (cœur et corps et savoir et intelligence et force et pouvoir) comme le chante Bernart de Ventadorn." Since *joi* can be best translated only by lengthy phrases, I have preferred to retain the Occitan word.

5 *romanz*: Levy *PD* gives for *romans*: 'langue vulgaire; écrit en langue vulgaire.' Levy *SW*, VII, 373b-374a, cites *"La parladura francesca val mais . . . a far romanz, retronsas et sirventes,"* from the *Razos de Trobar* of Raimon Vidal de Besalù (first half of the thirteenth century) and *"Vai sus Alis . . . / Pren lo romanz de Blancaflor. / Alis si leva tost e cor / Vas una taula on estava / Cel romans."* from *Flamenca* (ca. 1240), ll. 4477-4480. The *Cort d'Amor* was written most likely after the *Razos de Trobar* and probably before *Flamenca*. *Romanz* here, therefore, has its ordinary meaning of narrative poem written in the vernacular language in octosyllabic lines. Cf. also *FEW*, X, 453b and 455b, and especially P. Voelker, "Die Bedeutungsentwicklung des Wortes *Roman*," *Zeitschrift für romanische Philologie*, X (1886), 485-525. The word in Old Occitan was borrowed from French.

14 *Drut* is defined by Levy *PD* as 'amant, galant; fidèle, ami privé; homme courtois?' The second, third, and fourth meanings are preferable since the modern French word 'amant' and the equivalent English word 'lover,' imply an intimate physical relationship which would ordinarily include sexual consumation, which is probably *not* a necessary element in the medieval Occitan concept of *drut*. According to recent developments in the semantic study of this word, (cf. Ch. Camproux, *The Joy of Love of the Troubadours*, 2nd. ed., unpublished manuscript translation by L. Jones), *drut* refers to personal possessions in the legal domain of the lady, and thus the personal friends of the lady, or those admitted into her confidence. It appears therefore, that *drut* does *not* refer to a suitor, one who is seeking admittance to the lady's private circle of companions, but rather to one who has been accepted. Whether this acceptance involves anything more than attendance at her couchée or levée and similarly intimate services, depends entirely on the context in which the word appears and not on any meaning inherent in the word. As a result I have translated *drut* inconsistently, most often as 'lover' in the most general sense of 'one who loves' and occasionally as 'sweetheart' where lover seems a bit too strong.

22   *domna* is ambiguous here. It could refer either to the suitor's beloved, the lady, or it could refer to *Amor,* a feminine personification.

23   Eight twenties, viij.xx., or one hundred sixty (160), is a significantly large number implying 'a great many.' Cf. l. 59 *ha cent pulsellas,* where the specific number seems to have no particular significance except to emphasize quantity. Eight twenties corresponds to the English 'eight score.' It could also be read as twenty-eight, but this is less likely. Cf. l. 1697 of *Floire et Blanchefleur, édition critique avec commentaire* by Margaret Pelan (Paris: Les Belles Lettres, 1937), "En la tour sept-vint chambres a." Cf. also *FEW,* XIV, 444, and particularly the comment on p. 445. Our text contradicts von Wartburg's impression (n. 24) that the twenty system of counting was not rooted in the South of France and Upper Italy. On the contrary this attestation is even earlier than the first one given on p. 444a (1326) from the North (Tournai).

27-28   Cf. Arnaut Daniel (*Arnaut Daniel Canzoni,* ed. Gianluigi Toja, Florence: Sansoni, 1960, p. 316, xiii, "Er vei vermeills, vertz, blaus, blancs, gruocs," ll. 12-14): "C'Amors enquier los sieus d'aital semblan, / verais, francs, fis, merceians, parcedors / car a sa cort notz orguills e vol blandres."

30   *Amor,* translated as 'Love,' is a feminine noun and therefore the personification is a feminine character as clearly indicated by the epithet *la dousa et la bona.* For the sake of consistency this personification is treated as a feminine figure throughout. Cf. also ll. 48, 351, 353, 354.

39   *Fin'Amor* is untranslatable. Levy *PD* defines *fin* as 'fin, pur; vrai; accompli, parfait; fidèle; sur, certain.' The essence of the concept is 'perfect love' with all the implications of both perfection and love included in the definition; cf. Ch. Camproux, *Le Joy d'Amor, op. cit., passim.* For the sake of simplicity and clarity I have retained the Occitan phrase where it occurs in the text. 'Love' and *Fin'Amor* will refer to the same figure interchangeably, but I have followed the text in translating as 'Love' when the text bears simply *Amor.*

47   *Domneis* is untranslatable. The verb is *domnejar* which Levy *PD* defines as 'faire la cour aux dames, servir les dames; pratiquer la courtoisie (en parlant d'une femme); s'ébattre,' as a reflexive, 'parler d'amour, faire l'amour.' The noun *domnei,* m., is defined as 'la cour qu'on fait à une dame, service d'amour et de courtoisie,' and the noun *domnejador* refers to the 'galant, homme qui aime à courtiser les dames.' Levy *SW* cites Arnaut Daniel and Ademar Rocaficha and defines *domneis* as 'Herrin nennen, Herrin dienen; Minnespiel treiben.' The *FEW,* III, 124a, cites OFr *donoier* 'faire la cour aux dames, faire l'amour,' OOc *domnejar* 'id.; s'ébattre,' OFr *donoier* m. 'privauté de rire, baiser, etc., avec une dame, sans la dernière faveur'; OFr *donoi* 'plaisir amoureux, cour qu'on fait à une dame,' OOc *domnei*; OFr *donoiement,* OOc *domnejamen*; OFr *donoieor* 'amant, galant,' OOc *domnejador.*

The nearest possible English rendering of *domneis* would have to be 'privileged courtship,' which remains vague and stilted. It is impossible to translate as 'the service of love' since this is confusingly similar to *Corteszia* who represents both courtesy and courtship. For these reasons I have retained the Occitan *domneis.*

48   *Lo,* masculine singular pronoun, here refers to the feminine personification of Love/*Fin'Amor.* Cf. above notes to ll. 30 and 39.

51-54   Cf. Guillem de Saint Didier (in C. A. F. Mahn, *Die Werke der Troubadours in provenzalischer Sprache nach den Handschriften der Pariser*

Nationalbibliothek. Berlin and Paris, Klincksieck, 1846-1853, II, ix, "Malvasa m'es la moguda," ll. 36-37): "De cortes luoc mov la raiz / E.l jois qu'es dinz mon cor floritz."

52 Cf. Arnaut Daniel (*Canzoni, op. cit.,* p. 316, xiii, "Er vei vermeils, vertz, blaus, gruocs," ll. 8-11): "D'amor mi pren penssan lo cuocs / e.l desiriers doutz e coraus; / e.l mals es saboros q'ieu sint / e.il flama soaus on plus m'art."

53-54 Cf. Daude de Pradas (*Poésies de Daude de Pradas,* ed. A.-H. Schutz. Toulouse and Paris: Privat, Didier, 1933, pp. 51-52, xi, "En un sonet guay e leugier," ll. 5-10): "Dezir ai que.m ve de plazer, / E.l plazer mou del bon'esper, / E.l bon'esper de joi novel, / E.l joi novel de tal castel / Qu'eu no volh dir, mas a rescos, / A cels qui Amors ten joios.

61 *Amador* is defined by Levy PD as 'amant, amoureux, ami,' and in the second place as 'qui aimera; qui sera aimé; digne d'être aimé.' The only English word capable of rendering any of these ideas is 'lover' which unfortunately is fraught with connotations that practically exclude the last three interpretations. Within the context of the *Cort d'Amor,* by its very nature as an *art d'aimer,* futurity and possibility are repeatedly emphasized and 'qui aimera' and 'qui sera aimé' as well as 'digne d'être aimé' are probably intended and should be read into the single term 'lover.' Cf. note to l. 14 concerning *drut.*

71 Cf. Arnaut Daniel (*ed. cit.,* p. 222, v, "Lanquan vei fueill'e flor e frug," ll. 8-11): "Ar sai ieu c'Amors m'a condug / el sieu plus seguran castel / don non dei renda ni trahug, / ans m'en ha fait don e capdel."

72 This line is a repetition of l. 60.

73-74 Cf. *Floire et Blanchefleur, ed. cit.,* ll. 1748-1749: "De toutes parz est clos a mur / Tout paint a or et a azur."

76 Drudaria being the abstract idea of the relationship between *drut* and *druda* (cf. note to l. 14 above), it can be defined as 'the condition of having been admitted to the lady's private circle of intimate friends.' Cf. also l. 325.

91-92 Cf. Marcabru (*Poésies complètes du troubadour Marcabru,* ed. J.-M.-L. Dejeanne. Toulouse: Privat, 1909, V, "Al son desviat, chantaire," ll. 49-52): "L'amors don ieu sui mostraire / Nasquet en un gentil aire, / E.l luoc on ill es creguda / Es claus de rama branchuda."

97-98 Cf. Marcabru (*ed. cit.,* XXXVII, "Per savi.l tenc ses doptanssa," ll. 33-36): "Es de joi cim'e racina, / C'ab veritat seignoreis, / E sa poestatz sobranssa / Sobre mouta creatura."

98 For *destrenher* Levy *PD* gives: 'étreindre, presser, tourmenter; restreindre; empêcher; contraindre, forcer; obliger; rendre nécessaire; contraindre (t. de droit); maîtriser, assujettir, terminer, décider.' It is tempting to translate *destrenher* as 'torment' rather than 'rule,' but the context does not specifically permit this rendering. The various connotations of *destrenher* should be kept in mind nonetheless.

107 *Iohanitz* may refer to Johannes of Capua, a thirteenth century fabulist who wrote fables of Indian origin in Latin. "C'est seulement au XIIIe siècle que sous cette forme nouvelle [Indian fables converted into Latin fables] elles ont commencé à être connues en Europe et c'est un Juif italien converti au christianisme, appelé Jean de Capoue probablement de sa ville natale, qui, en donnant d'elles une version intitulée: *Directorium humanae vitae, alias parabolae antiquorum sapientium,* a peut-être le plus contribué à les vulgariser." (Léopold Hervieux, *Les Fabulistes latins depuis le siècle d'Auguste jusqu'à la fin du Moyen Âge,* Paris, 2nd. ed., 1893-1899, V, p. 3).

It has been impossible to locate any fable regarding an ant and a lion. Either this fable has been lost, or the author of the *Cort d'Amor* invented it and attributed it to Johannes in order to give it authority. The former is more likely.

108   *Que leons aucis la formitz* is ambiguous. It could be translated either as 'the lion kills the ant' or as the ant kills lions.' Grammatically either is correct, but ll. 115-116 indicate that the first reading is preferable.

178   *si dons*, although it is a masculine form, consistently refers to the lady in troubadour poetry and is synonymous with *sa domna*. Accordingly I have translated it as 'his lady.' By referring to his lady as 'my lord' the suitor hypothetically and temporarily placed himself in the position of vassal in terms of the feudal, social and legal hierarchies.

182   For *dir los bens* Levy *PD* also gives 'dire les messes pour un mort.'

186   Chabaneau interprets *mon* as derived from *multum* and not from *meum*.

189   Cf. Marcabru (*ed. cit.*, XV, "Cortesamen vuoill comenssar," ll. 19-24): "Mesura es de gen parlar, / E cortesia es d'amar; / E qui non vol eser mespres / De tota vilania.s gar, / D'escarnir e de folleiar, / Puois sera savis ab qu'el pes."

256   *Metas en orba*, 'to blind,' from *orbar*, v., 'aveugler' and *orp*, adj., 'aveugle.' Levy *PD* also gives 'non fondé en parlant d'une opinion?'. Hence the phrase could also be translated as 'discredits.'

273   Cf. note to l. 47 above.

275-276   Cf. Bernart de Ventadorn (*The Songs of Bernart de Ventadorn*, ed. Stephen G. Nichols, *et al.*, Chapel Hill: The University of North Carolina Press, 1965, p. 169, xliv, "Tant ai mo cor ple de joya," ll. 13-16): "Anar posc ses vestidura, / nutz en ma chamiza, / car fin'amors m'asegura / de la freja biza."

293-296   Cf. Peire Rogier (in Mahn, *Werke* I, p. 125, vii, "Senher Raymbautz, per vezer," ll. 26-28): "Cove que.s percas sai e lai / E tolha e do, si cum s'eschai, / Quan ve qu'es luecx ni sazos," and Peire Raimon de Tolosa (*Le Poesie di Peire Raimon de Tolosa*, ed. Alfredo Cavaliere, Florence: Olschki, 1935, p. 121, xviii, "Us noels pessamens m'estai," ll. 5-7): "E.m gart miels de far desplazer / E m'esfors en be captener / Quan vey que n'es luecx ni sazos."

301-304   The syntax here is confusing. It is perhaps a problem of ellipsis: 'both a fine mistress and that thing which pleases her most (her handsome lover in her arms) are welcomed through you (Sweet Company).' The intentional ellipsis is not unknown to troubadour poetry. Cf. Peire Cardenal: *Poésies complètes du troubadour Peire Cardenal (1180-1278)*, ed. René Lavaud (Toulouse: Privat, 1957), p. 160, xxviii, strophe ii. Cf. also l. 762 below.

315   Soredamors and Gawain make an astonishing appearance here since the other lovers mentioned (Floire and Blanchefleur, Tristan and Yseult) are well known couples, while Gawain and Soredamors are brother and sister (*Cliges*)! Once again a certain ambiguity allows the reader to accept these six characters as authorities on the subject of love as well as actual lovers.

316-317   These two famous couples often appear in troubadour poetry and the most complete reference to such lovers is found in a poem by Arnaut de Mareuil (*Les Saluts d'Amour du Troubadour Arnaut de Mareuil*, textes publiés avec une introduction, une traduction et les notes par Pierre Bec. Toulouse: Privat, 1961. *Salut* III, ll. 150-176): "Neih Leander Eros, / Ni

Paris Elenan, / Ni Pirramus Tisban, / Ni Floris Blancaflor, / Qe.n traich manta dolor, / Ni Lavina Eneas, / No neich Cleopatras / Cel qe fo reis de Tyr. / Non ac tan ferm desir, / Ni crei qe tant ames / Lo reis Etiocles / Salamandra tan be, / Ni tan per bona fe, / Ni anc Yseut Tristan, / Qe.n sofri maint afan, / Ni Berenguiers Quendis, / Ni Valensa Seguis, / Ni, pel meu essien, / Absalon Florissen, / Ni anc Itis, ço cre, / No amet Biblis re, / Avers so q'eu am vos / Ni nuls amans q'anc fos / No amet tant s'amia, / Ni no crei ke mais sia / Cors d'aman tant verais: / K'eu, Domna, no.m irais." Cf. Introduction, p. 37, n. 50, for a complete list of troubadour references to Tristan and Yseult.

327 *Dez* 'ten' was read by Constans *dui* 'two.' Levy noted (p. 238) that "ce sont les dix chevaliers qui ont été harangués par Amors: Jois, Solatz, Ardimens, Cortesia, Bon'Esperansa, Paors, Largueza, Domneis, Celamens et Dolsa Companha."

351 *leis,* feminine singular oblique stressed form, refers to *Amors.*

353 *lo,* masculine singular oblique unstressed form, refers to *Amors.*

354 *el,* masculine singular stressed form, refers to *Amor.*

369 *il,* masculine singular pronoun, refers to *Corteszia,* a feminine personification.

395-400 For the enemies of Love cf. Marcabru (*ed. cit.,* XL, ll. 15-35): "Cill son fals jutg'e raubador, / Fals molherat e jurador, / Fals home tenh e lauzengier, / Lengua-loguat, creba-mostier, / Et aissellas putas ardens / Qui son d'autrui maritz cossens; / Cyst auran guazanh ifernau."

"Homicidi e traïdor, / Simoniaic, encantador, / Luxurios e renovier, / Que vivon d'enujos mestier, / E cill que fan faitilhamens, / E las faitileiras pudens / Seran el fuec arden engau."

"Ebriaic et escogossat, / Fals preveire e fals abat, / Falsas recluzas, fals reclus, / Lai penaran, ditz Marcabrus, / Que tuit li fals y an luec pres, / Car fin'Amors o a promes, / Lai er dols dels dezesperatz."

396 This is possibly a reference to the burning of heretics in Occitania.

403-404 Cf. Daude de Pradas (*ed. cit.,* III, pp. 13-16, "Ben ay amors quar anc me fes chauzir," ll. 39-40): "Que.l dieus d'amor a ben per dreit jujat / Que dona deu son amic enriquir," and Uc de Bacalaria (in Mahn, *Werke,* II, iii, ll. 19-20): "Que segon jutjamen d'amor, / val mais quan la prec merceian." Cf. also l. 834 below.

417 *La Cortesa d'Amor lo pren*: Constans *La Cortesa d'amor lo pren.* Chabaneau believed that a new personification, *La Cortesa d'Amor,* "personnage différent de *Na Corteszia,*" was introduced here for the first time. Bartsch apparently agreed and printed *Na Cortezia d'Amor.* More recently Marc-René Jung, in his *Etudes sur le poème allégorique en France au Moyen Âge* (Berne: Francke, 1971), p. 151, n. 72, also agreed that a different character is signaled here. Chabaneau referred as evidence to l. 837: *La Cortesa d'Amor lo sona* (Constans *La Cortesa d'amor lo sona*), with the first 3 words in italics which he used to designate the allegorical personifications, indicating that he too considered this verse the second appearance of a character introduced in l. 417.

This reading is based on a misunderstanding of the world *la,* which is not the feminine definite article 'the,' but rather the adverb of place 'there.' The author of this text does not introduce personifications by means of a definite article, preferring as a rule, to use titles such as *Don Jois* (l. 109) or *Na Corteszia* (l. 364), or the proper name such as *Cortesia* (l. 181), *Bon'Esperansa* (l. 195) in direct address. In descriptive passages the same style is maintained: *Na Coindia* (l. 886). Only *la baillessa d'Amor* (ll. 1068, 1076, 1155) and *Plazers, lo senescals d'Amor* (ll. 897, 978), who bear legitimate functional feudal titles, are introduced by articles. In l. 417 *d'Amor* is not 'of Love,' but rather 'from Love' and so "The Courtesy of Love takes it" should instead be read: "There Courtesy takes it from Love."

Finally, the distinction between *Corteszia* and *La Cortesa d'Amor* required by these commentators is very difficult to grasp and they offer no satisfactory explanation.

427 Cf. Peire Rogier (in Mahn, *Werke*, I, 118, iii, "Al pareis sen de la flors," ll. 18-20): "Tro que lur domna.s n'irays, / E.l ris torna.ls pueis en plors."

451-452 Cf. Arnaut de Mareuil (*ed. cit.*, p. 143, xxiv, "Cui que Fin'Amors esbaudey," ll. 60-62): "Dona, leos ja s'afranquis et ieu on plus vos clam mercey / lo vostre fer cor s'afortis."

457 Cf. Bonifaci Calvo (in Mahn, *Werke*, II, 3, iii, "Temp e luec a mas sabers," ll. 11-13): "Quan de sos oils la ve rire / E pensar ab mainz sospirs, / Camjant mais de mil colors."

473-475 Cf. Guillem de Saint-Didier (in Mahn, *Werke*, II, 48, viii, "Estat aurai estas doas sasos," ll. 25-28): "Chanson non dic, domna, mas endret vos, / A cui non aus trametr'autre messatge / Mas los sospirs qu'eu fas de genoillos, / Mans jointas lai on sai vostr'estatge."

484-485 Cf. Daude de Pradas (*ed. cit.*, p. 45, x, "El temps que.l rossignol s'esgau," ll. 12-13): "aissi lonc temps mon cor en vuoill / que l'uoill m'en son tornat tot blau."

494-495 Cf. Gaucelm Faidit (*Les Poèmes de Gaucelm Faidit*, ed. Jean Mouzat. Paris: Nizet, 1965, p. 250, "Tant ai sofert longamen grand afan," ll. 19-24): "E pois mos cors e miei huoill trahit m'an / E ma mala dompn'e ma bona fes / Si que chascus m'agra mort si pogues, / Clamar m'en dei cum de mals baillidors; / E ja mos huoills, messongiers trahidors, / Non creirai mai, ni fiannsa ses gatge," and Daude de Pradas (ed. cit., p. 22, v, "Pois merces no.m val ni m'ajuda," l. 29): "Mos cors e miei huoill m'an trahit." Cf. also Folquet de Marseille (*Le Troubadour Folquet de Marseille,* ed. Stanislaw Stronski. Cracow, 1910, p. 12, i, ll. 1-3): "Ben an mort mi e lor / mei huel galiador, / per que.s tanh qu'ab els plor."

525-526 Cf. Guiraut de Calanso (in Mahn, *Werke*, II, pp. 31-32, iii, "El mon non pot aver," ll. 19-20): "Et en loc del jazer, / Prenc l'amor e.l solatz." Cf. also l. 538.

533 Cf. Guilhem IX (*Les Chansons de Guillaume IX, Duc d'Aquitaine (1071-1127)*, ed. A. Jeanroy. CFMA 9, 2nd ed., Paris: Champion, 1967, p. 25, x, "Ab la dolchor del temps novel," ll. 19-22): "Enquer me membra d'un mati / Que nos fezem guerra fi, / E que.m donet un don tan gran, / Sa drudari'e son anel." Cf. also l. 1134.

549-557 Cf. Guilhem IX (*ed. cit.*, p. 18, vii, "Pus vezem de novelh florir," ll. 25-30): "Ja no sera nuils hom ben fis / Contr'Amor si non l'es aclis, / Et als estranhs et als vezis / Non es consens, / Et a totz sels d'aicels aizis / Obediens."

561 *cembel* < *cymbalum*. Originally, from the idea of the cymbal, *cembel* came to signify a lure, a sign, a distraction, a sort of amusement, hence a gift. It referred also to the piece of leather in the shape of a bird used to attract a hunting hawk and lure, trap and artifice grew out of this more technical usage to refer to the small number of troops used to lure an enemy into an ambush. Cf. *FEW*, II, 2, 1611a. Finally it referred to the combat

itself, especially between small groups of men, and ultimately to jousting, tournament or military games. Levy *PD* cites two specific expressions: *bastir cembel,* 'engager le combat,' and *partir lo cembel,* 'séparer la mêlée.'

Curiously, the specific gifts mentioned in the following verse are all tokens of favor that were commonly worn in battle as insignias of a certain commitment. It is unusual here that these gifts are given by the lover to the lady since the reverse is more traditional, particularly as regards sleeves which were occasionally affixed to the lance itself as pennants.

564 *Ausiment,* from *auzir,* v. 'ouir, entendre, écouter,' is defined by Levy *PD* as 'ouie,' and probably means 'reputation.' Cf. for example, the proverb cited by the Monk of Montaudon (*Der Mönch von Montaudon, ein provenzalischer Troubadour, sein Leben und seine Gedichte,* ed. Emil Philippson. Halle: Niemeyer, 1873, p. 27, vii, "Ades on plus niu mais apren," l. 50): "Que bos pretz creis on plus loing es auzitz."

579-584 Cf. Lady H. (in *Les Poetesses provençales du moyen âge et de nos jours,* ed. Jules Véran. Paris: Quillet, 1946, pp. 101-104, "Rofin, digatz m'ades de cors," ll. 21-30): "A fin amic non tol paors, / Rofin, de penre jauzimens / Que.l dezirs e.l sobretalens / Lo destreing tan que per clamors / De si dons nominativa / Noi.s pot soffrir ni capdellar, / Qu'ab jazer et al remirar / L'amors corals recaliva / Tant fort que non au ni non ve / Ni conois quan fai mal o be."

592 *deu esser tenguda* is ambiguous. The context of this phrase, ll. 591-602, concerns the lady's grooming in which case *tenguda* might refer to her 'tenue' (i.e., behavior, deportment, carriage, bearing, good manners, dress or appearance). This would be reinforced by the image that follows in which both the posture and the behavior of the hawk carried on the fist and the care of the nobleman in protecting its plumage refer to the appearance of the lady. Verse 596 clearly continues this theme by repeating the verb *gardar* in reference to the lady's face. It is thus the lady's responsibility to behave like the nobleman (*se dona soin, gardar*) in terms of the hawk (*esser tenguda*).

On the other hand, *tenguda* read literally means 'held' and the subsequent simile literally refers to the manner in which the hawk is held, thus implying that the lady must be held by her lover in his arms as carefully as the hawk is held by the nobleman on his fist. However, the fact that this is the beginning of *Corteszia*'s speech advising the lady (preceded by a break in the manuscript separating it from her advice to the lover) would imply that the lady is responsible for the manner in which her lover holds her in his arms.

The third alternative is to translate *esser tenguda* as 'be treated' or 'be considered.' Levy *SW* VIII, 148b, 149a, cites Guiraut de Borneilh: "Que fol tenhatz celui / Que si mezeis destrui" (42, 56), and Appel's *Chrestomathie* (9, 156): "Senher Jozep es mot prozom / Et es tengutz, per ser[t], bon hom." Levy *SW* gives as definitions in these instances: 'halten für, erachten, betrachten als.' In the case of *deu esser tenguda,* the agent would then remain impersonal: everyone (including the lover and the lady herself) must treat *la dompna que vol esser druda* as carefully as a nobleman treats his hawk. Cf. also l. 608.

The ambiguity is apparently intentional and all three interpretations must be kept in mind.

625 This line is a repetition of l. 611.

633-634 Cf. Peire Rogier (*ed. cit.*, p. 123, VI, "Ges non puesc on bon vers falhir," ll. 4-6): "Qu'om non es tan mal ensenhatz, / Si parl'ab lieys un mot o dos, / Que, s'es vilas non torn cortes."

637 Cf. Raimbaut III, coms d'Aurenga (in Mahn, *Werke*, I, 69, ii, "A mon vers dirai chanso," ll. 36-37): "Quar en amar non sec hom drecha via, / Qui gent no sap sen ab foldat despendre."

640-642 Cf. Peire d'Alvernha (*Liriche*, ed. Alberto del Monte. Turin: Loescher-Chiantore, 1955. I, "Rossinhol el seu repaire," ll. 1-10): "Rossinhol, el seu repaire / m'iras ma dona vezer / e diguas li.l mieu afaire / et ill digua.t del sieu ver, / e man sai / com l'estai, / Mas de mi.ll sovenha, / que ges la / per nuill plai / ab si no.t retenha."

677-678 Cf. *Floire et Blanchefleur, ed. cit.*, ll. 2650-2651: "Les narilles avoit mielz fetes / Que s'il fussent as mains portretes," and ll. 2668-2669: "De cors est ele tant bien fete / Con s'ele fust as mains portrete."

680 *Sotz la bella boca*: *boca* 'mouth' was read by both Constans and Chabaneau as *bocla* or *bloca* 'buckle' and I have translated it following their proposed correction. The sense of 'below the pretty red mouth' could refer to the area of the chin, jaws, and throat. However, the correction of Constans and Chabaneau to 'buckle' does not change the number of syllables (9) and is more logical in the context. In l. 670 her chin is described as little, pretty, and round; in l. 672 her red lips are mentioned; in l. 675 her white neck. The area that would be *sotz la bella boca* is already well accounted for in these lines (ll. 670-675). The poet continues with references to her hands, gloves, purse, and belt in a logical earthward progression which is typical of these descriptions. Mention of the golden buckle would be here in proper sequence, especially since the next nine lines to l. 689 continue to describe her clothes and finally arrive at her feet. It is unusual that no reference is made to the breast since it is traditional in this kind of description. Cf. for example, Arnaut de Mareuil, *ed. cit.*, *Salut*, I, ll. 93-94, "Mento e gola e peitrina / Blanca co neus ni flor d'espina." In all other respects this portrait of feminine beauty is entirely typical of troubadour poetry.

698-699 In the middle ages gold was considered a shade of red, and therefore the ideal lady is auburn haired rather than blonde as gold seems to imply. Spring buds, rather than being necessarily green, are not infrequently brownish red, hence the comparison.

728 *Merce* is a feminine noun and therefore the personification is a feminine figure. Cf. l. 729 in which the past participle *vista* refers to *Merce*. However, in l. 733 *Aqest*, and in l. 739 *el*, both masculine pronouns, also refer to *Merce*. *El* could be a scribal error for which one could substitute *ill*, but if *aqest* were corrected to *aqesta*, it would add one syllable to the line. As in the case of *Fin'Amor* I have translated all pronouns referring to *Merce* as feminine for the sake of consistency.

791-798 Cf. Peire Vidal (*Poesie*, ed. D'Arco Silvio Avalle, Milan and Naples: Riccardo Ricciardi, 1960, xxxviii "Anc no mori per amor ni per al," ll. 17-24): "Bona Domna, vostr'home natural / Podetz si.us plai, leugeiramen aucir: / Mas a la gen vos faretz escarnir / E pois auretz en peccat criminal. / Vostr'om sui be, que ges nom tenc per mieu, / Mas ben laiss'om a mal senhor son fieu; / E val ben pauc rics hom, quan pert sa gen / Qu'a Daire.l rei de Persa fan parven." Cf. also Arnaut de Mareuil (*ed. cit.*, p. 116, xx, "E mon cor ai un novellet chantar," ll. 47-48): "Aucia me si no.m vol retener; / mas hieu l'afi que non l'estara ben," and Na Castelloza (in *Les Poétesses provençales, ed. cit.*, pp. 128-129, ll. 46-48): "...e si.m laissatz morir, / Faretz peccat, e serai n'en tormen, / E seretz ne blasmatz vilana-men," and Folquet de Marseilha (*ed. cit.*, p. 45, ix, "Amors, merce!; no mueira tan soven!" ll. 8-9): "Per qu'er peccatz, Amors, so sabetz vos, / si m'auciretz, pos vas vos no m'azir."

834 Cf. ll. 403-404.

837 *Lo*, masculine pronoun, refers to *Amors*, a feminine personification. Cf. l. 417.

872 *El*, masculine pronoun, refers to *Amors*.

879 *El*, masculine pronoun, refers to *Amors*.

899 *El*, masculine pronoun, refers to *Amors*.

902 This line states one version of a well known proverb. Cf. also Guilhem de la Tor (*Le Poesie di Guilhem de la Tor*, ed. Ferruccio Blasi. Genoa and Florence: Leo S. Olschki, 1934, 36, ix, "En vos eu ai mesa," ll. 44-45): "Car [en] suffren, / venz hom la gen."

903 *Rei*, masculine singular, refers to *Amors*.

905 Cf. Arnaut de Mareuil (*Les Poesies Lyriques*, ed. R. C. Johnston. Paris: Droz, 1935, p. 07, xvi, "Belh m'es lo dous temps amoros," ll. 36-42): "Contra.ls lauzengiers enueyos, / Mal parlans, per cui jois delis, / Volgra que celes e cobris / Son cor quascus dels amadors; / Que tals es fals lo segles a tener, / E ges ades non deu hom dire ver; / Soven val mais mentirs et escondires." Cf. also ll. 973 and 1050.

906 Cf. Bernat Marti (*Les Poésies de Bernat Marti*, ed. Ernest Hoepffner, CFMA 61, Paris: Champion, 1929, p. 7, ii, "A, Senhors, qui so cuges," ll. 55-56): "Lengua forcat son pejor / Que Judas qu'a trait son senhor," and (p. 29, viii, "Quant la pluei'e.l vens e.l tempiers," ll. 54-55): "Qu'ieu no.il serai pa mensongiers / Qant piegz seria qe Judas."

907 Cf. Bernart Marti (*ed. cit.*, p. 28, viii, "Qant la pluei'e.l vens e.l tempiers," ll. 17-18): "Per gelos ni per lauzengiers, / Cui mal focs las lengas abras!" and also Arnaut Daniel (*ed. cit.*, p. 364, xvii, "Si.m fos amors de ioi donar tant larga," ll. 41-42): "Fals lausengier, fuocs las lengas vos arga, / e que perdatz ams los huoills de mal cranc."

908 Cf. Peire Vidal (*Les Poésies de Peire Vidal*, ed. J. Anglade, 2nd. ed. Paris: Champion, 1966, p. 101, xxxii, "A per pauc de chantar no.m lais," ll. 9-11): "Qu'a Rom'an vout en tal pantais / L'Apostolis el.h fals doctor / Sancta Gleiza, don Deus s'irais."

931 Cf. Guillem de Cabestaing (*Chansons*, ed. Arthur Langfors. Paris: Champion, 1924, pp. 1-2, i, "Aissi cum selh que baiss.l fuelh," ll. 11-13): "Et anc l'amors per qu'ieu me muelh / Ab l'aigua del cor ma color / No fon per mi espandida."

939-940 Cf. Arnaut de Mareuil (*ed. cit.*, p. 59, x, "Aissi cum selh que anc non ac cossire," ll. 16-17): "Bona dompna, tant vos am finamen, / mos coratges no.is pot partir de vos."

942-953 Cf. Arnaut de Mareuil (*ed. cit.*, p. 54, ix, "Aissi cum cel c'am e non es amaz," ll. 29-35): "Soven m'aven, la nuoch can soi colgaz, / que soi ab vos per semblan en dormen; / adonc estau en tan ric jausimen, / ja non volr'esser mais residaz; / sol que.m dures aquel plazenz pensatz; / e can m'esveill, cuich murir desiran, / per qu'eu volgra aissi dormir un an."

959 Cf. Raimon de Miraval (*Les Poésies de Raimon de Miraval*, ed. L. T. Topsfield. Paris: Nizet, 1971, p. 297, xxxvi, "Contr'amor vau durs et enbroncs," ll. 29-32): "Si cum la ros'entre mil troncs / Es genser flors qe d'autres gras, / Entre las lausengiers trafas / Estai midonz en sa tenda." Cf. also Lanfranco Cigala (*Liriche*, ed. Gianluigi Toja, Florence: Sansoni,

1952, p. 58, vi, "Oi Maire, fillia de Dieu," l. 6): "Flors de roza ses spina."
964 *El* refers to *druda*. Read *ilh*.

981 Ch. Camproux, in his edition of the selected poems of Peire Cardenal (*Peire Cardenal, Troces Causits*, Montpellier: Centre d'Estudis Occitans, 1970, p. 55, n. 18), defined *legistas* as "oficiers de justícia, emplegats per los senhors o las ciutats que s'en servissián los clergues per sas condamnacions. Cf. per ex. *Cançon de la Crosada* II, 177, 53 e seg. 'Uns dels melhors legistas si que cascuns l'enten' que legis la condamnacion del pòble de Tolosa."

988-989 In his note to these verses, Constans remarked (p. 215) that they are an "allusion aux *Dits de Marcoul et de Salomon*, recueil de proverbes dont la première rédaction en francais remonte au XIIe siècle. A chaque sentence de Salomon, Marcoul, une espèce de Sancho Pança, répond par un proverbe populaire et souvent licencieux. De là l'idée de reciprocité exprimée de nos deux vers; mais les rôles sont ici renversés, et l'attaque est attribuée à Marcoul (Marcon)." Cf. Raimbaut d'Orange (*The Life and Works of Raimbaut d'Orange*, ed. W. J. Pattison. Minneapolis: University of Minneapolis Press, 1952, p. 79, iv (10), "Apres mon vers vueilh sempr'ordre," ll. 19-24): "Cil qi m'a vout triste-aslegre / sap mais qu'i vol sos ditz segre / Qe Salamos ni Marcouls / De fatz ric ab ditz entegre: / E cai leu d'aut en la pols / Qi.s pliu en aitals bretols." Cf. also *Histoire de la Littérature Française*, 23, pp. 688-689: "...on a supposé que le nom de Marculphe, Marcoul et Marcol, pouvait être un souvenir de celui de Marcus Caton, auquel on attribua dès premiers siècles de l'ère chrétienne le recueil de sentences morales en vers hexametres, souvent imprimés sous le nom de Denis Caton. Dans les sentences françaises en dialogue rimé, que des copistes attribuent à Pierre Mauclerc, Salomon représente le moraliste sage, et Marcoul le parodiste satirique."

998 Cf. Peirol (in Mahn, *Werke*, II, p. 5, iv, "Quoras que.m fezes doler," l. 40): "Cum fai l'aurs el fuec plus fis," and Peire Vidal (*ed. cit.*, xxxiv, "Neus ni gels ni plueja ni fanh," ll. 25-28): "Ab pauc de fuec romp l'aur e franh / L'obriers tro qu'el es esmeratz, / Don l'obra es plus bell'assatz: / Per que los loncs maltragz non planh," and Gaucelm Faidit (*ed. cit.*, p. 447, "Chant e deport, joi, dompnei e solatz," ll. 44-45): "...aissi for'afinatz / vas lieis, cum l'aurs s'afina en la fornatz."

1016-1017 Cf. Raimon de Miraval (*ed. cit.*, p. 266, xxxii, "Cel que no vol auzir chanssos," ll. 9-16): "De la bella, don sui cochos, / Desir lo tener e.l baisar, / E.l jazer e.l plus conquistar, / Et apres, mangas e cordos, / E del plus qe il clames merces; / Que jamais no serai conques / Per joia ni per entresseing, / Si so q'ieu plus vuoill non ateing."

1067 Chabaneau remarked (p. 95) that "La lacune ne doit pas être très considérable. Peut-être ne manque-t-il qu'un vers, dont le sens doit être *s'il ne se laisse émouvoir* ou *s'il ne devient amoureux*."

1078 *El*, masculine pronoun, refers to *Amors*.

1109 'Man' in this context means 'liege man,' 'vassal,' or 'servant.' *Amors* who is speaking is feminine.

1109 Cf. Arnaut de Mareuil (*ed. cit.*, p. 24, iv, "Us jois d'amor s'es e mon cor enclaus," ll. 39-42): "A! s'er ja temps qu'a dreit vos apelh domna, / qu'ie.us sia homs, mans juntas, lialmen, / e atressi cum bons senher acuelh / son lige ser, mi denhatz aculhir!"

1110 *Fin'Amor* stirs up a flame in the heart of *Fin'Amor*? Here the personification is referring to the concept that she represents, and revealing that she herself is vulnerable to love, not unlike Cupid pricking himself with one of his own arrows and falling in love with Psyche. Furthermore, it should not be surprising to find Love, a thirteenth century noble, speaking in the clichés of her day.

1128-1139 Cf. Daude de Pradas (*ed. cit.*, pp. 40-42, ix, "Trop ben m'estera si.s tolgues," ll. 25-32). The carpe diem theme along with the motif of the mirror is developed in this strophe.

1132 *El*, masculine singular, refers to the lady who looks in her mirror.

1160 This line refers to the famous *jazer* of the troubadours. Cf. Ch. Camproux, *op. cit.*, *passim*, and René Nelli, *L'Erotique des Troubadours* (Toulouse: Privat, 1963), p. 91.

1168-1180 Cf. Azalais de Porcaraigues (in Mahn, *Werke*, III, p. 177, "Ar em all freg temps vengut," ll. 33-45): "Bel amics de bon talan, / Son ab vos totz jorns en gatge, / Cortexa e de bel semblan; / Sol no.m demandes outrage, / Tost en venrem a l'assai, / Qu'en vostra merce.m metrai: / Vos m'avetz la fe plevida / Que no.m demandes faillida." Cf. also R. Nelli, *op. cit.*, p. 199, "... l'*asag* était une épreuve imposée à l'homme par la femme," and p. 200, "Le principe de l'*asag* consistait donc moins à mettre à l'épreuve la volonté, le stoicisme masculins qu'à manifester *in re* que, naturellement et spontanément, l'amour est chaste à ses débuts."

1182-1184 Cf. Peire Rogier (in Mahn, *Werke*, I, p. 118, ii, ll. 1-2): "Entr'ira e joy m'an si devis / Qu'ira.m tolh manjar e dormir."

1185 Constans placed the lacuna before this line.

1196-1203 Chabaneau noted (p. 96) that "notre auteur pensait ici certainement à la chanson de Perdigon, "Tot l'an mi ten amors d'aital faisso." The relevant lines are verses 10-18: "Be.m fetz amors l'usatge del lairo, / Quant encontra selhui d'estranh pahis, / E.l fai creire qu'alhors es sos camis, / Tro que li dis: 'Belhs amicx, tu me guida.; / Et en aissi es manta gens trahida / Qu'el mena lai on pueis lo lia e.l pren; / Et ieu puesc dir atressi veramen / Qu'ieu segui tant amor com li saup bo, / Tan mi menet tro m'ac en sa preizo."

1227-1229 Cf. Guilhem de Cabestanh (*ed. cit.*, pp. 19-20, vi, "Lo jorn qu'ie.us vi, dompna, premeiramen," ll. 22-24): E membre vos, si.us plai, del bon coven / Que me fezetz al departir saber, / Don aic mon cor adoncs guay e jauzen."

1292-1297 Cf. Peire Raimon de Tolosa (*ed. cit.*, p. 6, ii, "Ar ai ben d'amor apres," ll. 17-24): "Grant talent ai cum pogues / De ginols vas lieys venir, / De tan luenh cum hom cauzir / La poiria que.l vengues / Mas iuntas, far homenes, / Cum sers a senher deu far, / Et en ploran merceyar / Ses paor de gent savoya," and Raimbaut d'Orange (*ed. cit.*, p. 91, viii (21), "Braiz, chans, quils critz," ll. 49-51): "Humils, ses geing, / Domna.l vostre sers fals-faillitz / Merce vos quer."

1307 Cf. Arnaut de Mareuil (*ed. cit.*, p. 4, i, "La grans beutatz e.l fis ensenhamens," ll. 33-35): "Domna, genser qu'anc fos de nulhas gens / e la mielher de totas las melhors, / per vos morrai, so.m ditz ades paors." Cf. also p. 54, ix, "Aissi cum cel c'am'e non es amaz," l. 27): "mas eu soi cel que temen muor aman."

1448-1450 Cf. Guilhem de Cabestaing (*ed. cit.*, p. 1, i, "Aissi cum selh que baiss.l fuelh," ll. 9-10): "Ab dous esguart siey cortes huelh / M'an fait guai e fin amador," and (ll. 20-22): "Qu'als plus guays es lansa d'amor / Que fer al cor ses guandida / Ab plazens d'amistat." Cf. also Peire Raimon de Tolosa (in Mahn, *Werke*, I, p. 146, xiii, "Per qu'ieu li.m suy autreyatz e rendutz," ll. 6-7): "E pus tan gen / Nafret mon cor d'un esgart amoros," and Sordello (in Mahn, *Werke*, II, p. 248, ii, "Bel m'es ab motz leugiers de far," ll. 9-15): "Gen mi saup mon fin cor emblar / Al prion qu'ieu miriey sa faisso, / Ab un dous amoros esguar / Que.m lansero siey huelh lairo; / Ab selh esguar m'intret en aisselh dia / Amors pels huelhs al cor d'aital semblan / Qu'el cor en trays e mes l'a son coman," and Uc Brunet (in Mahn, *Werke*, III, pp. 206-207, i, "Cortezamen mov en mon cor mesclansa," ll. 4-8): "Quar en aissi sap ferir de sa lansa / Amors, que es us esperitz cortes, / Que no.s laissa vezer mas per semblans, / Quar d'huelh en huelh salh e fai sos dous lans, / E d'huelh en cor e de coratge en pes," and Folquet de Marseille (*ed. cit.*, p. 25, iv, "Us volers outracujatz," ll. 31-40): "Be.m parec necietatz / e trop sobrarditz volers / quan solamen us vezers / m'ac deceubut tan viatz / qu'escondudamens / mi venc al cor us talens / tals qu'ieu fui enamoratz, / mas puois m'es tan fort doblatz / que mati e ser / mi fai doussamen doler."

1458   Constans omitted this line.

1469-1474   Cf. Guilhem de Montanhagol (*ed. cit.*, p. 86, viii, "Non an tan dig li primier trobador," ll. 31-40): "D'una re fan donas trop gran follor / quar lor amor / menan ab tan loncx plays, / que quascuna pus ve son amador / fi ses error, / falh si l'alonga mais; / quar hom no viu tan quan faire solia, / doncx convengra que.l mals costums n'issis / del trop tarzar, qu'ieu no cre qu'om moris / tan leu com fai, si d'amor si jauzia."

1518   Aie probably was the daughter of duke Antoine d'Avignon and the niece of Charlemagne. She figures in the *chanson de geste Aye d'Avignon (publiée pour la première fois d'après le manuscrit unique de Paris* par F. Guessard et P. Meyer. Paris: 1861), a poem of 4136 alexandrines belonging to the cycle of Doon de Mayence. She figures also in the *chansons de geste Gui de Nanteuil* and *Parise la Duchesse*. Cf. F. Lot, "Notes historiques sur Aie d'Avignon," *Romania* 33 (1904), pp. 145-162, and especially E. Langlois, *Table des noms propres de toutes nature compris dans les chansons de geste* (Paris: Bouillon, 1904), p. 9, where one finds mention of two other women bearing this name: Aie, wife of Aimon de Dordon in the *chanson de geste Renaut de Montaudon*, and Aie de Montorie, wife of Terri in *Aiol*. Louis-Fernand Flutre in his *Table des noms propres avec toutes leurs variantes figurant dans les romans du moyen âge, écrits en francais ou en provencal et actuellement publiés ou analysés*, (Poitiers: Centre d'Etudes Supérieures de Civilisation Médievale, 1962), p. 7b, notes three other characters named Aie: the heroine of the *Roman de la Rose ou de Guillaume de Döle*, a woman in *Sone de Nausay*, and the epic heroine of *Richars li Biaus* by Maistre Requis.

Landri is even more difficult to identify, Langlois, *op. cit.*, pp. 391-392, recording 27 different characters by that name! (Flutre, *op. cit.*, records only two). Maurice Delbouille, in an article in the *Revue Belge de Philologie et d'Histoire*, V (1926), pp. 339-350, suggests that he is Landri le Timonier, hero of a lost poem known through the episode of Synagon in *Le Moniage Guillaume* and appearing in the *Couronnement de Louis*.

According to F. Lot, in "La Chanson de Landri," *Romania* 32 (1903), pp. 1-17, he would be Landri de Nevers, partisan of Girart de Rousillon and appearing in the *chanson de geste* by that name. Lot remarks that, in the introduction to his edition of *Aye d'Avignon, op. cit.*, Paul Meyer cited the following troubadour allusions:

      1. Arnaut de Mareuil: "Vostre hom sui, donna gaya, / E am vos mais que Landrics Aya."

2. Peire Raimon de Tolosa: "Plus fis ... que no fo Landrics a n'Aya."

3. Paulet de Marseilha: "Bella dompna plazens, ay / Dit soven quar ieu nous ai, / Quar vos am, que qu'ieu n'aya / Mais qu'Enricx no fes n'Aya."

Meyer also found two references in northern French literature:

1. *La Prise de Jerusalem*: "Baron, ceste chancons n'est mie de folie, / D'Auchier ne de Landri...."

2. Thibaut de Marly: "Ce que je vos vueil dire et ce qu'avez oï / Sachiez que ce n'est pas d'Auchier ne de Landri."

Lot continued (p. 10) "on le voit, ces allusions se réfèrent non pas à une, mais à deux compositions, l'une intitulée *Landri et Aye,* l'autre *Auchier et Landri.* De la première, qui n'a qu'un rapport de nom fortuit avec le roman d'*Aye d'Avignon,* nous savons seulement qu'elle avait pour sujet l'amour violent de Landri pour une certaine Aye." In note 3 of the same page he added, "les rapports que tente d'établir M. Birch-Hirschfeld entre ces deux compositions n'ont aucune vraisemblance ainsi que M. Paul Meyer l'a déjà fait observer," and he continued (p. 11), "les rapports entre Landri, comte de Nevers (m. 1028), et une certaine Aye, reposent-ils sur une réalité quelconque? C'est ce qu'il est impossible e'établir avec certitude. Je remarque seulement que ce nom d'Aye était extrêmement répandu dans le duché de Bourgogne au Xe siècle, surtout en Maconnais et Chaunois." Finally, he states (p. 12), "je laisse à la fantaisie du lecteur le soin de décider s'il y a quelque chose à tirer de ce fait que la femme d'une prédécesseur de Landri s'appelait Aye."

1521-1525 Cf. Aimeric de Peguillan (in Mahn, *Werke,* II, p. 165, vi, "Selh que s'irais ni guerray'ab Amors," ll. 15-16): "Quar selh qu'ama de cor non vol guerir / Del mal d'amor, tant es dous per sufrir," and Perdigon (*Les Chansons de Perdigon,* ed. H. J. Chaytor, CFMA 53, Paris: Champion, 1926, p. 1, i, "Los mals d'Amor ai eu ben totz apres," vv. 7-9): "pero si.l bes es tan dous e plazens qu'om es lo mals engoissos e cozens, / ans vuel non murir qu'eu ancar non l'atenda," and (p. 27, ix, "Be.m dizon, s'en mas chanssos," ll. 6-7): "qu'il auzon ben qu'ancse.m plaing / en chantan del mal d'amor," and Folquet de Marseilha (*ed. cit.,* p. 27, v, ll. 1-4): "En chantan m'aven a membrar / so qu'ieu cug chantan oblidar / mas per so chant qu'oblides la dolor e.l mal d'amor." Cf. also a discussion of the *mal d'amor* in the *Roman d'Eneas.*

1551-1554 Cf. Arnaut de Mareuil (*ed. cit.,* p. 73, xii, "L'ensenhamens e.l pretz e la valors," ll. 22-24): "Domna, nos trei, vos et ieu et Amors, / sabem tuch sol ses autra guirentia / cals fo.l covens...."

1584 *El,* masculine pronoun, refers to *Amors.*

1655 *Ill* is a feminine pronoun, but a masculine pronoun is required by the sense.

1660-1661 Cf. Peire Vidal (*ed. cit.,* xxv, "En una terr' estranha," ll. 49-53): "Quar pus qu'obra d'aranha / No pot aver durada / Amors pus es proada / Qu'ab ditz daur'ez aplanha / Tals qu'a.l cor de vilan escuelh."

1663-1669 Cf. Léopold Hervieux, *Les Fabulistes latins depuis le siècle d'Auguste jusqu'à la fin du Moyen Âge* (Paris: 1893-1899), II, p. 760, xiii. *Cervus* ad Fontem: "Cervics, bibens de fonte, cornua sua en eo magna vidit et insignia, et multum in eis gratulabatur. E, dum biberet, audivit tumultum venatorum et canum propium, quantum et fugit in densiorem silvam, ubi a vepribus et arborum ramiculis per cornua detentus est, ne trasire posset; et dixit; Heu! mihi, quia decor cornum meorum, in quo tantum superbivi, me cogit mori." Cf. also Guilhem de Montanhagol (*Les Poésies de Guilhem de Montanhagol, troubadour provençal du XIIIe siècle,* ed. Peter J. Ricketts. Toronto: Pontifical Institute of Mediaeval Studies, 1964, pp. 84-87, ix "Non estarai, per ome qe.m casti," ll. 27-45): "Mas eu fatz si com fe.l cers, qe, can vi / l'ombre dels bans en la fon bandejar, / de.s gran erguelh, tro qe pres a gardar / vas sos secs pes, e non s'amet aissi / com per los bans, car pario.l delgat; / pero los pes l'avion restaurat / tro.l feiron pueys los corns prendr'e aucir; / q'en lais per lei qe m'auci de desir mans de plazers q'amors d'autra.m daria." This poem is undatable but the editor suggests 1242-1250: In n. 40, p. 100 of his edition, the editor cites *Marie de France, Fables,* edited by A. Ewert and R. C. Johnston, Oxford, 1942, pp. 19-20; version by Phedrus: *Phaedri Fabulae Aesopiae,* edited by Iohannes Percival Postgate, Oxonii, 1919, Liber Primus, XII; for the version of Romulus, *Die Paraphrasen des Phraedrus und die Aesopishe Fabel im Mittelalter,* by Hermann Oesterley, Berlin, 1870, pp. 68-69; for *Ysopet-Avionnet: the Latin and French Texts,* eds. K. McKenzie and W. A. Oldfather, University of Illinois Studies in Language and Literature, V (Nov., 1919), no. 4, pp. 143-144. "Or la version de Guilhem offre vraisemblablement la même fable tire d'un fonds commun, sans doute, mais raccourcie. Il ne donne les détails ni de la fuite du cerf devant les chiens ni des difficultés du cerf à traverser le bois dans lequel ses cors sont pris. Chez Montanhagol, les pieds lui étaient utiles pour courir, tout maigres qu'ils étaient, tandis que ses cors le faisaient prendre et tuer. La version de Marie de France, dans laquelle le cerf admire ses cors, ne parle pas de ces 'jambes,' comme l'avait constaté Coulet. Il semble que Marie se soit inspirée d'un texte anglais, aujourd'hui perdu."

INDEX OF PROPER NAMES
(entries refer to line numbers)

GLOSSARY

(entries refer to line numbers)

adismar = *adesmar*, estimate: 1567.
ande, with (< *apud ab de*), cf. *FEW*, XXIV, 2, 63a: 1142.
aprodera = *apodera*, surpass: 1424.
aqesita, misspelling of *aqesta*: 999.
arozinatz = *arozina*, cf. textual note to 527.
assire = *asire*, compose: 1149.

bastarsa, misspelling of *bastarda*: 395.
bazaler = *bachaler*, bachelor: 1416.

catieu = *caitieu*, cf. also 241, 480, 763, 791: 233.
cembel, gifts, cf. translation note to 561.
cenbelin = *sebelin*, sable, cf. Levy *SW*, I, 539a: 761.
chadaus = *cada uns*, each, every: 283.
chiaj = *chiai*, 3rd. sing. pres. ind. of *cazer*, fall: 1418.
cimblos, misspelling of *cimbols*, cymbals: 888.
cobetsa = *cobeeza*, *cobeiteza*: 256. Cf. also 263, 1596.
conia = *esconja*, dismiss: 1044.
cortesa, cf. index of proper names.
cosapchatz = *cosa sapchatz*, as you know, cf. textual note to 1037.
cuza = *cuda*, 3rd. sing. pres. ind. of *cudar*, believe: 295.

dechaia = *decaza*, decline: 1060.
derer, behind, cf. *FEW*, III, 47b: 1691.
desenbria = *dezembria*, diminish: 1474.
destreis, 3rd. sing. pres. ind. of *destrenher*, constrain: 1720.
doin, misspelling of *don*, give: 300.
dra, misspelling of *dura*: 451.

eissa, fem. of *eis*, same, cf. *FEW*, IV, 808b, *per eissa maneira*, 'de cette
   façon': 268.
emdeven = *endeven*, arrives, happens, cf. textual note to 952.
enancha = *enansa*, advance: 1027.
enia = *enica*, irritation: 206.
enolt, from *enoldar*, enlace, cf. textual note to 662.
enpert = *en pert*, 1st. sing. pres. ind. of *perdar*: 1281.

enrabchar = *enrabjar*, enrage: 708.
envoza, misspelling of *envocar*, invoke: 54.
escanara, misspelling of *escarnara*, scrape or pare: 327.
eschai, from *escazer*, happen: 576, 769.
es conia = *esconjar*, dismiss: 1044.
escuoil = *escolh*, sort, type: 1672.

fluec, contamination of *fuec* with *flama*: 998.
fromitz = *formitz*, ant: 115.
fuel = *folh*, means, manner, role: 1141.

gad = *gap*, joke, raillery, cf. textual note to 390.
gaere = *gaire*, scarcely: 1004.
genchida, faire ⌒, resort to a subterfuge, refuse, cf. *FEW*, XVI, 555b: 1217.

ie = *i*, cf. textual note to 599.
iovecenlla, misspelling of *iovencella*, young girl, maiden: 1129.
ioza = *joia*: 53.

joas = *joias*: 1565.
jonrs, misspelling of *jorns*: 1603.

lapsapchia = *la sapchia*: 1245. Cf. also 1259.
lauries, misspelling of *lauriers*, laurel trees: 91.
lou = *loc*, from *locus*, cf. *FEW*, V, 392b, *aimer en bon lieu*, 'aimer une
    femme de bonne famille': 1269.
lous = *los*, art.: 1407.
luei = *lui*, pron.: 1022.
lu = *lo*, art.: 1293.

ma, see *plus*: 595.
malan = *malanha*, evil, rage: 1398.
malares = *malauros*, unhappy, unfortunate: 244.
manasas = *menasas*, menaces: 1712.
manent = *manen*, rich: 282.
meissaona = *meisona*, 3rd. sing. pres. ind. of *meisonar*, sow, cf. textual note
    to 156.
mercaanda = *mercanda* (noun), merchant: 828.
mie = *mieu*, my: 507.
miez = *mielz*, middle: 1220.
mota = *morta*, dead, cf. note to 1526.

nes = *neis*, same: 941.
nosa, 3rd. sing. pres. subj. of *nozer*, harm: 599.

orba = *orpa*, *metas en orpa*, to blind, cf. translation note to 256.
orus, misspelling of *ores*, cf. textual note to 1497.
oziman = *aziman*, diamond: 1067.

parleira, fem. of *parlier*, talkative: 1532.
parra, misspelling of *partra*, 3rd. sing. fut, ind. of *partir*, will leave: 1363.
peizura, contamination of *pejurar*, 'to worsen,' with *peitz*, 'pitch'? Cf. textual
    note to 1139.

pesz, sick, cf. *FEW*, VIII, 155a, *pietz estre* 'être en plus mauvaise santé'
(*Jaufré*): 140.
plus ma = *pluma*, feather: 595.
pn'es, scribal error for *n'es*: 1259. Cf. also 1245.

raza = *rosa*, rose: 959. Cf. textual note to 50 and *roesas* below.
repszas = *represzas*, blame, accuse: 1479.
ricedar, verb, enrich: 950. Ad *FEW*, XVI, 714 a?
roesas = *rosas*, rose: 50. Cf. also textual note to 50, and *ruosas*: 56, *roza*:
959, *ruesa*: 1261, *ruesza*: 1601 and *raza* above.

seingner = *senher*, seigneur, lord: 97. Cf. also *seignor*: 353, *seihner*: 992,
seiner: 838, 881, 1575, *seinher*: 1188, 1686, *seinhor*: 1021, 1126, 1293,
1645, *seinor*: 124, 127, 496, 979, *seinors*: 101, 277, 627, 1324, *sejnor*:
1431, *sener*: 1125, *senior*: 817, 871, 879, and *senor*: 1556.
seudadas = *soldadas*, prostitutes: 1701. Ad *FEW*, XI, 440b?
soclamada, sick, cf. textual note to 1522.
soenblan = *semblan*, opinion: 1465.

zinnosa = *ginhosa*, false: 1045.

NORTH CAROLINA STUDIES IN THE ROMANCE LANGUAGES AND LITERATURES

I.S.B.N. Prefix 0-8078-

Recent Titles

LUIS VÉLEZ DE GUEVARA: A CRITICAL BIBLIOGRAPHY, by Mary G. Hauer. 1975. (Texts, Textual Studies, and Translations, No. 5). *-405-5.*

UN TRÍPTICO DEL PERÚ VIRREINAL: "EL VIRREY AMAT, EL MARQUÉS DE SOTO FLORIDO Y LA PERRICHOLI". EL "DRAMA DE DOS PALANGANAS" Y SU CIRCUNSTANCIA, estudio preliminar, reedición y notas por Guillermo Lohmann Villena. 1976. (Texts, Textual Studies, and Translation, No. 15). *-415-2.*

LOS NARRADORES HISPANOAMERICANOS DE HOY, edited by Juan Bautista Avalle-Arce. 1973. (Symposia, No. 1). *-951-0.*

ESTUDIOS DE LITERATURA HISPANOAMERICANA EN HONOR A JOSÉ J. ARROM, edited by Andrew P. Debicki and Enrique Pupo-Walker. 1975. (Symposia, No. 2). *-952-9.*

MEDIEVAL MANUSCRIPTS AND TEXTUAL CRITICISM, edited by Christopher Kleinhenz. 1976. (Symposia, No. 4). *-954-5.*

SAMUEL BECKETT. THE ART OF RHETORIC, edited by Edouard Morot-Sir, Howard Harper, and Dougald McMillan III. 1976. (Symposia, No. 5). *-955-3.*

DELIE. CONCORDANCE, by Jerry Nash. 1976. 2 Volumes. (No. 174).

FIGURES OF REPETITION IN THE OLD PROVENÇAL LYRIC: A STUDY IN THE STYLE OF THE TROUBADOURS, by Nathaniel B. Smith. 1976. (No. 176). *-9176-2.*

A CRITICAL EDITION OF LE REGIME TRESUTILE ET TRESPROUFITABLE POUR CONSERVER ET GARDER LA SANTE DU CORPS HUMAIN, by Patricia Willett Cummins. 1977. (No. 177).

THE DRAMA OF SELF IN GUILLAUME APOLLINAIRE'S "ALCOOLS", by Richard Howard Stamelman. 1976. (No. 178). *-9178-9.*

A CRITICAL EDITION OF "LA PASSION NOSTRE SEIGNEUR" FROM MANUSCRIPT 1131 FROM THE BIBLIOTHEQUE SAINTE-GENEVIEVE, PARIS, by Edward J. Gallagher. 1976. (No. 179). *-9179-7.*

A QUANTITATIVE AND COMPARATIVE STUDY OF THE VOCALISM OF THE LATIN INSCRIPTIONS OF NORTH AFRICA, BRITAIN, DALMATIA, AND THE BALKANS, by Stephen William Omeltchenko. 1977. (No. 180). *-9180-0.*

OCTAVIEN DE SAINT-GELAIS "LE SEJOUR D'HONNEUR", edited by Joseph A. James. 1977. (No. 181). *-9181-9.*

A STUDY OF NOMINAL INFLECTION IN LATIN INSCRIPTIONS, by Paul A. Gaeng. 1977. (No. 182). *-9182-7.*

THE LIFE AND WORKS OF LUIS CARLOS LÓPEZ, by Martha S. Bazik. 1977. (No. 183). *-9183-5.*

"THE CORT D'AMOR". A THIRTEENTH-CENTURY ALLEGORICAL ART OF LOVE, by Lowanne E. Jones. 1977. (No. 185). *-9185-1.*

LANGUAGE IN GIOVANNI VERGA'S EARLY NOVELS, by Nicholas Patruno. 1977. (No. 188). *-9188-6.*

BLAS DE OTERO EN SU POESÍA, by Moraima de Semprún Donahue. 1977. (No. 189). *-9189-4.*

LA ANATOMÍA DE "EL DIABLO COJUELO": DESLINDES DEL GÉNERO ANATOMÍSTICO, por C. George Peale. 1977. (No. 191). *-9191-6.*

MONTAIGNE AND FEMINISM, by Cecile Insdorf. 1977. (No. 194). *-9194-0.*

SANTIAGO F. PUGLIA, AN EARLY PHILADELPHIA PROPAGANDIST FOR SPANISH AMERICAN INDEPENDENCE, by Merle S. Simmons. 1977. (No. 195). *-9195-9.*

When ordering please cite the *ISBN Prefix* plus the last four digits for each title.

Send orders to: University of North Carolina Press
Chapel Hill
North Carolina 27514
U. S. A.